TYNDALE OLD TESTAMENT COMMENTARIES

VOLUME 26

─── TOTC ───

OBADIAH, JONAH AND MICAH

Tyndale Old Testament Commentaries

Volume 26

Series Editor: David G. Firth
Consulting Editor: Tremper Longman III

Obadiah, Jonah and Micah

An Introduction and Commentary

Daniel C. Timmer

Academic

An imprint of InterVarsity Press
Downers Grove, Illinois

Inter-Varsity Press, England
36 Causton Street, London SW1P 4ST, England
Website: www.ivpbooks.com
Email: ivp@ivpbooks.com

InterVarsity Press, USA
P.O. Box 1400, Downers Grove, IL 60515, USA
Website: www.ivpress.com
Email: email@ivpress.com

Inter-Varsity Press, England, publishes Christian books that are true to the Bible and that communicate the gospel, develop discipleship and strengthen the church for its mission in the world.

IVP originated within the Inter-Varsity Fellowship, now the Universities and Colleges Christian Fellowship, a student movement connecting Christian Unions in universities and colleges throughout Great Britain, and a member movement of the International Fellowship of Evangelical Students. That historic association is maintained, and all senior IVP staff and committee members subscribe to the UCCF Basis of Faith. Website: www.uccf.org.uk.

InterVarsity Press®, USA, is the book-publishing division of InterVarsity Christian Fellowship/ USA® and a member movement of the International Fellowship of Evangelical Students. Website: www.intervarsity.org.

Scripture quotations are the author's own translation unless otherwise indicated.

The publisher and author acknowledge with thanks permission to reproduce extracts from the following: THE WEIGHT OF GLORY by C. S. Lewis copyright © C. S. Lewis Pte Ltd 1949. REFLECTIONS ON THE PSALMS by C. S. Lewis copyright © C. S. Lewis Pte Ltd 1958. Extracts reprinted by permission.

Every effort has been made to seek permission to use copyright material reproduced in this book. The publisher apologizes for those cases where permission might not have been sought and, if notified, will formally seek permission at the earliest opportunity.

First published 2021

Set in Garamond 11/13pt
Typeset in Great Britain by CRB Associates, Potterhanworth, Lincolnshire
Printed and bound in Great Britain by Ashford Colour Press Ltd, Gosport, Hampshire

Produced on paper from sustainable forests.

UK ISBN: 978–1–78359–976–9 (print)
UK ISBN: 978–1–78359–977–6 (digital)

US ISBN: 978–0–8308–4274–2 (print)
US ISBN: 978–0–8308–4276–6 (digital)

British Library Cataloguing-in-Publication Data
A catalogue record for this book is available from the British Library.

Library of Congress Cataloging-in-Publication Data
A catalog record for this book is available from the Library of Congress.

CONTENTS

General preface   vii
Author's preface   ix
Abbreviations   xi
Select bibliographies   xv

OBADIAH

Introduction   1
1. Authorship   2
2. Historical setting   2
3. Genre, structure and unity   7

Analysis   9

Commentary   11

JONAH

Introduction   31
1. Authorship and date   31
2. Historical setting   35
3. Genre, structure and unity   39

Analysis   45

Commentary   47

MICAH

Introduction 85
1. Authorship and date 85
2. Historical setting 87
3. Genre, structure and unity 91

Analysis 93

Translation 95

Commentary 107

GENERAL PREFACE

The decision to completely revise the Tyndale Old Testament Commentaries is an indication of the important role that the series has played since its opening volumes were released in the mid 1960s. They represented at that time, and have continued to represent, commentary writing that was committed both to the importance of the text of the Bible as Scripture and a desire to engage with as full a range of interpretative issues as possible without being lost in the minutiae of scholarly debate. The commentaries aimed to explain the biblical text to a generation of readers confronting models of critical scholarship and new discoveries from the Ancient Near East while remembering that the Old Testament is not simply another text from the ancient world. Although no uniform process of exegesis was required, all the original contributors were united in their conviction that the Old Testament remains the word of God for us today. That the original volumes fulfilled this role is evident from the way in which they continue to be used in so many parts of the world.

A crucial element of the original series was that it should offer an up-to-date reading of the text, and it is precisely for this reason that new volumes are required. The questions confronting readers in the first half of the twenty-first century are not necessarily those from the second half of the twentieth. Discoveries from the Ancient Near East continue to shed new light on the Old Testament, whilst emphases in exegesis have changed markedly. While remaining true to the goals of the initial volumes, the need for contemporary study of the text requires that the series as a whole be updated. This updating is not simply a matter of commissioning new volumes to replace the old. We have also taken the opportunity to update the format of the series to reflect a key emphasis from linguistics, which is that texts communicate in larger blocks rather than in shorter segments such as individual verses. Because of this, the treatment of each section of the text includes three segments. First, a short note on *Context* is offered, placing the passage under consideration in its literary setting within the book as well as noting any historical issues crucial to interpretation. The *Comment* segment then follows the traditional structure of the commentary, offering exegesis of the various components of a passage. Finally, a brief comment is made on *Meaning*, by which is meant the message that the passage seeks to communicate within the book, highlighting its key theological themes. This section brings together the detail of the *Comment* to show how the passage under consideration seeks to communicate as a whole.

Our prayer is that these new volumes will continue the rich heritage of the Tyndale Old Testament Commentaries and that they will continue to witness to the God who is made known in the text.

David G. Firth, Series Editor
Tremper Longman III, Consulting Editor

AUTHOR'S PREFACE

It is an honour to contribute this volume to the Tyndale series of
Old Testament commentaries. Not only is the series itself widely
respected, but the previous volume dealing with Obadiah, Jonah
and Micah was written by three very capable exegete-theologians
(David W. Baker, T. Desmond Alexander and Bruce K. Waltke)
who continue to advance evangelical scholarship in many ways. My
first expression of gratitude, therefore, is to Dr David G. Firth,
Series Editor, for the confidence in me he demonstrated by inviting
me to write this volume.

Each of the books that this commentary treats presents different
challenges to the reader. In keeping with the vision of the series I
have tried to make clear what the text means while making its
theology intelligible and providing a basis for further reflection by
readers who seek their own and others' spiritual transformation
under God's inspired word and by the Holy Spirit. One emphasis of
crucial interpretative and practical importance that is shared by all
three books is that one's identity is determined above all by one's
relationship to the living God. This was no less true centuries
before Jesus Christ's incarnation than it is now, and this truth
provides a wonderfully wide theological horizon in which even
books like Obadiah, which at first glance might appear to be
xenophobic or worse, find their place in relation to God's plan to
save people from every nation, tribe, people and language through
Jesus Christ (Gen. 12:3; Rev. 7:9). This emphasis on a God-defined
identity is particularly relevant in contexts where postmodern views
attempt to relocate identity to one's choices, ideology or actions.

The arguments and conclusions that this commentary presents have benefited enormously from interaction with students at Reformed Theological Seminary in Jackson, Mississippi, and more recently at the Faculté de théologie évangélique in Montreal, Quebec, Canada. I am grateful for their interaction in and out of class and for their willingness to explore these relatively unpopular books with me. I am likewise thankful to Mrs Laura Ladwig, Library Director at Puritan Reformed Theological Seminary, and Miss Kim Dykema, Assistant Librarian, for their unfailing help locating and obtaining resources that were essential to the writing of this commentary. I am also indebted to Drs David G. Firth and Philip Duce (IVP Senior Commissioning Editor) for their helpful feedback and flexibility as the volume came to completion and to Dr Rima Devereaux and Mrs Suzanne Mitchell for their expert, efficient help in preparing the manuscript for publication. Special thanks are also due to Puritan Reformed Theological Seminary, and especially to Dr Joel Beeke (President), Dr Michael Barrett (Academic Dean) and Dr Adriaan Neele (Director of the Doctoral Program), for creating an environment in which teaching, scholarship and the Christian life are integrated and inseparable and in which the time and support necessary for projects like this are available.

Lastly, and subordinate only to my grateful recognition that all these gifts and blessings come from the Triune God, I express my continuing and profound gratitude to Andreea, my wife of nearly twenty years. Her patience, perseverance, wisdom and love underlie this project and every other element of our life together. Our sons Nathan and Felix gave up some time with Papa so that I could finish this volume in a timely manner, and I owe both of them a large number of ping-pong matches in return. *Je vous aime!*

Readers should note that throughout this volume I use my own translation of Obadiah, Jonah and Micah rather than a standard one; the few times that a contemporary version is used, it is identified as such. I pray that this commentary will prove helpful to all who read the prophets with the desire to see, know and serve 'him of whom Moses, in the law, and the prophets wrote' (John 1:45).

Daniel C. Timmer

ABBREVIATIONS

AB	Anchor Bible
ABD	D. N. Freedman et al. (eds.), *The Anchor Bible Dictionary*, 6 vols. (New York: Doubleday, 1992)
ABS	Archaeology and Biblical Studies
ANEM	Ancient Near Eastern Monographs
ANET	J. B. Pritchard (ed.), *Ancient Near Eastern Texts Relating to the Old Testament*, 3rd edn (Princeton: Princeton University, 1969)
AOAT	Alter Orient und Altes Testament
AOTC	Apollos Old Testament Commentary
ASOR	American Schools of Oriental Research
ATANT	Abhandlungen zur Theologie des Alten und Neuen Testaments
ATD	Das Alte Testament Deutsch
AYBRL	Anchor Yale Biblical Reference Library
BASOR	*Bulletin of the American Schools of Oriental Research*
BBET	Beiträge zur biblischen Exegese und Theologie
BBR	*Bulletin for Biblical Research*
BHQ	Biblica Hebraica Quinta
BHS	K. Elliger and W. Rudolph (eds.), *Biblia Hebraica Stuttgartensia*, 5th edn (Stuttgart: Deutsche Bibelgesellschaft, 1997)
Bib	*Biblica*
BibInt	*Biblical Interpretation*
BINS	Biblical Interpretation Series

BN	*Biblische Notizen*
BZAW	Beihefte zur Zeitschrift für die alttestamentliche Wissenschaft
CBQ	*Catholic Biblical Quarterly*
CBQMS	Catholic Biblical Quarterly Monograph Series
CC	Continental Commentaries
CEB	Commentaire évangélique biblique
CHANE	Culture and History of the Ancient Near East
COS	W. W. Hallo (ed.), *The Context of Scripture*, 3 vols. (Leiden: Brill, 1997–2002)
CTJ	*Calvin Theological Journal*
DDD	K. van der Toorn, B. Becking and P. W. van der Horst (eds.), *Dictionary of Deities and Demons in the Bible*, 2nd rev. edn (Grand Rapids: Eerdmans, 1999)
EDB	D. N. Freedman (ed.), *Eerdmans Dictionary of the Bible* (Grand Rapids: Eerdmans, 2000)
Eng.	English
ErIsr	*Eretz-Israel*
FOTL	Forms of the Old Testament Literature
FRLANT	Forschungen zur Religion und Literatur des Alten und Neuen Testaments
HALOT	L. Koehler and W. Baumgartner, *The Hebrew and Aramaic Lexicon of the Old Testament*, Study Edition, 2 vols. (Leiden: Brill, 2001)
HCOT	Historical Commentary on the Old Testament
Heb.	Hebrew
Hen	*Henoch*
HS	*Hebrew Studies*
HSM	Harvard Semitic Monographs
HTKAT	Herders Theologischer Kommentar zum Alten Testament
HTS	*HTS Teologiese Studies*
HUCA	*Hebrew Union College Annual*
IEJ	*Israel Exploration Journal*
Int	*Interpretation*
ITC	International Theological Commentary
JAOS	*Journal of the American Oriental Society*
JBL	*Journal of Biblical Literature*

JBPR	*Journal of Biblical and Pneumatological Research*
JESOT	*Journal for the Evangelical Study of the Old Testament*
JETS	*Journal of the Evangelical Theological Society*
JHebS	*Journal of Hebrew Scriptures*
JNSL	*Journal of Northwest Semitic Languages*
JSOT	*Journal for the Study of the Old Testament*
JSOTSup	Journal for the Study of the Old Testament Supplement Series
JSS	*Journal of Semitic Studies*
LAI	Library of Ancient Israel
LHBOTS	Library of Hebrew Bible and Old Testament Studies
NAC	New American Commentary
NICOT	New International Commentary on the Old Testament
NIDOTTE	W. A. VanGemeren (ed.), *New International Dictionary of Old Testament Theology and Exegesis*, 5 vols. (Grand Rapids: Zondervan, 1997)
NSBT	New Studies in Biblical Theology
OTL	Old Testament Library
OtSt	Oudtestamentische Studiën
PBM	Paternoster Biblical Monographs
RB	*Revue biblique*
RIMA	The Royal Inscriptions of Mesopotamia, Assyrian Periods
SAAB	*State Archives of Assyria Bulletin*
SBLSym	SBL Symposium Series
ScrHier	Scripta Hierosolymitana
SHS	Scripture and Hermeneutics Series
StOr	*Studia Orientalia*
TDOT	G. J. Botterweck, H. Ringgren and H.-J. Fabry (eds.), *Theological Dictionary of the Old Testament*, 15 vols. (Grand Rapids: Eerdmans, 1975–2015)
Them	*Themelios*
THOTC	Two Horizons Old Testament Commentary
ThTo	*Theology Today*
TOTC	Tyndale Old Testament Commentary
TynBul	*Tyndale Bulletin*

UF	*Ugarit Forschungen*
VT	*Vetus Testamentum*
VTSup	Supplements to Vetus Testamentum
WBC	Word Biblical Commentary
ZAW	*Zeitschrift für die alttestamentliche Wissenschaft*
ZECOT	Zondervan Exegetical Commentary on the Old Testament

Bible versions

ESV	The ESV Bible (The Holy Bible, English Standard Version), copyright © 2001 by Crossway, a publishing ministry of Good News Publishers. Used by permission. All rights reserved.
LXX	Septuagint (pre-Christian Greek version of the Old Testament)
MT	Masoretic Text (the standard Hebrew text of the Old Testament)

SELECT BIBLIOGRAPHIES

Obadiah

Anderson, B. A. (2011), *Brotherhood and Inheritance: A Canonical Reading of the Esau and Edom Traditions*, LBHOTS 556 (London: Bloomsbury).

Arieh, I. B. (1995), 'The Edomites in Cisjordan', in D. V. Edelman (ed.), *You Shall Not Abhor an Edomite for He Is Your Brother: Edom and Seir in History and Tradition*, ABS 3 (Atlanta: Scholars), pp. 33–40.

Assis, E. (2006), 'Why Edom? On the Hostility Towards Jacob's Brother in Prophetic Sources', *VT* 56: 1–20.

—— (2014), 'Structure, Redaction and Significance in the Prophecy of Obadiah', *JSOT* 39: 209–221.

Ataç, M.-A. (2010), *The Mythology of Kingship in Neo-Assyrian Art* (Cambridge: Cambridge University Press).

Becking, B. (2016), 'The Betrayal of Edom: Remarks on a Claimed Tradition', *HTS* 72: 1–4.

Beitzel, B. J. (1992), 'Roads and Highways', *ABD* 5.776–782.

Ben-Yosef, E., T. E. Levy, T. Higham, M. Najjar and L. Tauxe (2010), 'The Beginning of Iron Age Copper Production in the Southern Levant: New Evidence from Khirbet al-Jariya, Faynan, Jordan', *Antiquity* 84: 724–746.

Ben Zvi, E. (1996), *A Historical-Critical Study of the Book of Obadiah*, BZAW 242 (Berlin: de Gruyter).

Bienkowski, P. (2001), 'New Evidence on Edom in the Neo-Babylonian and Persian Periods', in J. A. Dearman and

M. P. Graham (eds.), *The Land That I Will Show You: Essays on the History and Archaeology of the Ancient Near East in Honor of J. Maxwell Miller*, JSOTSup 343 (Sheffield: Sheffield Academic), pp. 198–213.

Block, D. I. (2013), *Obadiah: The Kingship Belongs to YHWH*, ZECOT (Grand Rapids: Zondervan).

Botta, A. F. and M. I. Rey (2018), 'Obadiah: Judah and Its Frenemy', in C. A. Rollston (ed.), *Enemies and Friends of the State: Ancient Prophecy in Context* (Winona Lake: Eisenbrauns), pp. 385–394.

Bryce, T. (2012), *The Routledge Handbook of the Peoples and Places of Ancient Western Asia: The Ancient Near East from the Early Bronze Age to the Fall of the Persian Empire* (London: Routledge).

Burnett, J. S. (2016), 'Transjordan: The Ammonites, Moabites, and Edomites', in B. T. Arnold and B. A. Strawn (eds.), *The World around the Old Testament: The People and Places of the Ancient Near East* (Grand Rapids: Baker Academic), pp. 309–352.

Clines, D. J. A. (1989), *Job 1 – 20*, WBC 20 (Dallas: Word).

Cogan, M. (2000), *1 Kings: A New Translation with Introduction and Commentary*, AB 10 (New York: Doubleday).

Cresson, B. C. (2000), 'Edom', *EDB*, pp. 372–373.

Crowell, B. L. (2008), 'A Reevaluation of the Edomite Wisdom Hypothesis', *ZAW* 120: 404–416.

Diakanoff, I. M. (1991), 'ערי מדי: The Cities of the Medes', in M. Cogan and I. Eph'al (eds.), *Ah, Assyria! Studies in Assyrian History and Ancient Near Eastern Historiography Presented to Hayim Tadmor*, ScrHier 33 (Jerusalem: Magnes), pp. 13–20.

Dick, M. B. (2005), 'The Poetics of the Book of Obadiah', *JNSL* 31: 1–32.

Dykehouse, J. (2013), 'Biblical Evidence from Obadiah and Psalm 137 for an Edomite Treaty Betrayal of Judah in the Sixth Century B.C.E.', *Antiguo Oriente* 11: 75–128.

Edelman, D. V. (1995), 'Edom: A Historical Geography', in D. V. Edelman (ed.), *You Shall Not Abhor an Edomite for He Is Your Brother: Edom and Seir in History and Tradition*, ABS 3 (Atlanta: Scholars), pp. 1–11.

Gelston, A. (2010), *The Twelve Minor Prophets*, BHQ 13 (Stuttgart: Deutsche Bibelgesellschaft).

Glazier-McDonald, B. (1995), 'Edom in the Prophetical Corpus',
    in D. V. Edelman (ed.), *You Shall Not Abhor an Edomite for He
    Is Your Brother: Edom and Seir in History and Tradition*, ABS 3
    (Atlanta: Scholars), pp. 23–32.
Goldsworthy, G. (2000), *Gospel and Wisdom*, in *The Goldsworthy
    Trilogy* (Exeter: Paternoster).
Haag, H. (1977), 'חמס', in G. J. Botterweck, H. Ringgren and
    H.-J. Fabry, *Theologisches Wörterbuch zum Alten Testament*, 9 vols.
    (Stuttgart: Kohlhammer), 2.1050–1061.
Hilber, J. (2012), 'The Culture of Prophecy and Writing in the
    Ancient Near East', in D. Magary and J. K. Hoffmeier (eds.),
    with a foreword by J. Woodbridge, *Do Historical Matters Matter
    to Faith? A Critical Appraisal of Modern and Postmodern Approaches
    to Scripture* (Wheaton: Crossway), pp. 219–242.
Jenson, P. P. (2009), *Obadiah, Jonah, Micah: A Theological Commentary*
    (London: T&T Clark).
Jeremias, J. (2007), *Die Propheten Joel, Obadja, Jona, Micha*, ATD 24.3
    (Göttingen: Vandenhoeck & Ruprecht).
Knauf, E. A. (1992), 'Teman', *ABD* 6.347–348.
Levy, T. E., M. Najjar, J. van der Plicht and N. Smith (2005),
    'Lowland Edom and the High and Low Chronologies:
    Edomite State Formation, the Bible and Recent Archaeological
    Research in Southern Jordan', in T. Levy and T. Higham (eds.),
    The Bible and Radiocarbon Dating: Archaeology, Text and Science
    (London: Equinox/Acumen), pp. 129–163.
Lipiński, E. (1973), 'Obadiah 20', *VT* 23: 368–370.
Lipschits, O. (2003), 'Demographic Changes in Judah between
    the Seventh and the Fifth Centuries B.C.E.', in O. Lipschits
    and J. Blenkinsopp (eds.), *Judah and the Judeans in the
    Neo-Babylonian Period* (Winona Lake: Eisenbrauns),
    pp. 323–376.
Lundbom, J. (2004), *Jeremiah 37 – 52*, AB 21C (New York:
    Doubleday).
Magary, D. R. (1997), 'Obadiah: Theology of', *NIDOTTE*
    4.992–996.
Mason, R. (2000), 'Obadiah', in J. Barton and J. Muddiman (eds.),
    The Oxford Bible Commentary (Oxford: Oxford University Press),
    pp. 590–592.

Nogalski, J. D. (1998), 'Obadiah 7: Corruption or Politically
    Charged Metaphor?', *ZAW* 110: 67–71.
—— (2012), 'Not Just Another Nation: Obadiah's Placement
    in the Book of the Twelve', in R. Albertz, J. Nogalski and
    J. Wöhrle (eds.), *Perspectives on the Formation of the Book of the
    Twelve: Methodological Foundations, Redactional Processes, Historical
    Insights*, BZAW 433 (Berlin: de Gruyter), pp. 89–107.
Parker, K. I. (1992), 'Solomon as Philosopher King? The Nexus
    of Law and Wisdom in 1 Kings 1–11', *JSOT* 53: 75–91.
Perdue, L. G. (1997), 'The Israelites and Early Jewish Family:
    Summary and Conclusions', in C. Meyer et al. (eds.), *Families
    in Ancient Israel, The Family, Religion and Culture* (Louisville:
    Westminster John Knox), pp. 163–222.
Podany, A. H. (2010), *Brotherhood of Kings: How International Relations
    Shaped the Ancient Near East* (Oxford: Oxford University
    Press).
Pons, M. V. (2014), 'The Origin of the Name Sepharad: A New
    Interpretation', *JSS* 59: 297–313.
Raabe, P. R. (1996), *Obadiah: A New Translation with Introduction
    and Commentary*, AB 24D (New York: Doubleday).
Renkema, J. (2003), *Obadiah*, trans. B. Doyle, HCOT (Leuven:
    Peeters).
Romerowski, S. (1989), *Les Livres de Joël et d'Abdias*, CEB 9
    (Vaux-sur-Seine: Edifac).
Rosen, S. A. (1992), 'Negeb', *ABD* 4.1061.
Seifrid, M. (2000), 'Righteousness, Justice and Justification', in
    T. D. Alexander and B. Rosner (eds.), *New Dictionary of Biblical
    Theology* (Downers Grove: InterVarsity Press), pp. 740–745.
Snyman, S. D. (1989), 'Cohesion in the Book of Obadiah', *ZAW*
    101: 59–71.
Tebes, J. M. (2009), 'The "Wisdom" of Edom', *BN* NF 143:
    97–117.
—— (2011), 'The Edomite Involvement in the Destruction of the
    First Temple: A Case of Stab-in-the-Back Tradition?', *JSOT* 36:
    219–255.
Timmer, D. C. (2015), *The Non-Israelite Nations in the Book of the
    Twelve: Thematic Coherence and the Diachronic-Synchronic Relationship
    in the Minor Prophets*, BINS 135 (Leiden: Brill).

—— (forthcoming c), 'Obadiah', in K. Dell and D. Lincicum
(eds.), *New Oxford Bible Commentary* (Oxford: Oxford University
Press).

Vanderhooft, D. (2003), 'Babylonian Strategies of Imperial
Control in the West: Royal Practice and Rhetoric', in
O. Lipschits and J. Blenkinsopp (eds.), *Judah and the Judeans
in the Neo-Babylonian Period* (Winona Lake: Eisenbrauns),
pp. 235–262.

van der Veen, P. (2014), 'Sixth-Century Issues: The Fall of
Jerusalem, the Exile, and the Return', in B. T. Arnold and
R. S. Hess (eds.), *Ancient Israel's History: An Introduction to Issues
and Sources* (Grand Rapids: Baker Academic), pp. 383–405.

van Wolde, E. (2002), 'A Leader Led by a Lady: David and Abigail
in 1 Samuel 25', *ZAW* 114: 355–375.

Wendland, E. R. (2014), 'The Rhetoric of Obadiah's "Day": Its
Structure and Significance', in *Prophetic Rhetoric: Case Studies
in Text Analysis and Transmission*, with a foreword by L. Zogobo,
SIL Publications in Translation and Textlinguistics 7
(Dallas: SIL International), pp. 103–141.

Williamson, H. G. M. (1999), 'Exile and After: Historical Study',
in D. W. Baker and B. T. Arnold (eds.), *The Face of Old Testament
Studies: A Survey of Contemporary Approaches* (Grand Rapids:
Baker), pp. 236–265.

Younger, K. L., Jr (1998), 'The Deportations of the Israelites',
JBL 117: 201–227.

Jonah

Abou-Assaf, A., A. Millard and P. Bordreuil (1982), *La Statue de
Tell Fekherye et son inscription assyro-araméenne* (Paris: Éditions
Recherche sur les Civilisations).

Abusch, T. (1999), 'Ishtar', *DDD*, pp. 452–456.

Ahlström, G. (1984), 'An Archaeological Picture of Iron Age
Religions in Ancient Palestine', *StOr* 55: 1–31.

Alexander, T. D. (1985), 'Jonah and Genre', *TynBul* 36: 35–59.

—— (1988), 'Jonah', in D. W. Baker, D. Alexander and B. Waltke,
Obadiah, Jonah, Micah, TOTC (Downers Grove: InterVarsity
Press), pp. 45–131.

Allen, L. C. (1976), *The Books of Joel, Obadiah, Jonah, and Micah*, NICOT (Grand Rapids: Eerdmans).

Aster, S. Z. (2007), 'Transmission of Neo-Assyrian Claims of Empire to Judah in the Late Eighth Century BCE', *HUCA* 78: 1–44.

Aurelius, E. (2003), 'Die fremden Götter im Deuteronomium', in M. Oeming and K. Schmid (eds.), *Der eine Gott und die Götter*, ATANT 82 (Zurich: TVZ), pp. 145–169.

Baker, D. W. (1992), 'Tarshish', *ABD* 6.331–333.

Benckhuysen, A. W. (2012), 'Revisiting the Psalm of Jonah', *CTJ* 47: 5–31.

Block, D. (1997), 'Nations/Nationality', *NIDOTTE* 4.966–972.

Bosma, C. J. (2013), 'Jonah 1:9: An Example of Elenctic Testimony', *CTJ* 48: 65–90.

Bottero, J. (2001), *Religion in Ancient Mesopotamia*, trans. T. L. Fagan (Chicago: University of Chicago Press).

Brenner, A. (1993), 'Jonah's Poem out of and within Its Context', in P. R. Davies and D. J. A. Clines (eds.), *Among the Prophets* (Sheffield: Sheffield Academic), pp. 183–192.

Butler, T. C. (2014), *Joshua 1 – 12*, WBC 7A, 2nd edn (Grand Rapids: Zondervan).

Byrne, J. M. (1997), *Religion and the Enlightenment: From Descartes to Kant* (Louisville: Westminster John Knox).

Cohen, A. and S. E. Kangas (eds.) (2010), *Assyrian Reliefs from the Palace of Ashurbanipal II: A Cultural Biography* (Hanover: University Press of New England), pp. 145–148.

Crossan, J. D. (1992), 'Parable', *ABD* 5.146–152.

Crouch, C. (2009), *War and Ethics in the Ancient Near East: Military Violence in Light of Cosmology and History*, BZAW 407 (Berlin: de Gruyter).

Day, J. (1990), 'Problems in the Interpretation of Jonah', in A. van der Woude (ed.), *In Quest of the Past: Studies on Israelite Religion, Literature and Prophetism*, OtSt 26 (Leiden: Brill), pp. 32–47.

Ehrenberg, E. (2008), 'Dieu et mon droit: Kingship in Late Babylonian and Early Persian Times', in N. Brisch (ed.), *Religion and Power: Divine Kingship in the Ancient World and Beyond*, Oriental Institute Seminars (Chicago: Oriental Institute of the University of Chicago), pp. 103–131.

Fales, M. (1982), 'The Enemy in Assyrian Royal Inscriptions: The Moral Judgment', in H. Nissen and J. Renger (eds.), *Mesopotamien und seine Nachbarn* (Berlin: Dietrich Reimer), pp. 425–435.

Fox, F. (1924), *Sixty-Three Years of Engineering* (London: John Murray).

Fuchs, A. (2011), 'Assyria at War: Strategy and Conduct', in K. Radner and E. Robson (eds.), *The Oxford Handbook of Cuneiform Culture* (Oxford: Oxford University Press), pp. 380–401.

Goswell, G. (2016), 'Jonah among the Twelve Prophets', *JBL* 135: 283–299.

Grayson, A. K. (1992a), 'Mesopotamia, History of (Assyria)', *ABD* 4.735–741.

—— (1992b), 'Nineveh', *ABD* 4.1118–1119.

—— (1993), 'Assyrian Officials and Power in the Ninth and Eighth Centuries', *SAAB* 7: 19–52.

—— (1996), *Assyrian Royal Inscriptions; Assyrian Rulers of the Early First Millennium BC II (858–745 BC)*, RIMA 3 (Toronto: University of Toronto Press).

Gut, R., J. Reade and R. M. Boehmer (2001), 'Ninive: Das späte 3 Jahrtausend v. Chr.', in J.-W. Meyer, M. Novák and A. Pruß (eds.), *Beiträge zur vorderasiatischen Archälogie: FS Winfried Orthmann* (Frankfurt am Main: Johann Wolfgang Goethe-Universität, Archäologisches Institut), pp. 74–92.

Hays, C. B., with P. Machinist (2016), 'Assyria and the Assyrians', in B. Arnold and B. Strawn (eds.), *The World around the Old Testament* (Grand Rapids: Baker), pp. 31–105.

Hendel, R. and J. Joosten (2018), *How Old Is the Hebrew Bible? A Linguistic, Textual, and Historical Study*, AYBRL (New Haven: Yale University Press).

Hunter, A. (2007), 'Inside Outside Psalm 55: How Jonah Grew out of a Psalmist's Conceit', in B. Becking and E. Peels (eds.), *Psalms and Prayers*, OtSt 55 (Leiden: Brill), pp. 129–139.

Iggers, G. G. and Q. Edward Wang (2008), *A Global History of Modern Historiography*, with contributions from Supriya Mukherjee (Harlow: Pearson).

Joosten, J. (2005), 'The Distinction between Classical and Late Biblical Hebrew as Reflected in Syntax', *HS* 46: 327–339.

Kaplan, J. and H. R. Kaplan (1992), 'Joppa', *ABD* 3.946.

Kaufman, S. A. (1992), 'Languages (Aramaic)', *ABD* 4.173.

Kim, H. C. P. (2007), 'Jonah Read Intertextually', *JBL* 126: 497–528.

Kuhrt, A. (1995), *The Ancient Near East, ca. 3000–330 BC*, 2 vols. (London: Routledge).

LaCoque, A. (2004), *Ruth*, trans. K. C. Hanson, CC (Minneapolis: Fortress).

Landes, G. M. (1967), 'Kerygma of the Book of Jonah: The Contextual Interpretation of the Jonah Psalm', *Int* 21: 3–31.

—— (1982), 'Linguistic Criteria and the Date of the Book of Jonah', *ErIsr* 16: 147–170.

Levine, B. A. and J.-M. de Tarragon (1993), 'The King Proclaims the Day: Ugaritic Rites for the Vintage', *RB* 100: 76–115.

Lichtert, C. (2003), 'Récit et noms de Dieu dans le livre de Jonas', *Bib* 84: 247–251.

Liverani, M. (2017), *Assyria: The Imperial Mission*, Mesopotamian Civilizations (Winona Lake: Eisenbrauns).

Longman III, T. (1996), 'Literary Approaches to Biblical Interpretation', in M. Silva (ed.), *Foundations of Contemporary Interpretation* (Grand Rapids: Zondervan), pp. 91–192.

Machinist, P. (1983), 'Assyria and Its Image in the First Isaiah', *JAOS* 103: 719–737.

Magonet, J. (1976), *Form and Meaning: Studies in Literary Techniques in the Book of Jonah*, BBET (Bern: Herbert Lang; Frankfurt: Peter Lang).

Marcus, D. (1999), 'Nineveh's "Three Days' Walk" (Jonah 3:3): Another Interpretation', in S. L. Cook and S. C. Winter (eds.), *On the Way to Nineveh: Studies in Honor of George M. Landes*, ASOR Books 4 (Atlanta: Scholars), pp. 42–53.

Millar, J. G. (2000), 'Land', in T. D. Alexander and B. S. Rosner (eds.), *New Dictionary of Biblical Theology* (Downers Grove: InterVarsity Press), pp. 623–627.

Miller, P. D. (1994), *They Cried to the Lord: The Form and Theology of Biblical Prayer* (Minneapolis: Fortress).

Moberly, R. W. L. (1998), '"God Is Not a Human That He Should Repent" (Numbers 23:19 and 1 Samuel 15:29)', in T. Linafelt and T. K. Beal (eds.), *God in the Fray: A Tribute to Walter Brueggemann* (Minneapolis: Fortress), pp. 112–123.

—— (2003), 'Jonah, God's Objectionable Mercy, and the Way
  of Wisdom', in D. F. Ford and G. Stanton (eds.), *Reading Texts,
  Seeking Wisdom: Scripture and Theology* (Grand Rapids: Eerdmans),
  pp. 154–168.

Möller, K. (2001), 'Words of (In-)evitable Certitude? Reflections
  on the Interpretation of Prophetic Oracles of Judgment', in
  C. Bartholomew, C. Greene and K. Moller (eds.), *After
  Pentecost: Language and Biblical Interpretation*, SHS 2 (Grand
  Rapids: Zondervan), pp. 352–386.

Moshavi, A. and T. Notarius (eds.) (2017), *Advances in Biblical
  Hebrew Linguistics: Data, Methods, and Analyses* (Winona Lake:
  Eisenbrauns).

Muldoon, C. L. (2010), *In Defense of Divine Justice: An Intertextual
  Approach to the Book of Jonah*, CBQMS (Washington DC:
  Catholic Biblical Association of America).

Niccacci, A. (1996), 'Syntactic Analysis of Jonah', *Liber Annus*
  46: 9–32.

Nielsen, K. (1997), *Ruth*, OTL, trans. E. Broadbridge (Louisville:
  Westminster John Knox).

Noegel, S. (2015), 'Jonah and Leviathan: Inner-Biblical Allusions
  and the Problem of the Dragon', *Hen* 37: 236–260.

Oppenheim, A. L. (trans.) (1969), 'Babylonian and Assyrian
  Historical Texts', *ANET*, pp. 265–317.

Pak, J. (2018), 'Self-Deception in Theology', *Them* 43.3:
  405–416.

Parker, B. J. (2011), 'The Construction and Performance
  of Kingship in the Neo-Assyrian Empire', *Journal of
  Anthropological Research* 67: 357–386.

Parpola, S. (1983), *Letters from Assyrian Scholars to the Kings
  Esarhaddon and Assurbanipal, Part II: Commentary and Appendices*,
  AOAT 5/2 (Kevelaer and Neukirchen-Vluyn: Butzon und
  Bercker and Neukirchener Verlag).

Plantinga, C., Jr (1995), *Not the Way It's Supposed to Be: A Breviary
  of Sin* (Grand Rapids: Eerdmans).

Pratt, R. L., Jr (2000), 'Historical Contingencies and Biblical
  Predictions', in J. I. Packer and S. K. Soderlund (eds.), *The Way
  of Wisdom: Essays in Honor of Bruce K. Waltke* (Grand Rapids:
  Zondervan), pp. 180–203.

Provan, I., V. Philips Long and T. Longman III (2015), *A Biblical History of Israel*, 2nd edn (Louisville: Westminster John Knox).

Radner, K. (2011), 'Royal Decision-Making: Kings, Magnates, and Scholars', in K. Radner and E. Robson (eds.), *The Oxford Handbook of Cuneiform Culture* (Oxford: Oxford University Press), pp. 358–379.

Reade, J. (2005), 'The Ishtar Temple at Nineveh', *Iraq* 67: 347–390.

Russell, J. M. (1998), 'The Program of the Palace of Assurnasirpal II at Nimrud: Issues in the Research and Presentation of Assyrian Art', *American Journal of Archaeology* 102: 655–715.

Saggs, H. W. F. (1984), *The Might That Was Assyria* (London: Sidgwick & Jackson).

Sasson, J. (1990), *Jonah*, AB 24B (New York: Abingdon).

Sauter, G. (2003), 'Jonah 2: A Prayer out of the Deep', in B. Strawn and N. Bowen (eds.), *A God So Near: Essays in Old Testament Theology in Honor of Patrick D. Miller* (Winona Lake: Eisenbrauns), pp. 145–152.

Schart, A. (2012), 'The Jonah Narrative within the Book of the Twelve', in R. Albertz, J. D. Nogalski and J. Wöhrle (eds.), *Perspectives on the Formation of the Book of the Twelve: Methodological Foundations, Redactional Processes, Historical Insights*, BZAW 433 (Berlin: de Gruyter), pp. 109–120.

Schaumberger, J. B. (1934), 'Das Bussedikt des Königs von Ninive bei Jonas 3, 7. 8 in keilschriftlicher Beleuchtung', *Miscellanae Biblica* 2: 123–134.

Schellenberg, A. (2015), 'An Anti-Prophet among the Prophets? On the Relationship of Jonah to Prophecy', *JSOT* 39: 353–371.

Schniedewind, W. (2005), 'Steps and Missteps in the Linguistic Dating of Biblical Hebrew', *HS* 46: 377–384.

Sheriffs, D. (1996), *The Friendship of the Lord* (Carlisle: Paternoster).

Shitrit, T. (2013), 'Aramaic Loanwords and Borrowing', in G. Khan (ed.) *Encyclopedia of Hebrew Language and Linguistics*, 4 vols. (Leiden: Brill), 1.165.

Smith, M. S. (2016), 'Ugarit and the Ugaritians', in B. Arnold and B. Strawn (eds.), *The World around the Old Testament* (Grand Rapids: Baker), pp. 139–167.

Stadel, C. (2013), 'Aramaic Influence on Biblical Hebrew',
   in G. Khan (ed.), *Encyclopedia of Hebrew Language and Linguistics*,
   4 vols. (Leiden: Brill), 1.162–165.
Stronach, D. and K. Codella (1996), 'Nineveh', in E. Meyers (ed.),
   The Oxford Encyclopedia of Archaeology in the Ancient Near East,
   5 vols. (New York: Oxford University Press).
Stuart, D. K. (2006), *Exodus*, NAC (Nashville: B&H).
Timmer, D. C. (2011), *A Gracious and Compassionate God: Mission,
   Salvation and Spirituality in the Book of Jonah*, NSBT 26 (Downers
   Grove: InterVarsity Press).
—— (2013), 'Jonah's Theology of the Nations: The Interface
   of Religious and Ethnic Identity', *RB* 120: 13–23.
—— (forthcoming a), 'Jonah, Book of', in G. K. Beale et al.
   (eds.), *Dictionary of the New Testament Use of the Old Testament*
   (Grand Rapids: Baker Academic).
—— (forthcoming b), *Jonas, Amos*, CEB (Vaux-sur-Seine:
   Edifac).
Vaillancourt, I. J. (2015), 'The Pious Prayer of an Imperfect
   Prophet: The Psalm of Jonah in Its Narrative Context',
   JESOT 4.2: 171–189.
Vanderhooft, D. (1999), *The Neo-Babylonian Empire and Babylon
   in the Latter Prophets*, HSM (Atlanta: Scholars).
van der Merwe, C. H. J., J. A. Naudé and J. H. Kroeze (2017),
   A Biblical Hebrew Reference Grammar, 2nd edn (London:
   Bloomsbury T&T Clark).
VanGemeren, W. (1991), 'Psalms', in F. Gaebelein (ed.), *Expositor's
   Bible Commentary*, 12 vols. (Grand Rapids: Zondervan),
   5.1–882.
Walton, J. (1992), 'The Object Lesson of Jonah 4:5–7 and the
   Purpose of the Book of Jonah', *BBR* 2: 47–57.
—— (2018), *Ancient Near Eastern Thought and the Old Testament*,
   2nd edn (Grand Rapids: Baker Academic).
Weissert, E. (1997), 'Royal Hunt and Royal Triumph in a Prism
   Fragment of Ashurbanipal', in S. Parpola and R. Whiting
   (eds.), *Assyria 1995* (Helsinki: Neo-Assyrian Text Corpus
   Project), pp. 339–358.
Wendland, E. (1996), 'Text-Analysis and the Genre of Jonah
   (Part 2)', *JETS* 39: 373–395.

—— (2014), 'Recursion and Variation in the "Prophecy" of Jonah: On the Rhetorical Impact of Stylistic Technique, with Special Reference to Irony and Enigma', in *Prophetic Rhetoric: Case Studies in Text Analysis and Transmission*, with a foreword by L. Zogobo, SIL Publications in Translation and Textlinguistics 7 (Dallas: SIL International), pp. 229–336.

Wilt, T. L. (1992), 'Lexical Repetition in Jonah', *Journal of Translation and Textlinguistics* 5.3: 252–264.

Wiseman, D. J. (1979), 'Jonah's Nineveh', *TynBul* 30: 29–52.

Yon, M. (1999), 'Ugarit', in Eric M. Meyers (ed.), *Oxford Encyclopedia of Archaeology in the Near East*, 5 vols. (Oxford: Oxford University Press), 5.255–262.

Young, I., R. Rezetko and M. Ehrensvärd (2008), *Linguistic Dating of Biblical Texts: A Survey of Scholarship, a New Synthesis, and a Comprehensive Bibliography*, 2 vols. (London: Equinox).

Youngblood, K. (2019), *Jonah*, ZECOT, 2nd edn (Grand Rapids: Zondervan Academic).

Younger, K. L., Jr (2003a), 'Kurkh Monolith (2.113A)', *COS* 2.263.

—— (2003b), 'Šamši-ilu: Stone Lions Inscription (2.115A)', *COS* 2.278.

—— (2007), 'Neo-Assyrian and Israelite History in the Ninth Century: The Role of Shalmaneser III', in H. G. M. Williamson (ed.), *Understanding the History of Ancient Israel* (Oxford: Oxford University Press), pp. 237–271.

Micah

Ahlström, G. (1984), 'An Archaeological Picture of Iron Age Religions in Ancient Palestine', *StOr* 55: 1–31.

Allen, L. C. (1976), *The Books of Joel, Obadiah, Jonah, and Micah*, NICOT (Grand Rapids: Eerdmans).

—— (1990), *Ezekiel 20 – 48*, WBC (Nashville: Thomas Nelson).

Anbar, M. (1994), 'Rosée et ondées ou lion et lionceau (Michée 5,6–7)?', *BN* 73: 5–8.

Andersen, F. I. and D. N. Freedman (2000), *Micah: A New Translation with Introduction and Commentary*, AB 24E (New York: Doubleday).

Aster, S. Z. (2007), 'Transmission of Neo-Assyrian Claims
    of Empire to Judah in the Late Eighth Century BCE', *HUCA*
    78: 1–44.
Averbeck, R. E. (1997a), 'טמא', *NIDOTTE* 2.365–376.
—— (1997b), 'Offerings and Sacrifices', *NIDOTTE* 4.996–1022.
—— (2011), 'Breath, Wind, Spirit and the Holy Spirit in the Old
    Testament', in D. Firth and P. D. Wegner (eds.), *Presence, Power,
    and Promise: The Role of the Spirit of God in the Old Testament*
    (Downers Grove: IVP Academic), pp. 25–37.
Baillie, J. (1996), *A Diary of Private Prayer* (New York: Fireside).
Barthélemy, D. (1992), *Critique textuelle de l'Ancien Testament*, vol. 3:
    Ézéchiel, Daniel et les 12 Prophètes (Fribourg: Éditions
    Universitaires; Göttingen: Vandenhoeck & Ruprecht).
Becking, B. (2002), 'The Gods, in Whom They Trusted . . .
    Assyrian Evidence for Iconic Polytheism in Ancient Israel',
    in B. Becking et al. (eds.), *Only One God? Monotheism in Ancient
    Israel and the Veneration of the Goddess Asherah*, Biblical Seminar
    77 (Sheffield: Sheffield Academic), pp. 151–163.
Ben Zvi, E. (1998), 'Micah 1.2–16: Observations and Possible
    Implications', *JSOT* 77: 103–120.
—— (1999), 'Wrongdoers, Wrongdoing and Righting Wrongs
    in Micah 2.1', *BibInt* 7: 87–100.
—— (2000), *Micah*, FOTL (Grand Rapids: Eerdmans).
Biddle, M. E. (2000), '"Israel" and "Jacob" in the Book of Micah:
    Micah in the Context of the Twelve', in J. D. Nogalski and
    M. A. Sweeney (eds.), *Reading and Hearing the Book of the Twelve*,
    SBLSym 15 (Atlanta: Scholars Press), pp. 146–165.
Block, D. I. (1997), *Ezekiel 1 – 24*, NICOT (Grand Rapids: Eerdmans).
—— (2011), 'The View from the Top: The Holy Spirit in the
    Prophets', in D. Firth and P. D. Wegner (eds.), *Presence, Power,
    and Promise: The Role of the Spirit of God in the Old Testament*
    (Downers Grove: IVP Academic), pp. 175–207.
Boda, M. J. (2016), *The Book of Zechariah*, NICOT (Grand Rapids:
    Eerdmans).
—— (2017), *The Heartbeat of Old Testament Theology: Three Creedal
    Expressions* (Grand Rapids: Baker Academic).
Bottéro, J. (2001), *Religion in Ancient Mesopotamia*, trans. T. L. Fagan
    (Chicago: University of Chicago Press).

Bretschneide, J. (2005), 'Life and Death in Nabada', *Scientific American* 15: 52–59.

Brueggemann, W. (1981), '"Vine and Fig Tree": A Case Study in Imagination and Criticism', *CBQ* 43: 188–204.

Butler, T. C. (1995), 'Announcements of Judgment', in D. B. Sandy and R. L. Giese, Jr, *Cracking Old Testament Codes* (Nashville: Broadman & Holman), pp. 157–176.

Butterworth, M. (1997), 'רחם', *NIDOTTE* 3.1093–1095.

Campbell, E. F. (1998), 'A Land Divided: Judah and Israel from the Death of Solomon to the Fall of Samaria', in M. D. Coogan (ed.), *Oxford History of the Biblical World* (New York: Oxford University Press).

Carpenter, E. and M. A. Grisanti (1997), 'פשע', *NIDOTTE* 3.706–710.

Carroll R., M. D. (2007), '"He Has Told You What Is Good": Moral Formation in Micah', in M. D. Carroll R. and J. L. Lapsley (eds.), *Character Ethics and the Old Testament: Moral Dimensions of Scripture* (Louisville: Westminster John Knox), pp. 103–118.

Chaney, M. L. (2014), 'The Political Economy of Peasant Poverty: What the Eighth-Century Prophets Presumed but Did Not State', *Journal of Religion & Society* 10: 34–60.

Chisholm, R. B. (1997), 'עוד', *NIDOTTE* 3.335–340.

Christensen, D. L. (2009), *Nahum: A New Translation with Introduction and Commentary*, AB24F (New York: Doubleday).

Clements, R. E. (1992), 'Woe', *ABD* 6.945–947.

Collins, C. J. (1997a), 'הדר', *NIDOTTE* 1.1013–1015.

—— (1997b), 'כבד', *NIDOTTE* 2.577–587.

Coomber, M. J. W. (2011), 'Caught in the Crossfire? Economic Injustice and Prophetic Motivation in Eighth-Century Judah', *BibInt* 19: 396–432.

Cox, G. (2013), 'The "Hymn" of Amos: An Ancient Flood Narrative', *JSOT* 38: 81–108.

Cuffey, K. H. (2015), *The Coherence of the Book of Micah: Remnant, Restoration, and Promise*, LHBOTS 611 (London: T&T Clark).

Dalley, S. (2004), 'Recent Evidence from Assyrian Sources for Judean History from Uzziah to Manasseh', *JSOT* 28: 387–401.

Dalley, S. (trans.) (2000), *Myths from Mesopotamia: Creation, the Flood, Gilgamesh, and Others*, rev. edn, Oxford World's Classics (Oxford: Oxford University Press).

Davies, E. W. (1989), 'Land: Its Rights and Privileges', in R. E. Clements (ed.), *The World of Ancient Israel: Sociological, Anthropological and Political Perspectives* (Cambridge: Cambridge University Press), pp. 349–369.

Day, J. (1992), 'Asherah', *ABD* 1.483–487.

Dempster, S. G. (2017), *Micah*, THOTC (Grand Rapids: Eerdmans).

Di Fransico, L. (2017), '"He Will Cast Their Sins into the Depths of the Sea . . ." Exodus Allusions and the Personification of Sin in Micah 7:7–20', *VT* 67: 187–203.

Ehrman, A. (1973), 'A Note on Micah vi 14', *VT* 23: 103–105.

Faust, A. (2018), 'Society and Culture in the Kingdom of Judah during the Eighth Century', in Z. I. Farber and J. L. Wright (eds.), *Archaeology and History of Eighth-Century Judah*, ANEM 23 (Atlanta: SBL), pp. 179–203.

Fiorello, M. (2014), *The Physically Disabled in Ancient Israel according to the Old Testament and Ancient Near Eastern Sources*, PBM (Milton Keynes: Paternoster).

Firth, D. G. (2009), *1 & 2 Samuel*, AOTC (Leicester: Apollos).

Floyd, M. (2000), *Minor Prophets: Part 2*, FOTL 22 (Grand Rapids: Eerdmans).

Follis, E. R. (1987), 'The Holy City as Daughter', in E. R. Follis (ed.), *Direction in Biblical Hebrew Poetry*, JSOTSup 44 (Sheffield: Sheffield Academic), pp. 173–184.

Fretheim, T. E. (1997), 'כפף', *NIDOTTE* 2.689.

Ganor, S. and I. Kreimerman (2019), 'An Eighth Century BCE Gate Shrine at Tel Lachish Israel', *BASOR* 381: 211–236.

Gelston, A. (2010), *The Twelve Minor Prophets*, BHQ 13 (Stuttgart: Deutsche Bibelgesellschaft).

Gignilliat, M. (2019), *Micah: An International Theological Commentary*, ITC (London: Bloomsbury T&T Clark).

Glenny, W. E. (2015), *Micah: A Commentary Based on Micah in Codex Vaticanus* (Leiden: Brill).

Gordon, R. P. (1978), 'Micah VII 19 and Akkadian *KABĀSU*', *VT* 28: 355.

Goswell, G. (2019), 'Davidic Rule in the Prophecy of Micah',
    JSOT 44: 153–165.
Grayson, A. K. and J. Novotny (2012), *The Royal Inscriptions of
    Sennacherib, King of Assyria (704–681 BC), Part 1* (Winona Lake:
    Eisenbrauns).
Greenwood, K. (2014), 'Late Tenth- and Ninth-Century Issues:
    Ahab Underplayed? Jehoshaphat Overplayed?', in B. T. Arnold
    and R. S. Hess (eds.), *Ancient Israel's History: An Introduction
    to Issues and Sources* (Grand Rapids: Baker Academic),
    pp. 286–318.
Hamilton, J. M. (1992), 'Adullam', *ABD* 1.81.
Hays, C. B., with P. Machinist (2016), 'Assyria and the Assyrians',
    in B. Arnold and B. Strawn (eds.), *The World around the Old
    Testament* (Grand Rapids: Baker), pp. 31–105.
Hess, R. S. (2007), *Israelite Religions: An Archaeological and Biblical
    Survey* (Grand Rapids: Baker Academic).
Hilber, J. (2012), 'The Culture of Prophecy and Writing in the
    Ancient Near East', in D. Magary and J. K. Hoffmeier (eds.),
    with a foreword by J. Woodbridge, *Do Historical Matters Matter
    to Faith? A Critical Appraisal of Modern and Postmodern Approaches
    to Scripture* (Wheaton: Crossway), pp. 219–242.
Horsnell, M. J. A. (1997a), 'כשׁף', *NIDOTTE* 2.735–738.
—— (1997b), 'קסם', *NIDOTTE* 3.945–951.
Japhet, S. (1993), *I & II Chronicles*, OTL (Louisville: Westminster
    John Knox).
Jenson, P. P. (1995), 'Models of Prophetic Prediction and
    Matthew's Quotation of Micah 5:2', in P. E. Satterthwaite,
    R. S. Hess and G. J. Wenham (eds.), *The Lord's Anointed:
    Interpretation of Old Testament Messianic Texts*, Tyndale House
    Studies (Carlisle: Paternoster), pp. 189–211.
—— (2008), *Obadiah, Jonah, Micah: A Theological Commentary*
    (New York: T&T Clark).
Jeppesen, K. (1984), 'Micah V in the Light of a Recent
    Archaeological Discovery', *VT* 34: 462–466.
Jeremias, J. (2007), *Die Propheten Joel, Obadja, Jona, Micha*, ATD 24.3
    (Göttingen: Vandenhoeck & Ruprecht).
Johnson, B. (1998), 'משׁפט', *TDOT* 9.86–98.
Jonker, L. (1997), 'רכב', *NIDOTTE* 3.1109–1114.

Joosten, J. (2013), 'YHWH's Farewell to Northern Israel (Micah 6,1–8)', *ZAW* 125: 448–462.

Katzenstein, H. J. (1992), 'Philistines', *ABD* 5.326–328.

Kessler, R. (2000), *Micha*, 2nd edn, HTKAT (Freiburg: Herder).

Kloner, A. (1992), 'Mareshah', *ABD* 4.523.

Knoppers, G. N. (2004), *I Chronicles 1 – 9*, AB 12 (New York: Doubleday).

Koehler, L. and W. Baumgartner (2001), *The Hebrew and Aramaic Lexicon of the Old Testament*, study edition, trans. M. E. J. Richardson (Leiden: Brill).

Lewis, C. S. (1958), *Reflections on the Psalms* (New York: Harcourt, Brace & World).

—— (2001), *The Weight of Glory and Other Addresses* (San Francisco: HarperOne).

Lipschits, O. (2003), 'Demographic Changes in Judah between the Seventh and Fifth Centuries B.C.E.', in O. Lipschits and J. Blenkinsopp (eds.), *Judah and the Judeans in the Neo-Babylonian Period* (Winona Lake: Eisenbrauns), pp. 323–376.

Littauer, M. A. and J. H. Crouwel (1992), 'Chariots', *ABD* 1.888–892.

Luc, A. (1997), 'חטא', *NIDOTTE* 2.87–93.

Luker, L. M. (1992a), 'Ephrathah', *ABD* 2.557–558.

—— (1992b), 'Moresheth', *ABD* 4.904–905.

McConville, J. G. (1984), *Law and Theology in Deuteronomy*, JSOTSup 33 (Sheffield: JSOT).

—— (2002), *Deuteronomy*, AOTC 5 (Leicester: Apollos).

McKane, W. (1998), *Micah: Introduction and Commentary* (Edinburgh: T&T Clark).

McNutt, P. (1999), *Reconstructing the Society of Ancient Israel*, LAI (Louisville: Westminster John Knox).

Manor, D. W. (1992), 'Chezib (place)', *ABD* 1.903–904.

Marrs, R. R. (1999), 'Micah and a Theological Critique of Worship', in P. Graham, R. R. Marrs and Steven L. McKenzie (eds.), *Worship and the Hebrew Bible: Essays in Honour of John T. Willis*, JSOTSup 284 (Sheffield: Sheffield Academic), pp. 184–203.

Mazar, A. (1990), *Archaeology of the Land of the Bible: 10,000–586 B.C.E.* (New York: Doubleday).

Mettinger, T. N. D. (1982), 'YHWH SABAOTH: The Heavenly King on the Cherubim Throne', in T. Ishida (ed.), *Studies in the Period of David and Solomon and Other Essays* (Winona Lake: Eisenbrauns), pp. 109–138.

Millard, A. (2012), 'From Woe to Weal: Completing a Pattern in the Bible and the Ancient Near East', in M. Boda and I. Provan (eds.), *Let Us Go Up to Zion: Essays in Honour of H. G. M. Williamson*, VTSup 153 (Leiden: Brill), pp. 193–201.

Miller, P. D. (2000), *The Religion of Ancient Israel* (Louisville: Westminster John Knox).

—— (2011), *Deuteronomy*, Interpretation (Louisville: Westminster John Knox).

Morrow, W. S. (2017), *An Introduction to Biblical Law* (Grand Rapids: Eerdmans).

Naudé, J. A. (1997), 'קדשׁ', *NIDOTTE* 3.877–887.

Nel, P. J. (1997), 'כבשׁ', *NIDOTTE* 2.596.

Nogalksi, J. D. (2010), 'Micah 7:8–20: Reevaluating the Identity of the Enemy', in R. Heskett and B. Irwin (eds.), *The Bible as Human Witness to Divine Revelation: Hearing the Word of God through Historically Dissimilar Traditions*, LHBOTS 469 (New York: T&T Clark), pp. 125–142.

O'Connell, R. H. (1997), 'משׁפחה', *NIDOTTE* 2.1139–1142.

O'Dowd, R. (2009), *The Wisdom of Torah: Epistemology in Deuteronomy and the Wisdom Literature*, FRLANT 225 (Göttingen: Vandenhoeck & Ruprecht).

Oppenheim, A. L. (trans.) (1969), 'Babylonian and Assyrian Historical Texts', *ANET*, pp. 265–317.

Pak, J. (2018), 'Self-Deception in Theology', *Them* 43.3: 405–416.

Paul, S. (1991), *Amos: A Commentary on the Book of Amos*, Hermeneia (Minneapolis: Augsburg Fortress).

Peterson, D. L. (1992), 'Eschatology (Old Testament)', *ABD* 2.575–579.

Prausnitz, M. W. (1992), 'Achzib', *ABD* 1.57.

Pritchard, J. B. (ed.) (1969), *Ancient Near Eastern Texts Relating to the Old Testament*, 3rd edn, with supplement (Princeton: Princeton University Press).

Provan, I., V. Philips Long and T. Longman III (2015), *A Biblical History of Israel*, 2nd edn (Louisville: Westminster John Knox).

Reicke, B. I. (1967), 'Liturgical Traditions in Mic. 7', *Harvard Theological Review* 91: 349–367.

Reimer, D. J. (2013), 'The Prophet Micah and Political Society', in R. P. Gordon and H. M. Barstad (eds.), *Thus Speaks Ishtar of Arbela': Prophecy in Israel, Assyria, and Egypt in the Neo-Assyrian Period* (Winona Lake: Eisenbrauns), pp. 203–224.

Renaud, B. (1977), *La Formation du livre de Michée: Tradition et actualisation* (Paris: J. Gabalda).

—— (1987), *Michée, Sophonie, Nahum*, Sources Bibliques (Paris: J. Gabalda).

Richelle, M. (2012), 'Un triptyque au cœur du livre de Michée (Mi 4–5)', *VT* 62: 232–247.

Rigney, J. (2018), *Lewis on the Christian Life: Becoming Truly Human in the Presence of God*, Theologians on the Christian Life (Wheaton: Crossway).

Roberts, J. J. M. (2018), 'Enemies and Friends of the State: First Isaiah and Micah', in C. A. Rollston (ed.), *Enemies and Friends of the State: Ancient Prophecy in Context* (Winona Lake: Eisenbrauns), pp. 329–338.

Romerowski, S. (1990), 'Que signifie le mot *ḤESED*?', *VT* 60: 89–103.

—— (2004), 'Prophétisme', in *Le Grand dictionnaire de la Bible* (Cléon d'Andran: Éditions Excelsis).

Schart, A. (1998), *Die Entstehung des Zwölfprophetenbuchs: Neubearbeitungen von Amos im Rahmen schriftenübergreifender Redaktionsprozesse*, BZAW 260 (Berlin: de Gruyter).

Schibler, D. (1989), *Le Livre de Michée*, CEB 33 (Charols: Edifac).

Seifrid, M. (2000), 'Righteousness, Justice and Justification', in T. D. Alexander and B. Rosner (eds.), *New Dictionary of Biblical Theology* (Downers Grove: InterVarsity Press), pp. 740–745.

Seow, C. L. (2011), 'Elihu's Revelation', *ThTo* 68: 253–271.

Smith-Christopher, D. L. (2015), *Micah: A Commentary*, OTL (Louisville: Westminster John Knox).

Snell, D. C. (2011), *Religions of the Ancient Near East* (Cambridge: Cambridge University Press).

Suriano, M. (2010), 'A Place in the Dust: Text, Topography and a Toponymic Note on Micah 1:10–12a', *VT* 60: 433–446.

Thompson, D. (1997), 'לאה', *NIDOTTE* 2.748–749.

Timmer, D. C. (2011), *A Gracious and Compassionate God: Mission, Salvation and Spirituality in the Book of Jonah*, NSBT 26 (Downers Grove: InterVarsity Press).

—— (2015), *The Non-Israelite Nations in the Book of the Twelve: Thematic Coherence and the Diachronic-Synchronic Relationship in the Minor Prophets*, BINS 135 (Leiden: Brill).

—— (2016), 'Joshua', in M. V. Van Pelt (ed.), *A Biblical-Theological Introduction to the Old Testament: The Gospel Promised* (Wheaton: Crossway), pp. 159–176.

Ussishkin, D. (1980), 'The "Lachish Reliefs" and the City of Lachish', *IEJ* 30: 174–197.

—— (2014), 'Sennacherib's Campaign to Judah: The Archaeological Perspective with an Emphasis on Lachish and Jerusalem', in I. Kalimi and S. Richardson (eds.), *Sennacherib at the Gates of Jerusalem: Story, History, and Historiography*, CHANE 71 (Leiden: Brill), pp. 75–104.

van der Merwe, C. H. J., J. A. Naudé and J. H. Kroeze (2017), *A Biblical Hebrew Reference Grammar*, 2nd edn (London: Bloomsbury T&T Clark).

van der Woude, A. S. (1969), 'Micah in Dispute with the Pseudo-Prophets', *VT* 19: 244–260.

VanGemeren, W. (1990), *Interpreting the Prophetic Word: An Introduction to the Prophetic Literature of the Old Testament* (Grand Rapids: Zondervan).

van Rooy, Harry F. (1997), 'בוך', *NIDOTTE* 1.619.

Vargon, S. (2009), 'The Prayer for the Restoration of the Israelite Kingdom in the Book of Micah: Literary Analysis and Historical Background', in G. Galil, M. Geller and A. Millard (eds.), *Homeland and Exile: Biblical and Ancient Near Eastern Studies in Honour of Bustenay Oded*, VTSup 130 (Leiden: Brill), pp. 597–618.

Verderame, L. (2014), 'Astronomy, Divination, and Politics in the Neo-Assyrian Empire', in C. L. N. Ruggles (ed.), *Handbook of Archaeoastronomy and Ethnoastronomy* (New York: Springer), pp. 1847–1853

Verhoof, P. (1997), 'Prophecy', *NIDOTTE* 4.1067–1078.

Wagenaar, J. A. (2001), *Judgement and Salvation: The Composition and Redaction of Micah 2 – 5*, VTSup 85 (Leiden: Brill).

Walker, P. W. L. (2000), 'Jerusalem', in T. Alexander and
  B. Rosner (eds.), *New Dictionary of Biblical Theology* (Downers
  Grove: InterVarsity Press), pp. 589–592.
Walsh, C. (2000), *The Fruit of the Vine: Viticulture in Ancient Israel*,
  HSM 60 (Leiden: Brill).
Waltke, B. K. (1993), 'Micah', in T. McKomiskey (ed.), *The Minor
  Prophets: An Exegetical and Expositional Commentary*, 3 vols.
  (Grand Rapids: Baker Academic), 2.591–764.
—— (2007), *A Commentary on Micah* (Grand Rapids: Eerdmans).
Walton, J. (2012), 'The Decalogue Structure of the Deuteronomic
  Law', in D. Firth and P. S. Johnston (eds.), *Interpreting
  Deuteronomy: Issues and Approaches* (Downers Grove: IVP
  Academic), pp. 93–117.
—— (2018), *Ancient Near Eastern Thought and the Old Testament*,
  2nd edn (Grand Rapids: Baker Academic).
Wendland, E. R. (2018), 'A Discourse Structural Overview
  of the Prophecy of Micah, *The Bible Translator* 69: 277–293.
Wessels, W. J. (2003), 'Micah 7:8–20: An Apt Conclusion to the
  Book of Micah', *Verbum et Ecclesia* 24: 249–259.
—— (2009), 'Empowered by the Spirit of Yahweh: A Study
  of Micah 3:8', *JBPR* 1: 33–47.
Wöhrle, J. (2009), 'A Prophetic Reflection on Divine Forgiveness:
  The Integration of the Book of Jonah in the Book of the
  Twelve', *JHebS* 9: article 7.
Wolff, H. W. (1990), *Micah: A Commentary*, trans. G. Stansell,
  CC (Minneapolis: Augsburg).
Wright, C. J. H. (1997), 'נחל', *NIDOTTE* 3.77–81.
Yadin, Y. (1963), *The Art of Warfare in Biblical Lands: In the Light
  of Archaeological Study*, 2 vols. (New York: McGraw-Hill).
Younger, K. L., Jr (1998), 'The Deportations of the Israelites',
  JBL 117: 201–227.
—— (1999), 'The Fall of Samaria in Light of Recent Research',
  CBQ 61: 461–482.
—— (2003), 'Kurkh Monolith (2.113A)', *COS* 2.263.
—— (2018), 'Assyria's Expansion West of the Euphrates
  (ca. 870–701 BCE)', in Z. I. Farber and J. L. Wright (eds.),
  Archaeology and History of Eighth-Century Judah, ANEM 23
  (Atlanta: SBL), pp. 17–33.

Ziese, M. (2000), 'Jackal', *EDB*, p. 665.

Zobel, H.-J. (1998), 'משפחה', *TDOT* 9.79–85.

Zukerman, A. and I. Shai (2006), '"The Royal City of the Philistines" in the "Azekah Inscription" and the History of Gath in the Eighth Century BCE', *UF* 38: 729–778.

OBADIAH

INTRODUCTION

The book of Obadiah presents God's justice against sin, and his mercy in salvation, in two overlapping perspectives.[1] The first is tied to the state of Edom at the time of Judah's destruction by Babylon in 586 BC, when Edom's often adversarial relationship with its kinfolk reached its lowest point in Edom's violence against residents of Jerusalem fleeing death and destruction. The retribution that Edom will receive for these sins overlaps with God's definitive punishment of all sin in the Day of YHWH (in most modern versions, the Day of the LORD). This second perspective also involves his restoration of his people, which includes both Israelites and those on 'Mount Esau', in fulfilment of Genesis 12:1–3. Obadiah's message thus encourages the faithful, whether in Judah or in exile then or in any setting now, while warning the wicked (whether Israelite or not) to repent before the Day of YHWH falls upon them (Wendland 2014: 133).

---

1. I briefly sketch some of the lines I develop here in Timmer (forthcoming c).

1. Authorship

The prophet Obadiah, whose name means worshipper or servant of YHWH, is mentioned only here in Scripture (ten other Obadiahs appear in the OT, but none is likely the book's author). Nothing is known of him other than that he was a prophet (Jeremias 2007: 61). The connection between Obadiah's vision and YHWH's speech reflects the indispensable connection between YHWH and authentic prophets in ancient Israel (Deut. 18:15–22). Similarly, the essential and self-evident continuity between a prophet and his words, whether spoken or written, requires that we see the book as faithfully presenting the contents of Obadiah's vision, whether he or one of his close associates wrote it under inspiration.[2]

2. Historical setting

a. Origins

Significantly, Edom's existence as a people group can be traced back to Jacob's brother Esau. His request for 'red [ʾādōm] stew' (Gen. 25:30) gave rise to the epithet Edom (ʾĕdōm), and that title was later extended to the red-soiled region where he settled (Gen. 32:3) and to his descendants (Gen. 36) (Burnett 2016: 329). The primary relevance of this tie between Jacob and Esau for the interpretation of Obadiah is that nations with a common ancestor (Isaac) are to treat each other as 'brothers', and this figures in Obadiah's condemnation of Edom (v. 10).

b. Rocky relationship

Edom's territory lay south of the Dead Sea and the territory of Moab. It was bounded by the Arabah on the west and the Arabian Desert on the east (Edelman 1995: 3). As early as the late second millennium it developed a large-scale metal production industry

---

2. A commitment to preserving the prophet–text link is evident across the Ancient Near East; see Hilber 2012 and note the similar conclusion of Ben Zvi (1996: 13), on the basis of the book's opening line. Raabe (1996: 94–95) offers a thorough discussion of the term 'vision'.

alongside its even older and largely nomadic agricultural and shepherding economy (Burnett 2016: 331). This significant industry, which thrived first in the twelfth to eleventh centuries and again in the tenth to ninth centuries, 'could only have been organized by a complex polity', to which passing reference is perhaps made in Genesis 36:21 (Levy et al. 2005: 158). By about 800 BC, Edom had become a vassal of the Neo-Assyrian Empire, but the effective absence of Assyria from the region for the next seventy or so years allowed Judah to occasionally reassert control over parts of Edom's territory (2 Kgs 8:22; 14:7, 22; 16:6; 2 Chr. 28:16–17) until Assyria returned in the late 730s. From that point onwards, Edom remained a vassal until the end of Assyrian control of the Levant a century later (Edelman 1995: 1).

Edom's participation in the Assyrian Empire enhanced its integration in international trade, which travelled along 'the King's Highway' that passed through Edom's territory as well as other southern routes.[3] Its increased economic success from the mid eighth century onwards reflects increased political organization centred on the Edomite Plateau (Burnett 2016: 336). The Edomite state was relatively decentralized and consisted primarily of 'small agricultural villages', which accounts for the minimal quantity of epigraphic (written) remains that have been discovered at its more developed sites (Crowell 2008: 413).

Alongside occasional conflict between Judah and Edom, includ-ing Edom's attack on Arad around 700 BC and significant incursions into Judean territory around the end of the seventh century (van der Veen 2014: 397), Edom's proximity to Judah also made possible more peaceful interaction, including mutually beneficial trade.[4] This general proximity echoes more formal alliances of 'brotherhood' that first appeared between second-millennium kings and later continued between smaller states (Podany 2010: 307), and it is pos-sible that such a formal agreement existed between Judah and Edom (Dykehouse 2013). Be that as it may, the brotherhood of their

---

3. Cresson 2000: 372; Burnett 2016: 335–36. Maps of these routes can be found in Beitzel (1992: 779–780).

4. Glazier-McDonald 1995: 27; and in more detail, Arieh 1995.

respective ancestors entailed even greater obligations. This explains Obadiah's exclusive focus on Edom, while Babylon is referred to only obliquely despite being almost entirely responsible for Jerusalem's destruction.[5]

c. The fall of Jerusalem

The sometimes bellicose and sometimes peaceful relationship between Judah and Edom was definitively undone by Edom's participation in the destruction of Jerusalem and its violence against its population. Obadiah's *you were like one of them!* (v. 11) compares the Edomites to the Babylonians, who had neither trade nor blood ties with Judah and who treated them as nothing more than an enemy to be destroyed. The intensity and focus of Edom's aggression against Jerusalem in the context of the latter's fall to Babylon in 586 were unprecedented (cf. esp. Ezek. 35:5), and that event is accordingly much more plausible as the general setting for the book of Obadiah than are earlier conflicts between the two states (cf. 2 Kgs 8:22; 14:7, 22; 16:6; 2 Chr. 28:16–17).[6] Although Edom had recently expressed interest in opposing Babylon once it had taken over Assyria's imperial project in the Levant (Jer. 27:1–11), this never came about, and soon the political calculus changed radically.

Judah's first rebellion as a vassal of Babylon in *c.*601, under Jehoiakim (608–598 BC; 2 Kgs 24:1), resulted in a punitive attack and deportation of its elite as well as much material wealth during the reign of his successor Jehoiachin (597; 2 Kgs 24:10–16). Zedekiah (596–586) also rebelled against Babylon (2 Kgs 24:20), and the consequences were disastrous. The king's family was slain, the king was blinded and imprisoned in Babylon, Jerusalem and its temple were destroyed along with the Judean cities of Lachish and Azekah, and

---

5. See the longer discussion of why Obadiah 'singled out' Edom in Ben Zvi 1996: 230–246, who helpfully critiques the idea that Judeans, especially after 586, had a special hatred for Edomites (p. 235).

6. For a nuanced proposal for a ninth-century date, see Romerowski 1989: 209–223.

a sizeable fraction of Jerusalem's population was exiled (2 Kgs 25) (van der Veen 2014: 383).

The possibility that Edom was a vassal of Babylon before (note Babylon's apparent use of soldiers from other vassal states in 2 Kgs 24:1–2, c.601) and after the fall of Jerusalem (note Babylon's destruction of Edom around 553, perhaps punishment of an unfaithful vassal) is congenial to the inference that Edom participated in or facilitated Judah's destruction as a vassal of Babylon.[7] It is also possible that Edom did what it did as an independent state, since such political motivation was not a necessary prerequisite for Edomite participation in Judah's downfall.

Despite the unsurpassed importance of Edom's extreme violence against Judah in 586, the relationship between the two states or at least between some of their citizens during that period was not always adversarial. For example, Jeremiah 40:11 mentions the presence of Judeans in Edom, Moab and Ammon. Although there is no indication of how long Judeans had been in those locations, it is likely that at least some of them had fled there to escape Babylon's retribution, and this compels us to recognize that not all Edomites were driven by hatred or disdain for their Judean kinfolk.[8] Various historiographic scenarios might explain the co-existence of these two attitudes (and possibly more), and we should avoid the assumption that Edomite violence against Jerusalem's fleeing population in 586 was the result of a long-standing and strategic Edomite involvement with the Babylonian siege or against the Judean state, something the Old Testament nowhere suggests. It is far more likely that Obadiah (like Lam. 4:21–22; Ps. 137:7) refers to a relatively small and unorganized series of events that involved some, but hardly all, of the Edomite population.[9]

---

7. So Burnett 2016: 338; van der Veen 2014: 397. Contrast Bienkowski 2001: 211, who thinks it 'survived as an independent state' and was annexed only in 553 by Nabonidus. Vanderhooft (2003: 242) considers the continuation of a general submission of states outside the coastal zone likely.

8. Lundbom (2004: 113) assumes these Judeans fled in response to Babylon's advance towards Jerusalem.

9. Romerowski (1989: 211) notes this as well.

Several factors must be kept in mind in this regard, not least the opportunistic and occasional nature of Edom's aggression against Judah. First, the biblical accounts report that Judeans fled Jerusalem only once the Babylonian siege ended (and perhaps before it began). Furthermore, Edom's relatively decentralized government makes possible scenarios in which Edomite participation in the attack on Jerusalem was limited to one or more regional populations, presumably those nearest Jerusalem (and thus quite far from Edomite administrative centres). The 'complex situation between the lowlands and highlands of Edom' (Levy et al. 2005: 160) means that some Edomites may have acted as described in Obadiah apart from the involvement of Edom's king and whatever military force he controlled. Finally, Edom's stereotyped identity in Obadiah cautions us against inferring that a majority of Edomites were involved in the events Obadiah describes (recall that Judeans were living in Edom immediately after Jerusalem's fall according to Jer. 40:11).[10] Whatever the precise details of this complex historical situation, Burnett notes that Edom's 'active participation in the Babylonian destruction of Jerusalem' would have been an opportunity to expand its control of trade and territory 'toward the west and north' (Burnett 2016: 338).

d. After 586 BC

Once the Babylonians had destroyed much of Jerusalem and deported the most useful levels of its society to serve the empire elsewhere, Nebuchadnezzar appointed Gedaliah as governor (2 Kgs 25:22). His assassination by a group of Judeans opposed to Babylonian control (cf. Jer. 41:1–2) ended his tenure after only a few months, and in response Babylon deported still more Judeans (Jer. 52:30). Despite the large-scale destruction of Jerusalem, there is some evidence that a cult continued on the site of the temple.[11]

---

10. Contrast the more sceptical views of Becking (2016) and Tebes (2011). Ben Zvi (1996: 238) proposes that 'the code term "Edom"' involves a particular dimension or portrayal of Edom that includes its fraternal ties to Judah as well as its wisdom, pride and opposition to YHWH.

11. See Lipschits 2003: 344–345.

Archaeology also shows that Edomites and other surrounding people groups gradually moved into Judah's former territory (Williamson 1999: 253), something that Obadiah's vision of restoration presumes (Obad. 17–21) (Assis 2014: 220).

3. Genre, structure and unity

a. Genre

Obadiah contains only two types of literature: oracles of judgment (vv. 2–4, 5–9, 10–14) and an oracle that promises deliverance for (restored) Judah and judgment for *all the nations* (vv. 15–21). Except for the first verse, the entire book is presented as YHWH's direct speech.

b. Structure and unity

In addition to its introduction, Obadiah consists of three separate oracles and a final announcement of salvation. The three oracles present different perspectives on Edom: its punishment at the hands of other nations for its pride (vv. 2–4 and 5–9) and its punishment for participating in Judah's destruction (vv. 10–14). The last section (vv. 15–21) announces YHWH's judgment against all nations that oppose him (including Edom as described in Obadiah) as part of the restoration of a renewed Israel in the Day of YHWH. Assis (2014) plausibly argues that these sections were composed at different times (just before, immediately after, and a few decades or so after the fall of Jerusalem in 586 BC) and that these different settings lie behind the different perspectives of verses 2–9, 10–14 and 15–21. The theme of YHWH's sovereign justice against sinful entities, first focused on Edom but gradually expanding to include all those who refuse to recognize YHWH's sovereignty, very effectively unites these units, and is reinforced by the prominence of Edom in all three sections.[12]

---

12. Other proposals for the book's structure are surveyed by Snyman (1989).

ANALYSIS

A. Introduction (1)
B. First oracle against Edom (2–4)
C. Second oracle against Edom (5–9)
D. Third oracle against Edom (10–14)
E. Announcement of salvation and judgment in the Day of YHWH (15–21)

COMMENTARY

A. Introduction (1)

Context

The book opens by linking its content to the prophet who received the *vision* that it transmits. The Hebrew text tradition places Obadiah immediately after Amos, which offers a contrasting but not disharmonious perspective on *Edom*, which is defined rather differently there (Amos 9:11–12).[1] More salient, however, is the way that Obadiah's opening verse sets the horizon for the rest of the book by revealing that YHWH will take definitive action against Edom.

Comment

1. The contents of the book are presented as the *vision* of Obadiah, without restricting that experience of divine revelation to what the prophet sees. This is borne out by the fact that what follows is verbal, and indeed a quotation: *Thus says YHWH of Hosts concerning Edom.* God, in turn, quotes an anonymous group that has heard him speak:[2] *We have heard a report from YHWH, and an envoy has been sent among the nations.* Finally, the envoy is quoted: *Rise up! Let's*

---

1. See Nogalski 2012, although the redactional processes he proposes are speculative.

2. Block (2013: 53) notes that the speaker may be an 'editorial "we", or Obadiah speaks as a representative of a group, perhaps of the people as a whole, or of a cadre of faithful followers of YHWH in post-fall Jerusalem'. Renkema (2003: 117) proposes that Obadiah sees himself as the recipient of Jeremiah's prophecy, which thus came to both prophets.

rise up against her for war! The following schematic illustrates these levels of discourse:

> *The vision of Obadiah.* (Author/prophet)
>> *Thus says the Lord YHWH concerning Edom:* (Prophet)
>>> *'We have heard a report from YHWH, and an envoy has been sent among the nations:* (Group)
>>>> *"Rise up! Let's rise up against her for war!"'* (Envoy)

Meaning

This elaborate presentation of the envoy highlights the interplay of YHWH's sovereignty and omniscience (YHWH introduces the report and all that it contains) and the decision of the nations (including the envoy) to wage war against Edom (*Let's rise up*).[3]

B. First oracle against Edom (2–4)

Context

The first oracle of judgment against Edom (vv. 2–4) emphasizes that the actions of the nations mentioned in verse 1 are the means by which YHWH himself will inflict judgment upon Edom. It focuses on Edom's pride, a sin which inevitably involves disregard for God's immeasurable greatness and unlimited power.

Comment

2–3. Beginning in verse 2, YHWH's pre-eminent role and agency are emphasized as he speaks in the first person to Edom. Verses 2 and 4b present the punishment for Edom's pride as described in verses 3 and 4a.[4] Verse 2 begins with a focus particle, *Look!*, that gives weight to what follows while establishing a perspective for the reader by focusing attention on God's agency.[5] YHWH promises that his actions against 'Edom' will make it insignificant and utterly despised on the international scene. This new status is the undoing

---

3. Raabe (1996: 99) structures the text similarly.

4. Wendland (2014: 107) notes this A-B-B'-A' structure in vv. 2–4.

5. Jenson (2009: 13), following Adele Berlin; similarly, Renkema 2003: 122.

or deconstruction of what Edom has made itself to be, as it were, described in verse 3. Edom's self-image is the quintessence of pride, which inevitably involves self-deception: its presumptuousness has deceived it.[6] In Edom's case this self-deception is expressed in terms of its geographical location, the height of which gives rise to its presumptive security. Hidden in the rocky terrain of its plateau and 'elevated' beyond the reach of danger, Edom thinks, *Who can bring me down to the ground?* The question is rhetorical, and the presumed answer is, 'No-one can.'[7] Edom's pride knows no bounds, and involves autonomy, self-determination and outright untouchability! This view of itself, and not its political factors or features alone, defines the *Edom* that YHWH identifies as his enemy in the first two-thirds of Obadiah (vv. 2–14), and prepares the reader for the strong parallel between Edom so described and the other *nations* in the last third of the book (vv. 15–21).

4. YHWH replies immediately to Edom's blatant denial of his supremacy, not to say his very existence, in verse 4. He asserts emphatically that no matter how high Edom believes itself to be, it is not beyond his reach. *Should you raise yourself like an eagle, should you place your nest among the stars, from there I will bring you down! Utterance of YHWH.* The rhetoric of the verse artfully raises Edom far above the rocks of verse 3: first to the height of the eagle, and then superlatively to the stars, far beyond the reach of any animal or human (and thus tantamount to an attempt to claim divine status).[8] *I will bring you down*, says YHWH, even *from there*, be it ever so high! God's response completely reverses Edom's elevation while putting the lie to its proud claim that no-one can bring it down. This outcome expresses YHWH's just judgment against an entity he describes as 'trusting in topography rather than in divine power, as foolishly attempting to trespass the limitations of human existence, and accordingly, as an enemy of YHWH' (Ben Zvi 1996: 68). The closing

---

6. Renkema (2003: 124) translates the term in question as 'over-confidence'.

7. Magary (1997: 992) draws attention to the use of rhetorical questions here and in vv. 5 (twice) and 8, as does Wendland (2014: 108).

8. Note Gen. 11:1–9; Isa. 14:12–15; and the discussion in Raabe 1996: 133.

affirmation at the end of verse 4 that this prediction comes from
YHWH makes it all the more certain.

Meaning
God will punish Edom's self-adulatory pride, which has deceived
it into believing it is untouchable and beyond the reach of any
power, human or divine. YHWH's response asserts his uniqueness and unlimited power, and demonstrates that no sin will go
unpunished indefinitely, no matter how powerful the human
perpetrator(s) might be.

C. Second oracle against Edom (5–9)

Context
Since no new condemnation is introduced in verses 5–9, the
punishment predicted there continues the emphasis of verses 2 and
4b.[9] Pride is thus still at issue, but this unit focuses on its manifestation in Edom's ill-placed trust in its allies and in its own wisdom
and might. The passage develops the judgment gradually, from loss
of property (vv. 5–6) to loss of territory (v. 7) and finally to the
destruction of Edom's wise men and its military force (vv. 8–9).[10]

Comment
  5. Verse 5 introduces two activities in which some but not all of
something valuable is taken or removed. Normally, since thieves
are not intent on removing all material wealth from the place they
rob, they take only what they want or need. Similarly, grape
harvesters normally do not remove every last grape, whether by
expediency or in fulfilment of YHWH's command to leave something behind for the poor (Lev. 19:10).[11] Edom's case will be quite

---

9. Wendland (2014: 109) suggests a break after v. 10, which would make
   YHWH's destruction of Edom in vv. 5–9 the consequence of its
   participation in the 'violent' destruction of Jacob in v. 10.
10. Romerowski (1989: 257) notes that both groups in vv. 8–9 were
    responsible, each in its own way, for the protection of Edom.
11. Both cases are emphatically normal: 'Would not this be the case?'

different, as the interjection *How you are cut off!* placed between these two images of limited loss shows.[12]

6. Contrary to what is usual or normal, this verse foretells that *nothing* will be left of Esau (a synonym for Edom, as noted above[13]). Here only the image of theft is used to depict Edom's loss, perhaps because it requires no personification (unlike the metaphorical vineyard) or because it is more violent. Edom will be ransacked and its *hidden things*, that is, its valuables, will be found by the thieves.

7. To the surprise of the reader and Edom alike, verse 7 identifies those responsible for this complete emptying of Edom as its allies! These enemies, who overlap with the *nations* summoned by the envoy in verse 2, are characterized as fundamentally deceptive and exploitative. While playing the role of Edom's allies, they plot and plan the demise of their Edomite victim. These false appearances add the elements of surprise and betrayal to the expulsion of Edom from its land (v. 7a). The same group which claimed to be Edom's friends (literally *men of its peace*) deceives and overcomes it (v. 7b), using their support (*bread*) as a trap for it (v. 7c).[14] Since Babylon was responsible for Edom's fall, it may be among the allies in view here (cf. its destructive attacks in 553/552).[15]

---

12. Notably, the Hebrew term that introduces the phrase expresses shock or sadness, not elation or derision. See the discussion in Renkema 2003: 136–137.

13. Raabe (1996: 144) suggests a connotation based on Esau's loss of his birthright to the deceptive Jacob that presages the focus on Edom's mistreatment of Judah in vv. 10–14.

14. Noting the domain of covenant/treaty relationship in v. 7a–b, Nogalski (1998: 70) suggests that *bread* is 'a synonym to "covenant" and "peace"'. This puts the matter too strongly, but the more general idea of support offered to a superior or equal is surely present (cf. 1 Sam. 21:3; 25:11), and the concept of covenant or treaty is clearly present in the context; Raabe (1996: 153) extends the argument to other passages. Raabe (1996: 154) derives the word translated *trap* from another root and translates this line as 'will establish a place of foreigners in your stead'.

15. Romerowski (1989: 251–252) notes that Arab tribes also drove some of the remaining Edomites out of their territory in the late sixth century and later.

Whatever the case, the fact that these nations have been able to hoodwink Edom reveals that Edom *has no understanding*. This situation, like Edom's supposed security in the heights of its plateau, reveals another dimension of Edom's fatal misinterpretation of reality (and of itself), for wisdom involves living in the light of the order that YHWH has built into the creation and maintains in history (Goldsworthy 2000: 490; Seifrid 2000). A few references to Edomite wisdom, some quite uncertain, are scattered across the Old Testament but shed no light on what Obadiah may refer to (1 Kgs 4:30–31;[16] Eliphaz, Job 2:11; 15:17–19;[17] Jer. 49:7, on which Obadiah may depend). Similarly, a few partially preserved texts of varying date related to Edom may hint at a literary interest in wisdom there.[18] The connection in the Old Testament between wisdom and mining (Job 28:1–12) and metallurgy (Exod. 31:1–5; 1 Kgs 7:14) is more certain, and is directly relevant in the light of Edom's extensive metalworking industry, which was the largest source of copper in the Levant.[19] The immediate context, however, adds further specificity to this wisdom by connecting it with Edom's relationships, first of all with other parties, and ultimately with YHWH (similarly, Abigail, 1 Sam. 25; Solomon, 1 Kgs 5:12).[20]

8. The focus on wisdom in verse 8 connects it to the last line of verse 7 (*understanding* appears in both verses), but the subject changes from the negative evaluation of Edom (v. 7) to the announcement of its destruction (vv. 8–9). Similarly, *that day* refers back to the

---

16. Reading 'Edomite' rather than 'all the men' requires emending the text without good reason, as Cogan notes (2000: 222). However, Edom may well be included in 'all the peoples of the east' in 1 Kgs 4:30.

17. Cf. Clines 1989: 57.

18. See the brief survey in Tebes 2009: 105–106. Crowell (2008) strongly doubts that there was an Edomite literary wisdom tradition.

19. Cf. Ben-Yosef et al. 2010. The possible connection between Punon and the bronze serpent in the OT may reflect this. Punon, often thought to be an Edomite site, is mentioned at the same point in the itinerary of Num. 33:42–43 as the episode of the bronze serpent in Num. 21:4–9 (so Tebes 2009: 108).

20. On Abigail, see van Wolde 2002, and on Solomon, Parker 1992.

events sketched in verses 6–7, and so connects God's judgment described here to what the nations will do to Edom. In this way YHWH's involvement (*I*, v. 8) overlaps with and supervenes the military actions described in verses 6–9. God commits emphatically to destroying *the* [supposedly] *wise* and even *understanding* itself (i.e. wisdom) from Edom and Mount Esau.[21]

9. The consequence of Edom's being deprived of wisdom is nothing less than its total defeat, with the *mighty men* of Teman (perhaps a region of Edom rather than a city, exact location unknown; Knauf 1992; Bryce 2012: 699) *terrified* and every man being cut down (v. 9).[22] The focus on the Edomite political and military apparatus rather than on the entire population is important, and reflects Obadiah's consistent focus on the spiritual and moral flaws of pride, violence and self-dependence that characterize the power structures and ideology that God will destroy.

Meaning

Edom's political alliances, like its trust in its advisors and its military might, demonstrate that its confidence is misplaced. Its sustained disregard for the God of Israel, who rules over all nations, makes its failure inevitable and expresses YHWH's just judgment of human pride and self-sufficiency.

D. Third oracle against Edom (10–14)

Context

The third oracle against Edom shifts the focus of condemnation to its mistreatment of Judah. The oracle's narrow focus presumes that this particular episode in the political–military existence of Edom is representative, even definitive, of it. That categorization simultaneously excludes a significant number of Edomites from

---

21. *Mount Esau*, like Esau in v. 6, probably anticipates the focus on the Edom–Judah relation discussed in vv. 10–14, as suggested by Ben Zvi (1996: 121).

22. The violence of this last line is substantially reduced if *by slaughter* is moved to the beginning of v. 10, as Renkema (2003: 156–158) suggests.

this condemnation, specifically those not involved in the violence
against the escapees from Jerusalem.

Comment

10. The offence is summarized in one strong Hebrew word,
violence, and the punishments in two Hebrew words each, *covered in
shame* and being *cut off for ever*. *Violence* refers to 'cold-blooded and
unscrupulous violation of the personal rights of others, motivated
by hatred and greed and often accompanied by brutal, physical
violence',[23] and puts the 'Edom' in view here in a very unfavourable
light.

Given the gravity of this behaviour, it is all the more striking
that Edom perpetrated it against *your brother, Jacob*. Edom's posture
reveals an egregious lack of love for its kinfolk.[24] Being *covered in
shame* complements the idea that Edom will be despised (v. 2) but
makes Edom the subject of the verb rather than the object of the
other's spite. More importantly, this shame reveals that Edom
will realize 'its own sin, guilt and folly' (albeit too late) (Jenson
2009: 20). Finally, being *cut off* echoes the same punishment in
verse 9 but also anticipates the description of Edom's violence
against Judah in verse 14 that employs the same verb.

11. God develops the critique of Edom's unbrotherly conduct
by arguing that its behaviour, described in detail in verses 12–14,
makes it like the nations that attacked Jerusalem (i.e. not like Judah,
but rather like its enemies) *even though its fraternal relationship is real
and entails relational obligations of kindness and faithfulness*.[25] As much as
the following verses emphasize Edom's active participation in the
destruction of Jerusalem, verse 11 condemns it for passivity and
toleration of the nations' aggression against Judah. The setting is
the day when Edom stood idly by while strangers carried away

---

23. Haag 1977: 1056, translated and cited by Renkema 2003: 159.

24. See Perdue 1997, esp. pp. 166–167.

25. This point is also made by Botta and Rey (2018: 388), although their
    explanation of it as nationalism overlooks Obadiah's idealized
    presentation of Judah.

Jerusalem's wealth[26] and foreigners entered its gates and cast lots to distribute the plunder. On *that day . . . you were just like one of them.*[27] Edom's lack of fraternal love and concern for Judah is inseparable from its disregard for YHWH as the deity in covenant with Judah (note *my people* in v. 13).[28] It is perhaps for this reason that this is the second and last time that Obadiah refers to Judah as Edom's *brother.*

12–14. The next three verses present a comprehensive rejection of Edom's behaviour. The list of eight actions or attitudes exceeds by one the Old Testament's classically complete list of seven (gloat, rejoice, boast, enter, gloat, loot, stand, hand over). These activities touch nearly every dimension of human existence: 'eyes (seeing), mouth, foot (entering), hand (reaching out), heart (to rejoice)' (Dick 2005: 16). The prohibitions are definitive of these Edomites, as much in grammar as in their number and variety, and simultaneously condemn them on those grounds (Renkema 2003: 171).

Verse 12 focuses on Edom's attitudes: *gloating over* the misfortune of *your brother*, rejoicing when Judah perishes, and boasting in the *day of [their] distress.* In the absence of love, Edom's hatred and pride flourish. Verse 13 repeats the command not to gloat (this time without identifying Judah as Edom's brother, as in v. 12) and adds entering the gate (of Jerusalem) and looting its wealth.[29] All three lines end with *in the day of his/their calamity*, showing that a proper interpretation of Judah's pitiful situation should have elicited radically different actions on the part of Edom. Verse 14 completes the list by drawing the reader's gaze to the most inhuman dimension of Edom's violence: neither attitudes (vv. 12, 13b) nor plundering (v. 13a, c), but *cutting down* and handing over to the

---

26. The same term can be translated 'leaders'; cf. Renkema 2003: 164; Block 2013: 72; and *HALOT* 1.311.

27. The two-colon structure of v. 11, with the three lines concerning non-Israelites as an expansion on the first colon, is defended by Dick (2005: 15).

28. This makes Assis's theory (2006: 14) that Judah's anti-Edomite sentiment was driven by the fear that 'God had now chosen Edom as his people in place of Israel' quite unlikely.

29. On the grammatical issues surrounding the plural verb 'stretch out', see Ben Zvi 1996: 156–157.

equally violent enemy Jerusalem's *escapees* and *survivors*.[30] This critical
moment should have elicited compassion more than any other, as
dishevelled and distressed Judeans fled from violence and ruin, but
the Edomites who strategically positioned themselves at a cross-
roads treated their relatives with utter disdain and spite.

Meaning
Edom's violence against its Israelite kinfolk epitomizes its self-
centred commitment to its own interests before all else, even when
that involves a flagrant lack of pity and heartless opportunism.
YHWH's justice, complemented by his covenantal commitment to
his people, expresses his strong condemnation of such violence and
ensures that such wrongs will not go unpunished.

E. Announcement of salvation and judgment in the Day of YHWH (15–21)

Context
The limited, non-eschatological punishment of Edom described in
terms of military defeat, political disintegration and shame and
scorn is distinct but not entirely separate from the Day of YHWH
that will come upon all nations. Edom is addressed in the second
person for the last time in verses 15–16, and that section serves as
a transition between these two stages of judgment, the first of
which typifies or presages the second.[31]

Comment
   15. Building on the unsparing violence that Edom exercised and
countenanced against Judah (esp. v. 14), verse 15 completes the

---

30. Raabe (1996: 187) notes that the possessive pronoun 'its' in v. 14
    refers back to 'my people' in v. 13. The pronouns thus preserve
    the connection between YHWH and his people and highlight the
    theological dimension of Edom's offence.

31. This understanding of the contribution of vv. 15–16 in particular is
    widely held; cf. Romerowski 1989: 270, 272–273; Jeremias 2007: 71;
    and many others.

presentation of Edom's punishment by affirming that it will be proportional to its crimes: *as you did, so it will be done to you! Your recompense will return on your head!* Unlike Edom's violence against Judah, YHWH's violence against Edom will be measured and just, and will be a foretaste of the just judgment he brings about on the world as a whole.

Verse 15 introduces this final divine judgment as *near* but, in contrast to the focus on Edom until now, as including *all the nations*. Since this category includes Edom, it eliminates the basic distinction between Edom and the *strangers* and *foreigners*, and indeed between *all* nations (the absence of any reference to Israel or Judah as a nation in this section is significant). Yet Edom remains a distinct entity among the *nations* because of its unique relationship and history with Judah.[32]

16. This verse includes the book's first reference to a second-person plural addressee. Since this group is said to have *drunk on my holy mountain*, that is, Jerusalem, it most likely refers to Edom, or perhaps to Edom and the Babylonians.[33] Edom (and perhaps others) drank, literally or metaphorically, in celebration of Jerusalem's destruction (cf. *rejoice* in v. 12 and *gloat* in vv. 12, 13).[34] The operative element here is comparison: *as* these victors drank on *YHWH's* holy mountain, a setting which underlines their rejection of his kingship, *so* 'all the nations' who treat God with the same disdain will drink in a still more intense way (*continually*) – but not wine! The contents of this *cup* end these rebels' very existence (*they will be as though they have never been*), showing that this cup is nothing other than YHWH's wrath poured out (cf. Ps. 75:8;

---

32. See in more detail Ben Zvi 1996: 181; Timmer 2015: 67–69.

33. Furthermore, Edom is the most recent (and second-person) addressee, in v. 15. The plural *you* is almost certainly not a reference to Judah, since this would be the only case in which Obadiah associates sin with Judah (albeit indirectly, via its punishment).

34. In a rough analogy, depictions of Neo-Assyrian royal lion hunts, in which the lion represents the king's enemies, concluded with a libation in honour of the gods. See Ataç 2010: 18–19.

Hab. 2:16; etc.).[35] The destiny of God's inveterate enemies is un-qualified destruction.

17. In contrast to this complete destruction of YHWH's enemies, Mount Zion is presented as the only place where *escape* from this final judgment can be had (v. 17).[36] This implies a radical transform-ation of Zion's fate, for in Obadiah's day the city lay destroyed and profaned, and death rather than deliverance had met its population. Similarly, as a *holy* location, this restored Jerusalem excludes sin (contrast Mount Esau in the present, and the sins of which the Edomites whom Obadiah condemns are guilty). Only by being sinless can this restored Jerusalem be immune from judgment, for sin is the only feature that Obadiah invariably connects to judg-ment (cultic purity or holy status is not in view).[37] Put otherwise, the characterization in verse 16 of those whom YHWH will destroy as those who live as if he did not matter means that the sole criterion for survival in this context is not Israelite ethnicity or nationality, but submission to and reconciliation with YHWH as king, as symbolized by the image of coming under his rule.

18. The last line of verse 17 (*The house of Jacob will repossess its possessions*) should be taken with verse 18. Its primary focus is restored Israel's repossession of its land, a topic to which verses

---

35. See the exhaustive discussion in Raabe 1996: 206–242.

36. The singular noun favours an abstract sense. Raabe (1996: 242) contends that when the noun is indefinite or does not connect to a grammatical element designating a people group, it is abstract, i.e. 'escape, deliverance'. Renkema (2003: 198) translates with the abstract 'escape' as well.

37. Renkema (2003: 200) is thus probably incorrect to limit the holiness to the city in the abstract. Note the same situation in similarly eschatological settings, e.g. Isa. 4:3; 25:6–8; 35:10. Obad. 17 indeed predicates that the *mountain* will be holy (or, with Block 2013: 90, 'there shall be holiness'), but this implies that the human beings who are there must also be holy, and in Obadiah sin is the only mechanism that separates sinners (especially Edom as characterized in vv. 2–14) from those who are holy (especially restored Judah as it is characterized in vv. 15–21).

19–20 will return. But in the light of Edom's implied residence in Judean territory, Edomites must first be expelled.[38] These lines present the dominance of YHWH's renewed people (in context, those who come to Mount Zion and submit to him) over the *house of Esau*, which throughout Obadiah has been defined as a sort of case study of proud, self-sufficient, violent humanity.[39]

19. The sub-unit made up of verses 19–21 brings to their peak God's twin commitments to judge sin and to deliver his people. The sixth-century struggle between Edom and Judah recedes before a comprehensive perspective that includes both local/national and global/international aspects. On the one hand, this sub-unit draws heavily on the conquest and settlement period in the early history of Israel, and so focuses on the 'possession' of the areas that make up the land promised to Abraham (cf. Gen. 15:7). On the other hand, the future repossession of the land that verses 19–20 present as a recapitulation of early Israel's settlement in the land is the outcome of the Day of YHWH against *all the nations* introduced in verse 15 and unpacked on a global level in verses 16–18. The geography of the world in verses 19–21 is thus presented in terms of Israel as the locus of YHWH's eschatological kingdom. This kingdom/world consists only of Mount Zion (v. 21, already defined by *escape* in v. 17) and what lies outside it (destruction, vv. 16, 18; note that Mount Esau is integrated in YHWH's kingdom, vv. 19, 21). The perspectives of verses 15–18 and 19–21 are thus complementary.

One key difference between the era of Joshua and this new era, complicated by the fact that Obadiah does not actually describe the

---

38. MT's 'their possessions' should probably be retained over against 'those who dispossessed them', but the difference between the two is minimal given the focus on Edom in the next verse. For arguments in favour of retaining the MT reading, see Renkema 2003: 202–203; for arguments to the contrary, see Gelston 2010: 91. Ben Zvi (1996: 189) prefers keeping both options open to maintain the ambiguity he sees at various points in the text.

39. Mason (2000: 591) speaks of Edom in this context as 'a symbol . . . of certain sinful human characteristics' and of such persons as having no place in YHWH's kingdom.

restoration of the people of God that occurs between the exile and the eschatological return he associates with the Day of YHWH, is the absence of sin from this new land/kingdom/world. In the Day of YHWH section (vv. 15–18), YHWH's righteous rule involves both destruction of sinful *nations* (v. 16), typified by the *house of Esau* (v. 18), and the rescue (*escape*) of an unidentified group that comes to Zion (v. 17), where holiness characterizes both city and people. In other words, the *sole criterion* for expulsion from, or participation in, God's kingdom is whether sin still separates one from him. By contrast, the Israel that entered Canaan was not without sin (recall Achan, Josh. 7), a fact to which the following few centuries under the judges bore witness. The reuse of the settlement period as a paradigm for Israel's eschatological restoration highlights continuity and development in terms of the divine promise of land, but significant discontinuity with respect to those who inhabit it.

A second important difference between past and future is the fact that the coming kingdom is emphatically YHWH's (v. 21). At the end of the book of Judges, Israel had fallen into a worsening spiral of egregious sin, the consequences of which entailed not only spiritual deadening but terribly destructive civil war. The author notes at several points, including the last verse of the book, that this was so because Israel did not have a king (Judg. 21:25). In Obadiah, by contrast, sin is absent from the repossessed land, including its population.

In verses 2–14, Obadiah focuses primarily on the presence (however temporary) of Edomites in Jerusalem and by extension in Judah.[40] Yet the geographic focus of verses 19–20 widens far beyond the southern kingdom to include the entire land promised to Abraham in all but the most extensive of its descriptions (cf. Gen. 15:18, 'from the River of Egypt to the great river, the river Euphrates'; also Gen. 28:14). Verse 19 presents the repossession of the land in terms of Judeans (all four groups that are subjects of the verb 'dis/possess' reside in Judean territory) taking control of areas that, seen from the vantage point of Judah, are to its south (*Esau*), west

---

40. As such, Edom's possession of Judah's land is a rejection of YHWH's allocation of it to his people (Anderson 2011: 191).

(*Philistines*), north (*Ephraim, Samaria*) and east (*Gilead*).[41] A schematic presentation of the text shows this clearly (terms implied but not grammatically present in the Hebrew text are in parentheses):

(Those in) the Negeb will possess	Mount Esau,
(Those in) the Shephelah (will dispossess)	the Philistines,
(Those in the Shephelah) will possess	the land[42] of Ephraim and the land of Samaria,
(Those in) Benjamin (will possess)	Gilead.[43]

20. Verse 20 presents a complementary view while adding further detail and emphasis. First, it states that northern (Israelite) and southern (Judean) *exiles* will repossess the land, implying their return, restoration and reunification (cf. Deut. 30:1–10; Ezek. 36:16–36; 37:15–28).[44] Second, naming regions at the extreme north and south of the historical land of Israel emphasizes the extent of renewed Israel's land.[45] Zarephath lies to the north of Tyre and outside Israelite territory proper. The Negeb refers to a triangular area with its southern point touching the Gulf of Aqaba (Eilat) and its sides extending north-west to the Mediterranean coast (at Rephiah) and north-east to the lower extremity of the Dead Sea (Rosen 1992: 1061). A schematic of the verse is helpful once again:

---

41. Raabe (1996: 258) also notes that v. 19 focuses on Judah.

42. Hebrew *śādeh* can be translated 'land' (*HALOT* 2.1307–1309).

43. Following some of the structural observations of Ben Zvi (1996: 201), and his critique of common alternatives (pp. 204–210).

44. Obad. 20a is the only element that includes northerners, who are, however, undoubtedly involved in the restoration of Israel/Judah due to the mention of *the house of Joseph* in v. 18. The emphasis here is thus not on their possible northern-Israel origin, but on their being *former* exiles, implying return and restoration (cf. Deut. 30:1–10).

45. It may also expand it somewhat, in light of Deut. 2:2–8.

The exiles of this territory[46]	(will possess) (among) the
of the Israelites	Canaanites as far as Zarephath,
The exiles of Jerusalem	will possess the cities of the
which are in Separda[47]	Negeb.

Although the word translated *Canaanites* (as in Neh. 9:24) can also mean 'traders' (Prov. 31:24), the prominence of the settlement period as a paradigm for Israel's restoration favours interpreting it as Canaanites here.[48] Since the Israelites (northern kingdom) were exiled only to Assyria, not to Canaanite territory, two possibilities exist in the light of the verse's problematic syntax. If it is read as 'The exiles of this territory of the Israelites (among) the Canaanites (will possess)', the reference is most likely to Israel's early loss of territory during the settlement period (a phenomenon notably limited to the northern tribe of Dan, Judg. 1:34–36).[49] If, more plausibly, it is read as 'The exiles of this territory of the Israelites (will possess) (among) the Canaanites', the reference would refer to Israelite exiles to Assyria, which complements nicely the focus on the southern kingdom in the next line.[50]

The *exiles of Jerusalem* can refer only to a southern (Judean) population, whose sole destination was Babylon. Several possible referents exist for the Hebrew text's *sĕpārad*. First, 'Shaparda' is mentioned in the annals of the Assyrian king Sargon II as one of

---

46. So Ben Zvi 1996: 220–221, based on the analogy of 1 Kgs 21:23. Contrast Renkema (2003: 211), who (like some others) reads 'Halach' here.

47. See the literature cited in Ben Zvi 1996: 212 n. 46.

48. Ben Zvi (1996: 222 n. 81) sees this reference as anticipating 'the language reminiscent of the period of the Judges in Obad 21'.

49. Ben Zvi's suggestion (1996: 224) that the possession of the cities of the Negeb not by those of the Negeb but by returned exiles is 'anomalous' fails to appreciate the unity of the restored people of God in Obadiah. The image is not of separate subgroups living in separate territories, but one people, made up of *currently dispersed* groups, being *reunited* in one land.

50. Raabe (1996: 262) includes the Babylonian deportations of Judah.

six regions in the easternmost part of his empire that he conquered in his sixth year (722–705, thus 716) (Diakanoff 1991: 16–17). This location coincides with the testimony of the book of Kings, which telescopes several Assyrian deportations of (northern kingdom) Israelites in 2 Kings 17:6; 18:11 as 'settling them in Halah, on the Habur, the river of Gozan and in the towns of the Medes' (Younger 1998: 215–224). However, it is difficult to harmonize what seems to be an explicit reference to exiles from Judah with a destination clearly associated with exiles from Israel.[51] Second, and more plausibly, Sardis, located in western Anatolia and the capital of the kingdom of Lydia during the seventh and sixth centuries, eventually became part of the Persian Empire that integrated the Babylonian Empire to which Judeans had been exiled.[52] Furthermore, it is referred to as Seph(a)rad in an inscription from the city's necropolis. It is thus more likely that Obadiah's reference anticipates (or reflects) the deportation of Judean exiles to Babylonia after 586, and later to Asia Minor.[53]

21. The focus on Zion and YHWH's kingship in verse 21 continues the conceptual overlap between the land-focused restoration sketched in verses 19–20 and the global Day of YHWH in verses 15–18. Verse 21 presents one more significant modification of an earlier paradigm, the covenant with David, and melds it with the two models of kingdom-establishment presented in verses 15–18 and verses 19–20. While God had committed to ruling his people through David and his descendants (2 Sam. 7), divine discipline could interrupt that vice-regency, as Judah's exile clearly shows. Furthermore, the Old Testament reminds the reader in various ways that the throne of Israel was and is YHWH's; he was and remains its only King (1 Sam. 8; 1 Kgs 3:7; 1 Chr. 28:5; 29:23;

---

51. Understanding Shaparda as the destination of the *exiles of Jerusalem* has some plausibility in the light of Obadiah's emphasis on renewed 'Israel' as including both the northern and southern kingdoms (cf. Jacob and Joseph in v. 18).

52. See Bryce 2012: 618. The identification of Seph(a)rad with a location in Spain is unlikely; see Pons 2014.

53. See Lipiński 1973: 368, 370.

Mal. 1:14). In the closing verse of Obadiah, YHWH's kingship realizes the hope expressed in the book of Judges for a king who could guide Israel in covenant obedience even as it transcends the hope for a merely human Davidide to rule YHWH's kingdom. This tension is evident in the presence of *saviours*[54] on Mount Zion who are involved in the administration of justice and perhaps deliverance but who do not share the royal role that belongs exclusively to YHWH: 'the dominion will belong to YHWH'.[55]

Perhaps the most surprising statement in the entire book is the assertion that these judge-like figures will bring (under God) justice and/or deliverance to Mount Esau. The context leaves little doubt that the Edomites who reside in this place have survived the Day of YHWH against the nations (contrast those who did not, in v. 18) and are now members of YHWH's kingdom (cf. Amos 9:11–12).[56] Their preservation, especially in a role that represents the nations, contrasts with the destruction of other non-Israelites in verse 16 and other Edomites in verse 18. Like the restored and returned exiles of Judah and Israel, these Edomites are in a radically new and different relationship with God and consequently with his people.

Meaning

The final section of Obadiah connects the local judgment against Edom to God's commitment to restore and deliver Israel, settling

---

54. There is no reason to modify MT in the light of LXX, especially because the reuse of the settlement period highlights connections to earlier 'saviours' such as Othniel (Judg. 3:9) and Ehud (3:15); Shamgar (3:31), Gideon (8:22), Tola (10:1), Samson (13:5, qualified by 'begin to') and YHWH (10:13) are all said to 'save' Israel (Heb. *yāšaʿ*), and all the judges were raised up by YHWH to 'save' Israel (2:16, 18). The root *šāpat* is also used in Judges of Othniel (3:10), Deborah (4:4), Tola (10:2), Jair (10:3), Jephthah (12:7–8) and others, and YHWH is 'the Judge' (11:27).

55. Block's translation (2013: 103), although he asserts that the 'saviours' rule (p. 102). Note a similar situation in Mic. 5:5–6, where YHWH's eschatological Davidic ruler 'delivers' restored Israel from Assyria with the cooperation of 'seven shepherds and eight princely men'.

56. The interpretation of Renkema (2003: 220) also moves in this direction.

them in his land and ruling over them there while simultaneously destroying their enemies and bringing his blessing to the nations through his restored people (Gen. 12:1–3; Pss 10:16; 22:27–28). The section sketches in bold colours the culmination of YHWH's worldwide exercise of judgment and deliverance in the Day of YHWH. With sinners removed from his temple-like kingdom, which is characterized by holiness, YHWH's reign is fully established over his purified and multi-ethnic people (Rom. 2:28–29), who inherit, as Abraham's seed, the kingdom that cannot be shaken (Heb. 11:10; 12:28).

JONAH

INTRODUCTION

The book of Jonah is a carefully constructed yet wonderfully simple and theologically powerful work. Its power is due to several features. It is set in the tumultuous eighth century BC, when the northern kingdom of Israel was for a time free from the menacing presence of Neo-Assyria and later saw that threat return stronger than before. The main character, the prophet Jonah, acts in extremely unusual ways that first subtly, and then explicitly, bring him into conflict with the very God who sent him to Nineveh. The non-Israelite characters, for their part, also act in very unusual ways that further reveal the character of all the actors: the sailors and Ninevites, Jonah, and God himself. All this is presented with humour, occasional sarcasm, and a focus that forces the book's reader to align himself or herself with the God of Israel, even if that means deconstructing a more comfortable, self-serving pseudo-theology.

1. Authorship and date

The book of Jonah is a narrative about the prophet whose name it bears rather than a collection of the prophet's oracles, as is the case with other prophetic books. The anonymous author reports that *the word of YHWH came to* Jonah, and always speaks of the prophet in the third person. It is of course possible that Jonah himself (assuming that after the events the book recounts he repented of the theology and behaviours that he displays in the book) wrote the book to challenge such views. However, since the book makes no claims as to its author, we must leave the question open.

In terms of the book's main character, we know very little about the prophet Jonah or of the precise dates of his ministry. His prophecy that Israel's territory would be restored was fulfilled during the reign of Jeroboam II (2 Kgs 14:25), and the lacklustre geopolitical situation that oracle addressed ties the prophecy to a period near the beginning of his reign (789–748 BC) (Provan, Long and Longman 2015: 328). The books of Jonah and Kings both identify the prophet as the son of Amittai, and the fact that both assign to Jonah the same father and the same (quite rare) role of prophet makes it essentially certain that they refer to the same individual. To this scarce data 2 Kings 14:25 adds that Gath-Hepher, a short distance to the west of the Sea of Galilee, was Jonah's home town.

Because the book is anonymous, we cannot establish the date of its composition in relation to the prophet, other than to say that the author wrote some time after Jonah had gone to Nineveh. The date of the book's composition must therefore be approximated on the basis of the book's language and message. A first type of linguistic evidence involves the book's use of words or meanings of words that are thought to have entered the Hebrew language after a particular point in time. For example, if Jonah contains a number of words or meanings drawn from or influenced by Aramaic, which became the lingua franca of the Levant from roughly the seventh century onwards, one might propose that the book was composed in the seventh century or later (Kaufman 1992: 173).[1] However, there are only a few examples of potential Aramaisms in the book, notably the verb 'think' in 1:6 and the noun 'edict' in 3:7. Since these and a few other examples are not part of a larger pattern in

---

1. In this section I draw on some of the arguments in Timmer (forthcoming b).

Jonah that would reflect consistent Aramaic influence on the author's language, their importance as a means of dating the book is rather limited (Stadel 2013: 162). This is all the more true since in the eighth century, Jonah's home town of Gath-Hepher was not far from nearby states where Aramaic was spoken (e.g. Aram/ Damascus) (Shitrit 2013: 165; Stadel 2013: 164), and the 'influence of Aramaic on Hebrew was exerted over a very long period' (Hendel and Joosten 2018: 83).

Evidence based on the appearance of new (later) meanings for existing (older) words is also quite rare in Jonah, and is disputed.[2] Similarly, some argue that a word such as 'journey/visit' in 3:4 is late since (in that case) it appears elsewhere only in Nehemiah 2:6, Ezekiel 42:4 and perhaps Zechariah 3:7 (Muldoon 2010: 53; *HALOT* 1.552). One must ask, however, how to determine the earliest date at which a word entered the Hebrew of a particular author. If we assume initially that Ezekiel was the first to use it (early sixth century), why could not someone else have used it before Ezekiel? Since recent research on the development of Biblical Hebrew has not clearly settled the question of how to distinguish the classical Biblical Hebrew that an eighth-century author would have used from later stages of the language elsewhere in the canon, these linguistic details do not provide a satisfactory basis for dating the book either.[3]

Syntax, the relation of words and groups of words in a text to one another, offers another kind of data. Since syntax involves large-scale, supra-verbal relationships, its data comes from numerous points in the text and can provide a better overall impression of the text's linguistic profile when data based on individual words is not readily available. It is therefore notable that the syntax of Jonah

---

2. The argument for a later date on this basis is made by Day (1990): 34–36. Contrast the arguments against this conclusion by Landes (1982).

3. Hendel and Joosten (2018: 82) classify the Hebrew of Jonah as transitional. For arguments against dating biblical texts on linguistic grounds, see Young, Rezetko and Ehrensvärd 2008. For arguments to the contrary, see Moshavi and Notarius 2017.

reflects the syntax of classical (pre-exilic) Biblical Hebrew.[4] While it is possible for later scribes to have made a text seem (superficially) older than it is by using earlier terms and expressions, this kind of archaizing is easily detected (Schniedewind 2005: 383). By contrast, it is much more difficult for a later scribe to mimic the syntax of an older stage of language (Joosten 2005: 329). Since the syntax of the book of Jonah as a whole is clearly early, while the evidence tied to individual words is relatively isolated and less widespread, the weight of the evidence favours dating the book's composition before Judah's exile in 586.

Jonah's message, which is inseparable from the Neo-Assyrian Empire, presents a different sort of information that sheds light on the most likely time for the book's composition. Since this empire flourished from the late ninth to the late seventh century, its prominence in the book argues for dating its composition to that period or shortly thereafter. It is of course possible to write historically (that is, significantly later) of Neo-Assyria or another empire, but it is a quite different thing to do so in a way that captures accurately the empire's unique historical and ideological profile.[5] Since Assyria had posed a danger to the northern kingdom since as early as the battle of Qarqar in 853, when Ahab contributed '2,000 chariots, (and) 10,000 troops',[6] the punch of Jonah's story would be felt most keenly by an audience familiar with Neo-Assyria, whether in the northern or southern kingdom. This argument cannot by itself rule out the possibility that the book was composed later. It does, however, reinforce the linguistic data that favour a pre-exilic date for the book's composition.

---

4. 'If, as is usually assumed, Jonah is a late composition imitating the language of the 8th century prophet whose name it bears, one has to say that the imitation is superb from the point of view of syntax' (Niccacci 1996: 32).

5. See, for Assyria, Liverani 2017; for Babylon, Vanderhooft 1999; and for Persia, Ehrenberg 2008.

6. From the Kurkh Monolith of Shalmaneser III, inscribed shortly after the battle of Qarqar in 853. See Younger 2003a.

2. Historical setting

There is no doubt that the book of Jonah is set in the Neo-Assyrian period, and more specifically in the early or mid eighth century (cf. 2 Kgs 14:25). By this time, the Assyrian Empire had existed in various forms for roughly one thousand years. After the empire's 'old' and 'middle' stages, the Neo-Assyrian Empire arose near the end of the tenth century under Ashur-Dan II (934–912 BC) (Grayson 1992a). His military campaigns pursued the recovery of territory lost to the Arameans to Assyria's south-west, and so brought Assyria into the Levant and into proximity to Israel. Assyria's movement towards Israel continued during the reign of Adad-Nirari (911–891), who extended the empire's control to its north-west (modern Turkey) in an effort to establish reliable access to natural resources (Saggs 1984: 71). By the time of Shalmaneser III (858–824), Assyria's reach extended all the way to Israel, and it was able to compel Tyre, Sidon and 'Jehu (the man) of Bit-Humri (Omri)'[7] to become the empire's vassals. In this role these states functioned rather like provinces of the empire while retaining limited political independence. They were expected to contribute soldiers to its campaigns and to make regular payments (precious metals or other goods) to the royal treasuries, failing which they would be susceptible to severe punishments, including military invasion and deportation of the population. The Black Obelisk, from the time of Shalmaneser, shows Jehu or his representative bowing before the Assyrian king during a diplomatic visit in which such taxes were paid.[8]

Assyria's military might and calculated use of brutality made rebellion a very dangerous option for its vassals.[9] The empire's

---

7. The Black Obelisk epigraphs read: 'I received tribute from Jehu (Iaua) of Omri (Humri): silver, gold, a gold bowl, a gold tureen, golden vessels, gold pails, tin, the staffs of the king's hand, (and) spears' (Grayson 1996: text 8).

8. Images of the obelisk are available in the 'Collection online' at the British Museum, <https://www.britishmuseum.org/collection/search?title=The%20Black%20Obelisk>.

9. See Fuchs 2011, esp. pp. 396–399.

force and tactics were guided by a royal ideology that laid upon the king the obligation to subjugate the entire world on behalf of the national god Assur, who was at the summit of the Assyrian pantheon and so laid claim to worldwide rule. In short, 'It was the king's duty to explore, overcome, and incorporate [all non-Assyrian territories] into the realm of Ashur' (Parker 2011: 363). In this ideology, the Assyrian king's warfare brought to reality the kingship of Assur and led to the only stable social order.[10] Non-Assyrian states that resisted peaceful or coerced subjugation to the empire were thus believed to be in direct opposition to the empire's gods, and so merited the sharpest reprisals.[11]

This religiously based strategy of imperialism was solidly in place by the early ninth century, as the annals of Shalmaneser III (858–824) show. In his 'throne inscription', he introduces himself in typical fashion as

> the legitimate king, the king of the world, the king without rival, the 'Great Dragon', the (only) power within the (four) rims (of the earth), overlord of all the princes, who has smashed all his enemies as if (they be) earthenware, the strong man, unsparing, who shows no mercy in battle.
> (Oppenheim 1969: 276)

In an inscription dedicated to the events of his first year on the throne, he recounts his victory over Ahuni and the town of Bur-mar'ana in these terms: 'I stormed and conquered (it). I slew with the sword 300 of their warriors. Pillars of skulls I erec[ted in front of the town]'. His taking of the fortified town of Lutibu develops the emphasis on violence further:

> I inflicted a defeat upon them. I slew their soldiers with the sword, descending upon them like Adad when he makes a rainstorm pour down. In the moat (of the town) I piled them up, I covered the wide plain with the corpses of their fighting men, I dyed the mountains

---

10. Following Crouch 2009: 27.
11. See Fales 1982: 425–435.

with their blood like red wool . . . I erected pillars of skulls in front
of his town, destroyed his (other) towns, tore down (their walls) and
burnt (them) down.
(Oppenheim 1969: 277)

In a similar way, bas-reliefs in the palace of Assurnasirpal (883–
859) at Nimrud present the king overseeing the attack against the
enemy.[12] The key themes of these bas-reliefs connect the ideology
of kingship discussed above with the well-being of the empire.[13]

As the overly optimistic account of the 853 BC battle of Qarqar
by Shalmaneser III reports, Israelite troops encountered Assyrian
violence on the battlefield, although additional campaigns in later
years were required to solidify Assyria's control of the area.[14] Israel
eventually became an Assyrian vassal in 841, and this status continued intermittently into the early eighth century (Provan, Long
and Longman 2015: 358, 360). In addition to these administrative and
political measures, Assyrian ideology and presence were mediated
by stelae placed along routes that Israelite envoys travelled on their
way to deliver tribute (Aster 2007: 22–23), Assyrian ideology was
reflected in early prophetic literature such as Isaiah (Machinist 1983),
and Assyrian motifs eventually appeared on seventh-century Judean
material culture (Ahlström 1984). These various avenues of transmission make it likely that Assyrian ideology was not unfamiliar to
some of the Israelite population by the time of Jonah's ministry.
Indeed, Jonah's refusal of YHWH's call to go to Assyria, and his fear
that Nineveh might somehow experience divine mercy and patience,
makes clear that he was fairly well aware of Assyria's ideologically
driven violence against Israel and other states in the Levant.

---

12. See the digital reconstruction of this palace at 'Digital Reconstruction
    of the Northwest Palace, Nimrud, Assyria', Metropolitan Museum of
    Art, <https://www.metmuseum.org/metmedia/video/collections/
    ancient-near-eastern-art/northwest-palace-nimrud>, and the
    discussion of the bas-reliefs in Cohen and Kangas 2010.
13. Russell (1998: 663) identifies the themes as 'military success, service
    to the gods, divine protection, and Assyrian prosperity'.
14. Oppenheim 1969: 279. See further the discussion in Younger 2007.

Our tentative dating of Jonah's ministry to the early or middle part of the eighth century suggests that he prophesied the renewal of Israel's control over its northern territories before that came about later in the reign of Jeroboam II. Although we do not know how long his ministry lasted, it is plausible to assume that he travelled to Nineveh around the same time, meaning near the middle of the eighth century. This period would have been a particularly opportune moment for Nineveh's population to respond to a threat of divine judgment, for several reasons.

First, during roughly the period covered by the reign of Jeroboam II, the Assyrian Empire suffered from internal instability and a degree of political disintegration. In the last few decades of the ninth century, revolts had delayed and jeopardized the coming to the throne of Shamshi-Adad V (823–811) (Kuhrt 1995: 490). During the first half of the eighth century, a handful of magnates and regional rulers controlled the various regions of the empire, but the status quo was one of maintaining and defending the empire rather than expanding it as before (Saggs 1984: 82). Saggs notes that three of these 'over-mighty governors' left records of their political and military exploits in the same way that Assyrian monarchs had done. Šamaš-resh-usur, governor of Suhu and Mari, recounts that he was the first to establish beekeeping, and that he understood 'how to do the melting out of the honey and wax' and wanted to be remembered as the one who 'introduced bees' (Saggs 1984: 83). Another regional governor, Šamši-ilu, decorated his palace with two large lion sculptures that resembled the leonine images that represented the Assyrian king (Weissert 1997) and adapted the literary style of Assyrian royal annals for his own inscriptions (Younger 2003b).

In addition to the interruption of the imperial project that this political fragmentation produced, Assyria suffered a series of misfortunes near the middle of the eighth century, being 'plagued by epidemics, famines, revolts and succession problems for almost forty years' (Kuhrt 1995: 492).[15] These events, individually and

---

15. The eponym list for the ninth year of Ashur-Dan III (772–755, thus 763) records an eclipse, interpretations of which typically predicted

especially when taken together, would have been interpreted as signs of coming disaster, making Jonah's threat of judgment quite plausible.[16] This reduces, if only a little, the surprise the modern reader might feel when reading of the city's readiness to take seriously a message of divine judgment from a novel source.

3. Genre, structure and unity

a. Genre
The literary genre of the book of Jonah has long been debated. The debate is not merely academic, for the genre which the reader assigns to Jonah (consciously or not) determines how it is read and thus what it means.[17] Some propose that it is like a comedy because of its depictions of the ridiculous behaviour of the prophet and the surprising reactions of the sailors and Ninevites.[18] Others take it as a parable (i.e. non-historical), with Jonah representing Israel and the sailors and Assyrians representing non-Israelites,[19] that critiques Israelite attitudes towards foreigners and an unhealthy pride in their status as God's chosen people. In some cases, these suggestions are also driven by the conviction that it is impossible that Jonah could have survived 'three days' in the entrails of a large fish. We will first consider the primary objections to reading the book as a historical narrative, then consider the plausibility of

---

the death of the king, the taking of the throne by 'a worthless fellow', floods, or devastation of the land by the gods; cf. Wiseman 1979: 46, 50, with reference to the *Enuma Anu Enlil* series of omens.

16. Popular sentiments resembled these more official religious gestures. A text representing unofficial or personal religion, found in Nineveh and Assur and dated from the century after Jonah, contains 'prayers for appeasing the heart of an angry god' and asks that the god's 'heart [might] rest and that the god would be reconciled to me'; see Hays 2016: 71–72.

17. See the extensive literature and interpretative choices in Goswell 2016: 283 n. 1.

18. For example, Schart 2012.

19. For example, Allen 1976: 175–181; Schellenberg 2015.

reading the book as something other than a humorous, genuinely unusual, but factual historical narrative.

Over the last few centuries modern thought has come to a settled rejection of the supernatural in general (Byrne 1997: 230–231) and of supernatural causation in historical reconstruction in particular, meaning anything that would break the sequence of (natural, material) cause and effect (Iggers and Wang 2008: 22–23). However, it was very much the norm in the Ancient Near East to assume that the divine world was connected to and present in the physical world.[20] We must therefore recognize that an anti-supernatural reading of Jonah goes against the grain of the text and (if the book is indeed a historical narrative) rejects its most important truth claims by removing God from the scene.[21]

There are also indications in the book itself that favour reading it as a genuine historical narrative.[22] The historical nature of God's call to Jonah to prophesy in 1:1 is comparable to other calls to prophetic activity that are part of historical literature elsewhere in the Old Testament. These include cases in which the sending is followed by supernatural events that confirm the authenticity of the prophet (Moses to the Israelites, Exod. 3:7–10; 4:27–31; Moses to Pharaoh, Exod. 7:1–5; Elisha to Ahab, 1 Kgs 17:1–16), as well as cases without immediate miraculous confirmation (Jehu to Baasha, 1 Kgs 16:1–4; Isaiah before Ahaz, Isa. 6 – 7; Jeremiah to Judah, Jer. 1:4–10).[23]

The nature of God's intervention in history in the book of Jonah also presents nothing that is without precedent elsewhere in the Old Testament. In addition to calling a prophet to prophesy, God

---

20. See, for example, Bottero 2001: 58–77.

21. The prominence of the apparently supernatural in Jonah thus relativizes the importance of non-supernatural anecdotes which demonstrate the possibility of surviving ingestion by a whale. Fox (1924) records that a sailor who fell overboard from a whaling vessel survived approximately twenty-four hours in a whale before being extracted when the whale was captured.

22. See the additional arguments brought by Alexander (1985).

23. This paragraph develops a briefer argument by Alexander (1988: 76).

controls the forces of nature (the storm in 1:4; cf. rain in 1 Kgs 18:41–46), tells the prophet what to say (Jon. 1:2; cf. God's instructions to Elijah, 1 Kgs 21:17–19), repeats the call to prophesy (Jon. 3:1; cf. God's command to Elijah at Horeb, 1 Kgs 19:15–18), and carries on a veritable dialogue with the prophet that brings to light issues of fundamental importance for God's purposes through the prophet (Jon. 4:1–11; cf. Elijah and God in 1 Kgs 19:9–14; Moses and God in Exod. 33:13–23). Furthermore, in distinction from the invented characters that appear in parables, which are typically much shorter than the book of Jonah, Jonah's home town and most notably his father are identified in 2 Kings 14:25.[24] Jesus' statement to the scribes and Pharisees that they would witness only the 'sign of Jonah' (Matt. 12:38–42) compares his time in the grave to Jonah's time in the fish (12:40) and Jonah's ministry to his own, which is 'greater' (12:41). It also affirms that the Ninevites repented in response to Jonah's preaching (12:41) and that they would rise up and condemn Jesus' generation in the judgment alongside the 'queen of the South' (12:42), whose presence in Israel's history is unequivocally affirmed in 1 Kings 10.

Taken together, these considerations give the reader of Jonah good reason to understand the book as a historical narrative. The elements of humour, sarcasm and surprise that the book shows hardly overturn this classification, whether one compares it with narratives elsewhere in the Old Testament or with later historical literature.

b. Structure and unity

The structure and unity of the book of Jonah are interrelated. As is the case with all literary works, readers have discerned a variety of structures in the book of Jonah. With few exceptions, these proposals are not mutually exclusive, and demonstrate the various ways in which the different parts of this short book are interconnected rather than undermining each other. Here we will briefly

---

24. Setting aside 'parables-as-proverbs', genuine parables in the OT include Judg. 9:7–15; 2 Sam. 12:1–4; 14:4–7; 2 Kgs 14:9; Isa. 5:1–6; Ezek. 15:1–5; 17:3–10; cf. Crossan 1992.

discuss a variety of structural elements as they relate to the book's unity.

First, the book of Jonah naturally falls into two parts, each of which is introduced by God's call to the prophet to go to Nineveh (1:1; 3:1).[25] These sections have similar (although not identical) structures: God calls the prophet to go to Nineveh, Jonah travels (away from, or towards, that destination), Jonah's interaction with non-Israelites leads to striking religious change among them, and Jonah prays to God in a way that reveals radical self-centredness (Alexander 1988: 68).

Attention to the narrative dynamics of each half of the book reveals this same structure, with one notable modification. In both halves, the stage is set (1:1–4a; 3:1–3b) and a 'pre-peak episode' brings God's mercy to the foreground (1:4b–17b; 3:3c–10) before the 'peak episode' develops that focus further in relation to Jonah (1:17c – 2:10; 4:1–4) (Youngblood 2019: 43–45). This rhetorical structure suggests that 4:5–11 can be seen as a separate section in which an object lesson permits a closer analysis of the book's main event: the demonstration of God's rich mercy to Nineveh, and of the prophet's unprecedented reaction to it.

The correspondence between the two halves of the book not only highlights its unity; it promotes comprehension of the whole by encouraging the reader to compare elements in the two parts of the book.[26] For example, the contrasting responses to the divine calls in 1:1 and 3:1 invite the reader to wonder what prompts Jonah to comply with the divine command in 3:1, especially in the light of 4:2. Again, the positive responses of the sailors to Jonah's few words invite comparison with the Ninevites' repentance in chapter 3. These connections at the level of plot elements are complemented by a plethora of connections at the level of individual words and phrases that pepper the book.[27]

---

25. The statement in 3:1 that the call there is the *second time* demands that the two halves of the book be seen in chronologically interrelated 'chapters' in the life of Jonah.

26. Wendland 2014, with a summary on p. 245.

27. See Magonet 1976: 13–38; Wilt 1992; Wendland 2014.

Most critiques of the book's unity focus on the prayer or psalm in chapter 2.[28] A number of interpreters have argued that it fits poorly in its context because it presents the prophet as pious rather than rebellious, or because much of the psalm's vocabulary does not appear elsewhere in the book, or simply because such a lengthy poetic section supposedly jars with its narrative context. Here the observations above regarding the book's structure are helpful, not least because they remind us that a coherent work need not be flat, woodenly repetitive or without complexity. The contrast between the prophet's self-presentation as pious in Jonah 2 invites comparison with the disobedient prophet of chapter 1 and with the vociferous prophet of chapter 4. Such comparison enriches the interpretation of the book, as we shall see, rather than presenting the reader with contradictory characterizations of the prophet. The different vocabulary of the psalm is almost inevitable in the light of its nature as poetry, and is heavily indebted to several biblical psalms, notably Psalms 31, 42, 69 and 107.[29] These parallels invite the reader to compare Jonah's prayer with those of the psalmists, and to compare the prophet with them (Timmer 2011: 87–88; Timmer forthcoming a). Finally, the objection that the psalm as poetry fits poorly with its surrounding narrative frame can be dismissed as arbitrary, not least because other biblical narratives include similarly significant poems (e.g. Gen. 49:2–27; Exod. 15:1–18; Deut. 32:1–43; 33:1–29; Judg. 5:2–31; 1 Sam. 2:1–10; 2 Sam. 22:2–51).[30]

These considerations vindicate the evangelical commitment to take Scripture as a whole, and its individual books, as rich, varied but ultimately unified compositions in the light of their ultimate authorship by the same God. In what follows, the following structure will guide our discussion, and reflects the book's unity and complexity (notice the unique element 'D' in the second part of the book).[31]

---

28. Landes (1967) summarizes a century or more of such arguments.

29. See Magonet 1976: 44–50, 65–84; Kim 2007; Noegel 2015.

30. For further development of some of the points made here, see Vaillancourt 2015.

31. This structure reflects especially the reasoning of Wendland (1996: 373), but also that of Youngblood (2019: 43–45), as noted above.

ANALYSIS

1. FIRST COMMISSION, DIVINE MERCY TO NON-ISRAELITES, JONAH'S RESPONSE (1:1 – 2:10)

   A. First divine commission and Jonah's disobedience (A) (1:1–3)

   B. Jonah and the non-Israelite sailors (B) (1:4–16)

   C. Jonah's deliverance and response/prayer (C) (1:17 – 2:10 [Heb. 2:1–11])

2. SECOND COMMISSION, DIVINE MERCY TO NON-ISRAELITES, JONAH'S RESPONSE (3:1 – 4:11)

   A. Second divine commission and Jonah's obedience (A') (3:1–3a)

   B. Jonah and the Ninevites (B') (3:3b–10)

   C. Nineveh's deliverance and Jonah's response/prayer (C') (4:1–4)

   D. YHWH contests Jonah's response (D) (4:5–11)

COMMENTARY

1. FIRST COMMISSION, DIVINE MERCY TO NON-ISRAELITES, JONAH'S RESPONSE (1:1 – 2:10)

A. First divine commission and Jonah's disobedience (A) (1:1–3)

Context

The book opens by introducing its principal human character – the prophet Jonah – and one of the two primary theological issues the book will explore: God's relationship to non-Israelites. This short section's statement that Nineveh was an *evil* city would have surprised none of its Israelite hearers or readers, but the same cannot be said for the prophet's response to YHWH's call. The opening verses of the book thus also present, more mysteriously, a second theological issue of central importance: what explains Jonah's decision to disobey God's command? The unit follows the conventions of standard Biblical Hebrew narrative, including the narrator's tendency to simply report events without explicitly commenting upon them.

Comment

1. As noted above, the book opens with a typical prophetic commission (cf. 2 Sam. 7:4; 24:11; 1 Kgs 12:22; 21:17; elsewhere in the Minor Prophets, Hos. 1:1; Joel 1:1; Mic. 1:1; Zeph. 1:1; Hag. 1:1; Zech. 1:1). In addition to identifying Jonah as a de facto prophet, this command carries divine authority and so obliges him to accept it. The identification of Jonah as *the son of Amittai* identifies him as the same prophet as the Jonah of 2 Kings 14:25. That connection highlights YHWH's compassion for the northern kingdom (2 Kgs 14:26–27), and echoes his compassion for Israel in slavery in Egypt (Deut. 26:7).

Although *the word of* YHWH is the normal way to introduce a prophetic call, in Jonah that divine name is also integrated in the author's careful use of different divine names in order to highlight human beings' relational distance from, or nearness to, God. The book of Jonah uses *YHWH* to express close relationship to the God of Israel, thus on the part of Jonah (1:9) but also (and more genuinely) on the part of the sailors (1:14, 16). The more generic term or title *God*, on the other hand, is used to refer to a false deity (1:5–6) or to the God of Israel whom the Ninevites come to know in some measure (3:5, 8, 9, 10). The fact that this careful use of different divine names corresponds to developments in the story illustrates one of the many ways in which diversity can enrich, rather than detract from, the coherence of the narrative (Lichtert 2003).

2. In 1:2 YHWH orders Jonah to go to Nineveh, *the large* [*gādôl*] *city*, and to call out *against it* because of its *evil* (*rā'*). The author of Jonah uses the terms 'large/great' and 'evil' with precision, as our exploration of the book will show, but only here and in 4:1 (with a different form of the same root) are they used together. This, along with the fact that God himself utters this very negative evaluation of one of Assyria's key cities, highlights its religious and moral degradation and the consequent danger of divine judgment.

This straightforward statement of the city's uncertain future would have seemed quite improbable to some of the book's original audience, and much more so to Assyrians (without forgetting the ominous nature of the calamities that befell parts of Assyria near the middle of the eighth century). Perhaps most importantly, since the late third millennium Nineveh was home to a temple of

Ishtar, an important goddess associated especially with love, fertility, storm and war.[1] That temple 'dominated' the hill at the city's centre, measuring roughly 300 × 150 feet (Reade 2005: 347, 365). As the location of Ishtar's throne, this temple was adorned by a number of stone monuments and alabaster wall panels portraying lion hunts in which Ishtar's help aided the king in vanquishing these symbols of chaos and danger, and was complemented by an impressive ziggurat (Reade 2005: 374, 378, 384). Nineveh's importance was further augmented by its having been a royal residence since the time of Shalmaneser I (1273–1244 BC) (Stronach and Codella 1996: 146). In the light of these and other factors, its size gradually increased over time, and by the early to mid eighth century it covered roughly 1230 acres (Grayson 1992b: 1119). Its size and religious and political importance probably account for Sennacherib's decision to make it the empire's capital city as of 705.

YHWH's condemnation of Nineveh and prediction of its downfall thus stand in tension with its illustrious past and present. Any who failed to recognize YHWH's unique deity would understandably wonder what, if anything, such a city had to fear from the deity of a distant, comparatively minuscule country like Israel. This tension is linked to another surprising dynamic in the book: God's willingness to show mercy to the undeserving. This appears first in his willingness to spare the sailors' lives, and then Jonah's life, and comes fully into view with his decision to rescind Nineveh's punishment once it repents.

3. Without explanation or evaluation, the narrator follows YHWH's command to Jonah in 1:2 with the statement in 1:3 that he rose up to *flee from the presence of YHWH* by heading to Tarshish, an evidently distant location somewhere in the Mediterranean (perhaps in modern Spain) (Baker 1992). As noted earlier, Jonah is the only prophet in the Old Testament who reacts to a divine commission in this way. The reader needs to wait until chapter 4 to discover the cause, but surely knows already that something is amiss – how can the prophet hope to escape YHWH's presence?

---

1. Gut, Reade and Boehmer 2001: 74–75. Abusch (1999: 452–456), describes Ishtar's variegated identity.

As a northerner, Jonah cannot intend to flee from the temple, which was located in Judah. It is more likely that he associated God's presence (only) with the promised land. Not only did the land of Israel 'belong' to YHWH (Lev. 25:23), but his presence in it meant that Israel's sin could render the land unclean and so jeopardize Israel's presence in it (Lev. 18:24–30) (Millar 2000). While believing that YHWH's deity was a reality only in the promised land reveals a deeply flawed and reductionist view of who YHWH is, Jonah confesses in 1:9 that YHWH made both the sea and the dry land. How might we explain these contradictory positions? Jonah's decision to flee from God's presence could be the bitter fruit of flawed theology if the confession of 1:9 is 'by rote' and mere 'dead orthodoxy'. The reality was probably more complex, however. Considering his prayer in chapter 2, it seems that Jonah's knowledge of YHWH is selective, since there YHWH's power is clearly not limited to the land of Israel. Returning to chapter 1, it would seem that Jonah chooses to ignore that reality, deceiving himself in order to create a way out. When confronted with an unacceptable divine command, flight seems possible (even if a one-in-a-million chance). When that attempt fails, Jonah undertakes still more desperate measures, as we will see.

Whatever the precise contours of his mental and spiritual states, Jonah does the only thing he thinks he can. He first makes his way to Joppa, a port that lay some 70 miles to the south-west of his home town (Kaplan and Kaplan 1992). There he finds a boat heading west, pays his fare (or perhaps books the ship itself; the text says he *paid its hire*) and goes below board for the trip.[2] The author repeats the prophet's intention to escape YHWH's presence, certainly a means of ridiculing Jonah's benighted scheme. This is the first, but certainly not the last, humorous element in the book.

Meaning
On one level, the meaning of this section is self-evident: the prophet Jonah, called to deliver a message of judgment against the prominent Assyrian city of Nineveh, refuses and attempts to flee from

---

2. On the question of the fare paid, see Youngblood 2019: 59.

YHWH's presence. No mystery attends YHWH's decision to have Jonah *cry out against* Nineveh considering its misdeeds, but the same cannot be said for the prophet's rejection of his call, a response attested nowhere else in the Old Testament. Thus, on another level lurk several questions which can be answered only in the light of the rest of the book, especially the reason for Jonah's disobedience. At this stage the reader suspects something is gravely wrong, both because Jonah disobeys a direct command from YHWH and because he seeks to flee from his presence. A final question concerns the role of Jonah in the story: what is the reader meant to learn from him? These questions, and still others, can be answered only by continuing to follow Jonah as he makes his way westwards.

B. Jonah and the non-Israelite sailors (B) (1:4–16)

Context
This unit explores both issues raised in the opening verses (God's relationship to non-Israelites and the cause of the prophet's mysterious disobedience), but provides clarity only on the former, leaving the latter for the end of the book. Jonah and the non-Israelite mariners are clearly meant to contrast sharply with one another in generally religious terms, but the author masterfully inverts this contrast over the course of the events he recounts so as to partially illuminate Jonah's state of heart and to show conclusively that non-Israelites are not excluded from God's gracious purposes. As is the case throughout the book, the author makes frequent use of humour, satire and irony in his presentations of the human characters.

As is the case with the book as a whole, this passage has been shown to have a number of structural levels or patterns, most of which identify 1:9–10 as its centre.[3] In what follows, we will note the most significant structural features without choosing one structure as definitive.

---

3. Magonet (1976: 57) sees a concentric structure bounded by the pattern of narrative, direct speech and prayer in 1:4–5a and 1:15–16.

Comment

4. The Hebrew syntax at the beginning of 1:4 indicates a break in the series of actions that began with Jonah 'rising' in 1:3. The purpose of the break is to introduce a new actor, who is none other than God. Whatever the reader might have made of Jonah's attempted flight in 1:3, this makes clear that it was futile. The author describes God's insurmountable interruption of Jonah's attempt to flee his commission in strong language: he *hurled a great* [*gādôl*] *wind* onto the ocean. The severity of the resulting storm threatens to break the ship apart, and so endangers the lives of all on board.

5. Rather than resolving this crisis right away, the narrator shifts the reader's attention first to the non-Israelite sailors, and through them to Jonah, before bringing both of those parties into relation to God as he reveals the outcome of this terrifying situation. The actions of the mariners are unsurprising, particularly because mariners in the Ancient Near East associated control of the sea with one or more gods. In the case of Ugarit, a city-state on the Mediterranean located roughly 250 miles north of Joppa that flourished in the period of about 1750–1190 BC, a temple of Baal easily visible from sea contained seventeen stone anchors (Yon 1999: 260; Smith 2016: 148–150). This reflects the belief of some mariners of the ancient Mediterranean that Baal controlled the seas, and thus held their fate in his hands.[4]

This situation is the first of a number of suggestive correspondences between Jonah and the Psalms, in this case Psalm 107, where sailors in similar circumstances cry out to YHWH (cf. Ps. 107:23, 25, 28–29).[5] At this point, although the sailors were looking to the

---

4. Levine and de Tarragon (1993: 109) explain that 'Upon his victory [over Yamm], Baal became ruler of the sea, not only of the heavens; he had become the deity to be worshiped by seafarers. The collection of anchors adorning the temple of Baal testifies to the temple's function both as lighthouse of sorts, guiding sailors to the shore, and as their safe haven, the residence of their protector deity, Baal.'

5. The narrative moves in the same order as parts of Ps. 107; cf. Timmer 2011: 68.

wrong deity for help, Jonah was not looking for help at all! Quite surprisingly, in the same way that he disappeared below deck as soon as he boarded (1:3), he remains not only out of sight, but in a sleep so profound that it is undisturbed by the chaos that has been unleashed around him! The author describes Jonah's condition as a state of 'stupor' or 'unconsciousness' in which Jonah is not only unaware of what is happening around him, but (as the text shows) unlikely to awake.[6] This almost incredible situation underlines Jonah's lack of concern for his own well-being and that of the crew as well as his radically stunted perception on all levels (Timmer 2011: 69).

6. The captain's terrified question in 1:6, which one must imagine involved shaking the prophet awake, confirms that Jonah's behaviour is inexplicable: *What are you doing sleeping?* He urges the prophet to follow the crew's example and to petition his (personal) *god* so that all those on board (*perhaps*) might be delivered from what appears to be a watery grave. Although arguments from silence must be handled with care, the fact that Jonah never prays during this sequence of events seems to confirm that he has no intention of dealing with YHWH, from whose gaze he hopes to escape. It also reveals a shocking lack of concern for the lives of those on board with him, a hint that his response to Nineveh's deliverance will amplify enormously.

7. The focus shifts from the silent prophet back to the sailors. As the storm continues to rage, they and the reader realize that their gods are either unwilling or unable to deliver them. Their decision to cast lots reveals, furthermore, that they now suspect that the storm has been sent as a punishment for the sin of one among them. Even though these sailors do not even know of YHWH's existence yet, he uses this means of determining guilt to draw attention to Jonah. The reader knows that Jonah has sinned in rejecting the divine commission and attempting to flee from God, but it is far from certain that God sent the storm as punishment for Jonah's sin. Only in 3:1–2, however, does the reader

---

6. See the root's other uses in Gen. 2:21; 15:12; Judg. 4:21; Ps. 76:6; Prov. 10:5; 19:15.

learn that YHWH's goal was to interrupt Jonah's flight and redirect him to Nineveh.

8. In 1:8 the sailors infer (correctly) that Jonah's *evil* (the same word as in 1:2) has brought the storm upon them, and they assume that Jonah knows this to be so. Although their questions seem to touch randomly on various domains of Jonah's life, and presumably reflect their alarm, the questions are probably intended to draw out which god or gods are behind the punishment (Youngblood 2019: 80).

9. Jonah's response goes in this direction, but the author significantly relegates his admission of guilt to a comment at the end of 1:10. By first quoting other elements of Jonah's reply in direct speech, the focus is placed on what the wayward prophet (and the author, for different reasons) considered most relevant or important.

Jonah mentions his ethnicity first, and then his religious identity, probably equating the two (i.e. being a Hebrew means revering YHWH).[7] Jonah's description of his religious identity is the first time that the sailors hear the name YHWH, and the events that follow reveal to them a faint outline of the same saving character that accompanied the revelation of that name to Israel in Egypt (cf. Exod. 6:7).[8] But more immediately, his response invites the reader to return to the questions that were already raised by the prophet's unexpected disobedience of the divine command to go to Nineveh.

To begin with, Jonah's true claim that YHWH made *the sea and the dry land* jars with his attempt to flee from such a deity, whose power and knowledge cannot be limited to a particular part of the globe.[9] Second, his insistence that he *reveres* YHWH, a standard way of expressing holistic and genuine piety in the Old Testament, is clearly incompatible with his behaviour. Thus, while his statement regarding his ethnicity is true, both of his theological statements

---

7. The interplay of ethnic and religious identity in the book of Jonah is discussed in Timmer (2013).

8. See further the comments of Stuart 2006: 169–173.

9. Note the other contexts in which this description with heaven, sea and sky occurs, as tabulated by Wendland (1996: 390).

(*I revere* YHWH . . . *who made* . . .) seem to be nothing more than theological formulas that he has memorized but never internalized.

10. As far as these truths seem from affecting Jonah, their significance for the sailors is readily apparent. Jonah's claim that YHWH, the sole creator of the cosmos, has authority over all that exists completes the removal of their mute and impotent gods from the scene. The statement that YHWH is *the God of the heavens* also challenged the sailors' existing religious convictions, specifically with respect to the weather, which they would attribute to a storm god such as Baal Shamem.[10] This monotheistic note is strengthened by another example of resonance with the Psalter. The phrase *made the sea and the dry land* finds its closest parallel in Psalm 95:5, which is 'the climax of a subversive polemic against the gods' (Bosma 2013: 78). As pertinent as this information was for the sailors, Jonah's past and present reflect his failure to reckon with the truth contained in his confession, and his subsequent actions reveal that he maintains this course regardless of the cost.

While Jonah remains existentially detached from the theological truth that he conveys to the sailors, their response is radically different. Upon hearing it (plus his confession of having attempted to flee from YHWH) they *feared with great fear* (*yir'āh gĕdôlâ*) and express disbelief at his actions.[11] In context, both reactions are to be understood as the result of their new-found knowledge of YHWH, against whom Jonah has sinned. This is the first of several indications that, against all odds, the sailors' knowledge of God is increasing.

11. The dread that the sailors feel grips them more and more strongly as the storm worsens, and drives them in 1:11 to ask Jonah what they can do to him as the guilty party so that all of them might live (not only do the sailors hesitate to throw Jonah overboard, but they refer to all on board as 'we/us' in 1:8). In keeping

---

10. This is still more likely if the sailors were Phoenician, as noted by
   Sasson (1990: 118), or were familiar with a different identity of Baal
   such as the one attested earlier at Ugarit (see above).

11. The rhetorical question refers to serious wrongdoing; see Gen. 3:13;
   12:18; 20:9; 26:10; 29:25; 44:15; Exod. 14:11; Judg. 8:1; etc.

with widespread religious beliefs in the Ancient Near East, the sailors presumed that some sort of divine retribution must be inflicted upon Jonah, and they were ready to do so (*what shall we do to you?*) (Walton 2018: 66–67, 284–288). The fact that they address their question to Jonah rather than to YHWH allows us to contrast Jonah's proposal with the outcome that YHWH brings about by direct divine intervention (cf. 1:17).

12. Jonah correctly recognizes that his misdeeds have brought the present distress upon the sailors. However, despite several echoes of different psalms so far, and many more which will come to expression in his prayer in chapter 2, Jonah's proposal is not repentance, or sacrifice (presumably at a more convenient time) or even prayer, but his own death! No less ironically, his experience at Nineveh shows that even a limited measure of repentance can be met with divine clemency. We are thus justified in wondering why Jonah would propose such a radical solution to the problem of his guilt and the danger posed by the storm. If we can peek ahead, as it were, to Jonah's self-analysis in 4:2–3, we learn that he prefers death to (the possibility of) Nineveh's repentance. This crucially important piece of evidence allows us to interpret his suggestion to the sailors as springing from the same root: it is his final attempt at evading YHWH's call to preach to Nineveh. The fact that the narrator delays this definitive revelation of Jonah's priorities until so late in the story suggests that there is some evidence for evaluating them critically here, but also shows that motives, priorities and ultimate commitments are often difficult to discern, whether in ourselves or in others.

13. Interestingly, even though the crew takes with utmost seriousness what Jonah says about YHWH, they are very sceptical that his self-imposed death penalty is just. Instead of implementing it (a very easy task), they do their utmost to bring the ship to safety, hoping to save themselves and Jonah (hardly an easy task). Despite the correctness of their moral instinct and their admirable reticence to end Jonah's life themselves (cf. 1:15), YHWH's sovereign decision to make the storm grow still worse prevents them from reaching land.

14. Unable to escape the storm, the sailors adopt what they conclude is the only possible course of action: throwing Jonah overboard. Yet they do not do so without seeking clemency and mercy from YHWH. The first prayer to YHWH that the book records is thus ironically from non-Israelites (cf. 1:6), and this creates another contrast between Jonah and the sailors.

The sailors' prayer in 1:14 is also the longest-quoted (direct) speech in this section. The fact that they pray to YHWH takes on added significance once the reader hears the echo of Psalm 50:14–16 in 1:16. Outside of legal texts, only a few texts use the pair 'offer sacrifices and pay/make vows' (e.g. 1 Sam. 1:21; Pss 50:14; 66:13; 116:14, 17, 18; Isa. 19:21). Of these, all but Isaiah 19:21 portray this behaviour as typical of faithful *Israelites* in the present. Psalm 50 is the most likely source of the echo here (if it antedates the book of Jonah) since its sharp distinction between faithful (50:5, 14–15) and unfaithful Israelites (50:16) parallels one of the primary emphases of this passage (Timmer forthcoming a).

Despite its urgency, the sailors' prayer to YHWH begins with a respectful tone, especially in the opening O (*ʾānāh*, indicating an 'urgent request'; van der Merwe, Naudé and Kroeze 2017: 335) and the *please* (*nāʾ*, expressing deference; ibid.). Because they believe that Jonah is guilty of a sin that merits death (see above), they ask YHWH not to hold them guilty of murder, that is, of shedding *innocent blood*, for throwing Jonah into the sea (cf. Deut. 19:10, 13; 21:8–9; 27:25; etc.).

The ground for the mariners' petition is recognition of YHWH's sovereignty (cf. 1:9): *You are YHWH; as you have pleased, so you have done.* Here more potential connections with the Psalms appear, especially Psalms 115:3 and 135:6. If the book of Jonah postdates the composition of these two psalms, this allusion draws into this context their strong critique of false gods. In any event, the sailors' own actions are a radical turn from false deities to YHWH, who alone can save.

15. Trusting that YHWH will deal justly with them, the sailors *hurl* (the same verb as in 1:4) Jonah into the sea, producing an immediate end to the storm. The shared verb and especially the shared emphasis on YHWH's sovereign control over the created order (cf. Gen. 8:1; Exod. 10:13; 14:21; Num. 11:31; Ps. 107:29) contribute to the unity of this section. Neither the sailors nor Jonah dared hope that he would survive being thrown overboard.

Whether the death penalty was indeed required will appear only later, when YHWH ends the storm without ending Jonah's life. As far as the narrative itself is concerned, the storm ends in response to the sailors' prayer, not as a result of Jonah's nearly fatal ordeal.

16. The sailors' response to their deliverance is the last step in their transformation from polytheists who know nothing of YHWH (1:5) into men who know of his sovereignty and worldwide rule (1:9–10) and who now are his authentic, fully committed worshippers. This verse makes the last step of this radical change clear by applying to the sailors two descriptions that are fundamental and defining for Israelites who genuinely know and live in a healthy relationship with YHWH.

The first description, 'to revere YHWH', is a concise description of someone who truly knows God, is reconciled to him through repentance, and lives in accord with his will. The concept expresses 'both the inward orientation and its practical outcome in behavior' (Sheriffs 1996: 164), and so excludes superficial orthodoxy, that is, holding beliefs that do not affect one's behaviour. This description of the sailors, which comes from the narrator and therefore is entirely reliable, contrasts with Jonah's claim to revere YHWH (1:9), which fails to convince because of his entrenched opposition to YHWH's will. The contrast is sharpened still further by the narrator's addition that these non-Israelites *revered YHWH with great reverence*, a phrase without parallel in the Old Testament. It is all the more striking in the light of the very limited religious knowledge these men had and the rapidity with which it bore fruit in their lives.

The second element of the narrator's description of the sailors that shows them to be genuine worshippers of YHWH is the affirmation that (presumably after reaching land) they *offered a sacrifice to YHWH and made vows*. These actions express a healthy, integral relationship with God in narrative contexts (1 Sam. 1:21) and prophecy (Isa. 19:21), and are frequently part of the vows to praise that appear in psalms and prayers throughout the Old Testament (e.g. Pss 50:14; 65:1–2; 66:13–15; 107:22; 116:12–14, 17–19).[12] These two descriptions

---

12. See Miller 1994: 130–133, 196–198.

of the sailors establish beyond doubt their new religious identity as a result of abandoning their gods and entering into an exclusive relationship with YHWH. This transformation is ironically the result of a rebellious prophet's refusal to bring a message of judgment against a foreign city out of fear that they would respond in repentance. In God's (sometimes humorous) providence, Jonah's feckless attempt at escape brings about the very thing he is committed to avoiding or impeding even at the cost of his life: the extension of YHWH's grace to non-Israelites. The fact that he remains ignorant of it (the sailors are presumably the referent of 2:8) only adds to the reader's delight.

Meaning

This section reveals two equally surprising responses to YHWH that the reader is invited to compare and contrast. Jonah, who knows a good deal about YHWH, understands that he is displeased by his disobedience, but claims to 'revere' YHWH as the creator and ruler of the heavens and the earth, all the while acting in ways that are radically inconsistent with his knowledge. His final attempt to evade his calling by having himself thrown into the sea demonstrates that he is willing to die rather than obey YHWH, a situation that cannot but leave the reader mystified (the reasons for this unparalleled rebellion will be revealed only in ch. 4).

The non-Israelite sailors, on the other hand, who have the most limited knowledge of YHWH one can imagine (ironically, it comes to them through Jonah's disingenuous profession of Yahwistic faith), yet respond to YHWH in ways that sharply contrast them with Jonah and put them on a par with the most pious of Israelites. This radical contrast prepares the reader for the subtle negative portrayal of Jonah in chapter 2, but also for the comparable response of the Ninevites to Jonah's message in the second half of the book. Finally, despite Jonah's plans, the sailors' conversion reveals that one of the book's main interests is the fact that non-Israelites can respond positively to God even before the dawn of the eschatological age in which prophetic books typically situate that almost unprecedented development.

C. Jonah's deliverance and response/prayer (C) (1:17 – 2:10 [Heb. 2:1–11])

Context

This unit shifts the focus from the sailors to Jonah, who was thrown into the sea in 1:15. Since the sailors were not able to rescue Jonah, it appears he had sunk under the waves before the storm had dissipated. After briefly describing his miraculous delivery by a fish, the bulk of the section presents Jonah's prayer before concluding with Jonah's indecorous exit from the fish and return to dry ground. Although the structure of the prayer is similar to that of biblical psalms of thanksgiving, it follows that pattern only loosely, yielding the following structure:[13]

1. Introduction (2:2): a summary of the psalm (problem→ prayer→ provision)
2. Lament (2:3–6a): the psalmist's problem is described
3. Proclamation (2:6b): praise of YHWH's mighty act of deliverance
4. Appeal (2:7): call to YHWH for help
5. Testimonial (2:8): recital of YHWH's greatness and glory (transformed into a condemnation of the ungodly)
6. Thanksgiving and vow (2:9): praise of YHWH and promise of concrete acts of worship

Comment

17. The author returns to Jonah where he left him in 1:15, that is, entering the water. The reader learns first that YHWH had already prepared a fish to swallow Jonah, and then that the fish became the vehicle for his rescue. The verb *prepare* (*mānâ*) also appears in 4:6, 7, 8, and these four passages establish a pattern in which God acts within the created order so as to achieve certain ends with respect to Jonah. Our conclusion that Jonah's suggestion that he be thrown overboard was illegitimate is confirmed by the fact that, rather than letting him drown, God delivers him from his self-imposed death

---

13. Here I follow Wendland (1996: 376), with some changes.

penalty. The phrase *three days and three nights*, in its only other use in the Old Testament (1 Sam. 30:12–13; similarly, its sole use in the NT, Matt. 12:40), is not necessarily a precise measurement of time. The phrase in 1 Samuel 30 involves the period during which a man without food and water survived, and the emphasis in Jonah may well be the same – Jonah cannot remain indefinitely in the fish's entrails. The similar phrase 'three days' is also flexible (cf. Josh. 1:11 and 3:2) and determined more by events than by the passage of time (cf. Josh. 2:22; 9:16).[14]

2:1. In any case, Jonah's time in the fish is important to the story only as the period during which he uttered the prayer that chapter 2 focuses on. As noted earlier, some interpreters think that since the prayer is uttered before Jonah is expelled from the fish, it sits uneasily in its context. But since the focus of the prayer is on the deliverance from drowning, not on Jonah's return to land, its placement is unproblematic. The prayer develops several themes that were introduced in chapter 1, often by alluding to psalms or by taking a very different perspective on the events of chapter 1 than that offered by the narrator. Jonah artfully captures the intensity of his experience by alternating between two all-important spheres, *the belly of Sheol* (the realm of the dead, and synonymously the place of his distress, the deep, the seas, etc.) and YHWH's presence (and synonymously, his temple and the place of sacrifice). Even though this psalm is awash with pious language, and even though at first glance it presents Jonah as a paragon of faith and fortitude, a careful reading shows it to be as surprising as the narrative into which it is integrated.

2. Throughout the prayer Jonah presents himself in language drawn from biblical psalms. This in itself is not terribly significant, but when one compares the beliefs and behaviours that led to Jonah's present situation, the fact that he is careful to describe his experience in terms used by those who suffer unjustly at the hands of the wicked shows that his understanding of himself and of his circumstances is terribly contorted. A first example appears in the

---

14. The use of three successive 'days' in Hos. 6:1–3 is also probably figurative.

orthodox language of the introduction (2:2), which is very similar
to Psalm 120:1, where the sufferer is being verbally attacked by
deceitful, bellicose enemies.[15] While Psalm 120 makes no connection between its author's trials and sin, Jonah's use of its language
in a context that is directly connected to his disobedience is
tantamount to a rejection of wrongdoing on his part.[16]

Jonah's focus on his cry for help also jars with the fact that
God had prepared the fish to deliver Jonah before he hit the water
(something the reader knows but which Jonah does not learn from
his very unexpected deliverance). Still more strangely, Jonah's
emphasis on his strong desire to live wholeheartedly rejects his
earlier and equally intense desire to die by drowning. Given his earlier willingness to die rather than go to Nineveh, the reader might
suspect that Jonah concludes that YHWH has forgiven him for his
rebellion and will simply let him skip going to Nineveh, as it were.
If so, the second commission in 3:1 will dash these hopes, and
Jonah's desire to die will return thereafter (4:3). We should also note
that Jonah's repeated attention to his presumed agency in bringing
about his deliverance (*voice* twice in 2:2; looking to YHWH's temple
in 2:4; remembering YHWH in 2:7) reveals a strongly egocentric
perspective in the most unsuitable of contexts. By contrast, that
God *heard* his voice is mentioned only once, here in 2:2 (cf. Ps. 31:22),
and the same element is artfully circumvented in Jonah 2:7 by the
statement that Jonah's petition made its way to YHWH's temple.

3. Jonah's very dubious interpretation of his recent experience
continues in the lament section of the prayer (2:3–6a). Perhaps the
most flagrant distortion of the events that led to his brush with
death and miraculous deliverance is Jonah's statement to YHWH in
2:3 that he *threw me into the sea*. Here again Jonah's language is very
similar to that used by genuinely pious biblical psalmists, and
Psalm 42:7 offers an exact parallel to his words here (*all your billows*

---

15. It is not certain that the references to Meschech and Kedar show
    that his enemies are non-Israelites; cf. VanGemeren 1991: 771.
16. The various connections between Jonah's prayer and the OT
    are explored in Brenner (1993); Hunter (2007); Benckhuysen (2012);
    Vaillancourt (2015); and Timmer (forthcoming a).

and waves pass over me). The contrast between the two individuals and their situations is highly ironic, however. The author of Psalm 42 laments the attacks of his godless enemies and the fact that he is far from the temple in Jerusalem, while Jonah's dilemma is the explicit result of his senseless attempt to flee from YHWH's presence! Jonah's self-justifying imagination reinterprets divine discipline of his disobedience as suffering common to the godly who endure unjustified oppression![17]

Being *surrounded* by *a river* may imply that Jonah saw his brush with death in the sea as a river ordeal, an Ancient Near Eastern judicial procedure in which the suspect was thrown into or required to traverse a river and taken to be innocent if he or she survived.[18] If Jonah understood his being thrown into the sea this way, he would almost certainly have interpreted his survival as divine confirmation of his innocence. Jonah's statement that the *waves* and *billows* are YHWH's is technically correct in the abstract, but here it most likely continues his attempt to attribute his current difficulties to YHWH's will (without any further explanation) rather than recognizing that he was responsible for his near death by drowning.

4. Jonah's attention shifts slowly away from YHWH, as the alleged cause of his problems, to himself. But even here the transition implicates YHWH: Jonah is *driven away* from God's sight by someone other than himself, and most likely by God. In this dire situation (which exists only in Jonah's imagination), he meditates on his steadfast faith as he looks *once again* towards YHWH's temple. Given Jonah's shaky understanding of YHWH's global reign and transcendence, it is much more likely that the Jerusalem temple, and not God's heavenly abode, is in view here. Ironically, however, this pious gaze is theologically impossible due to Jonah's refusal to repent. The prophet falls under prophetic condemnation, as it were, by approaching God without first cleansing his heart by repentance (cf. Isa. 1:12–15; Amos 4:4–5; 5:21–24). Even if Jonah had a clear image of the Jerusalem temple in mind, legitimate

---

17. This point is explored further by Sauter (2003).
18. This is suggested by Youngblood (2019: 111); contrast the opinion of Sasson (1990: 175–176).

access to it and to the presence of the God who resided there exists only in his imagination. This self-deception has already appeared at several points in Jonah's recent past.[19] He supposed that he could flee from YHWH's presence, he parrots orthodox Israelite theology while living in flagrant contradiction of it, he attempts to bring about his death at the hands of others to escape once and for all the call to speak against Nineveh, and once in the fish he attributes his difficulties to YHWH's mercurial or inexplicable treatment of him while denying any guilt or responsibility of his own. As with sin in general, this self-justifying tendency becomes more and more bizarre and implausible as time goes on and as Jonah refuses divine discipline and correction.[20]

5–6a. The prophet next shifts his focus from his faith back to the subject of his lament. These verses develop further the picture of his watery trial that began in 2:3–4a. The feature of depth is used to depict the trial's increasingly urgent nature, leaving behind the waves and billows on the surface of the sea and passing through the *deep* to reach the seabed. Jonah's very *life* (2:5a) is passing into the realms of the dead (cf. Sheol, 2:2), and the imagery of vegetation that wraps about him and gate-bars closing over him emphasizes that escape is impossible (2:6a).

6b. But at the last possible moment, in fulfilment of Jonah's hopes, YHWH intervenes! The prayer's proclamation section (2:6b) is one of the few independent poetic lines in the psalm, and like the last line of 2:9, it focuses attention on YHWH (Youngblood 2019: 104). While earlier YHWH was the cause of Jonah's ordeal (2:3), now it is YHWH who brings Jonah *up from the pit* by delivering him from death. Yet as powerful and true as this short proclamation is, it is the shortest section of the psalm, and Jonah's attention returns to his own activity for the rest of the psalm.

7. The appeal section in 2:7 does not focus on what Jonah said to YHWH in terms of a desperate prayer for deliverance, but instead on the fact that Jonah did so. He first sets the scene, describing

---

19. See the insightful treatment of self-deception by Pak 2018.

20. See the insightful and sobering analysis of sin offered by Plantinga 1995, esp. pp. 52–77.

the time of his prayer as the very last moments of his life, just before he would have drowned. Once again, nothing is said of the radical shift from his desire to die to his equally strong desire to avoid death. Jonah describes his prayer not in terms of its content, but in terms of its cause: *I remembered you*. The focus on the temple connects this verse to 2:4b, where the gaze towards the temple symbolizes the prayer that is answered here. As noted above, Jonah prefers to emphasize that *his* prayer was successful (*it came to you, into your holy temple*) rather than that God responded graciously to his prayer, despite the fact that this is the point in the psalm that depicts his brush with death in the most urgent terms.

8. The last few verses of the psalm, its testimonial (2:8) and thanksgiving sections (2:9), bring Jonah's self-congratulatory and self-centred view of God and himself to bear on the issue of non-Israelites by contrasting *those who hold to worthless gods* (2:8) with Jonah (2:9). This is highly salient in the light of Jonah's commission to go to Nineveh and the shocking response of the sailors to the meagre knowledge of YHWH they gained from him in chapter 1. But in contrast to other psalms that praise God for manifesting his glory, power, faithful love, amazing deeds and so on in the author's deliverance (Pss 30:11; 31:22; 34:7–9; 35:10; 40:5, etc.), the 'testimonial' is replaced by a condemnation of those who worship false gods (cf. Ps. 31:6). Jonah most likely has in mind the sailors, perhaps because he is unaware that the sea calmed once he was thrown overboard. But whether they, the Ninevites or non-Israelites in general are in view, the contrast clearly presumes that Jonah, because he has been delivered, is the polar opposite of such people and has himself experienced God's *faithful love* (*ḥesed*). The larger context in which Jonah constructs this flattering contrast invites the reader to draw the opposite conclusion. On the one hand, the sailors' new-found relationship with YHWH is undoubtedly genuine, and constitutes a revelation of his *ḥesed* to those who do *not* worship false gods (note Ps. 31:7, which follows a similar condemnation in 31:6). On the other hand, Jonah's deliverance is in large part a means to God's end: bringing a message of condemnation to Nineveh that will reveal his *ḥesed* to the most unpromising non-Israelites (Jon. 4:2).

9–10. The prayer's final verse (v. 9), the thanksgiving section, strengthens the reader's impression that this comparison is valid by putting on Jonah's lips a promise to offer *sacrifices* and pay *vows* that echoes key elements of what the sailors did in 1:16. There is no record later in the book that Jonah fulfilled his promises here, and since he does not repent here and later expresses profound animosity towards God's compassionate and gracious character, it is most likely that he never did in the time period the book covers. Be that as it may, the last line of the thanksgiving section reiterates one of the book's key themes, already evident in the deliverance of the sailors and now, no less spectacularly, in that of Jonah: *Deliverance belongs to* YHWH! Here, at least, Jonah's egoism and theological aberrations are temporarily out of view, and the rest of the book develops this theme in a way that is wonderfully surprising, even if it eventually brings Jonah into the depths of despair.

Whether or not *deliverance* for Jonah meant only rescue from drowning, it is clear that YHWH saved his life for a purpose. With the report in 2:10 that the fish unceremoniously deposited Jonah onto dry ground, the theme of prophetic commission has come full circle, and YHWH will soon repeat his call for Jonah to go to Nineveh.

Meaning

Jonah's deliverance demonstrates God's mercy to him despite his disobedience, but the prophet's prayer continues to develop the very strange disconnect between the theology that Jonah knows in his head and the attitudes of his heart that drive his actions. With great subtlety, the author juxtaposes Jonah's pious self-image with his self-absorption, his assumption of his own innocence and cavalier attribution of his troubles to God's carelessness or mistreatment of him, and his newly revealed disdain for those who, in his mind, do not share his orthodox religious beliefs. Despite its pious overtones, this depiction of the prophet is extremely negative, and is a very sharp warning to all who profess to know God. Jonah neither loves God (he would rather die than do what YHWH wants, for reasons revealed in ch. 4) nor loves his non-Israelite neighbour, whose unhappy fate he imagines and glibly contrasts with his own. Those who genuinely love God reflect his character and rejoice to see others receive and enjoy the grace they have received.

2. SECOND COMMISSION, DIVINE MERCY TO NON-ISRAELITES, JONAH'S RESPONSE (3:1 – 4:11)

A. Second divine commission and Jonah's obedience (A′) (3:1–3a)

Context

The second half of the book opens where the first left off, with Jonah called to go to Nineveh a second time. This time he obeys, and this sets the scene for his delivery of the divine message and Nineveh's response to it in the next unit.

Comment

1–2. In 3:1 the reader finds Jonah in an unknown location, having survived his ordeal only because of God's direct intervention and, it would appear, against his own wishes. The introduction of the second commission is almost identical to that of the first, in 1:1, and leads the reader to wonder how and why the second instalment in this strange story might differ from the first. The commission itself (3:2) differs from the first in 1:2 only in that it does not mention Nineveh's *evil* and the message is now *to* rather than *against* Nineveh. While these small differences soften slightly the tone of the second commission, there has of course been no change in Nineveh itself.

3a. Jonah's silent compliance with YHWH's command is radically different from his attempt at flight in chapter 1. God has not changed, Jonah's commission has not changed, and Nineveh has not changed, so the prophet's obedience must arise from a change in Jonah himself, but of what kind? Jonah is unaware of the radical spiritual transformation of the sailors and seems to believe that they are still far from God (2:8), so their positive response has not made him hope (or fear) that Nineveh might respond similarly. Indeed, knowing that Jonah hopes that Nineveh will be destroyed until the very end of chapter 3, the best explanation for his decision to comply with the second call to go to Nineveh is that he has no other choice. If God has used miraculous means to prevent him from ending his own life, Jonah apparently realizes that resistance is futile and so trudges off to Nineveh.

Meaning

Like the first section of the first half of the book, the events this short unit recounts are clear as such. Jonah obeys God's second call to go to Nineveh. But the significance of this new state of affairs remains unclear at this point: what drove Jonah to obey rather than disobey, as he did earlier? As is often the case in biblical narratives, the reader must interpret Jonah's actions here in the light of what he says and does in the rest of the book – has he really changed?

Before that question is answered, the author presents a second episode involving non-Israelites who respond positively to Jonah's message, again after hearing only very little of God. Like the sailors, the Ninevites are also a foil for Jonah, who superficially obeys here but whose heart, as chapter 4 shows, is at the farthest possible remove from genuine obedience.

B. Jonah and the Ninevites (B') (3:3b–10)

Context

The bulk of chapter 3 is structured like many biblical narratives.[1] It begins with an opening scene in which Jonah arrives at Nineveh (3:3), creates a crisis by means of the message of looming judgment

---

1. See Longman 1996: 152.

against the city (3:4), and then explores the climax of that crisis in 3:5–9. The two scenes that constitute the climax make up the longest section of the narrative and lead the reader to focus especially on how the city's ruler understood and responded to the situation. The city's very surprising collective response then leads to the unexpected resolution described in 3:10.

3:3b	Background: Nineveh's importance
3:4	Conflict generated: Jonah threatens divine judgment of Nineveh
3:5	First perspective on climax: Nineveh repents
3:6–9	Second perspective on climax: Nineveh's king repents and orders repentance
3:10	Resolution: YHWH spares repentant Nineveh

Comment

3b. The reader knows from 1:2 that Nineveh is *large* and *evil*. To this information 3:3b adds, first, that Nineveh was *large to God* (some Bible versions translate this phrase as 'extremely large' or the like), underlining that, for better or worse, it is important to God (cf. 4:11).[2] Second, the city's physical size is emphasized by the phrase *a three-day walk*, which like other biblical references to distance in relation to three days (e.g. Gen. 30:36; Exod. 3:18; 5:3; 8:27; Num. 10:33; 33:8) is probably an approximate and contextually nuanced expression for 'a reasonably long time'.[3] As such, it impresses upon the reader the impressive scale of Nineveh.

---

2. Translating *'ĕlōhîm* as 'gods' is grammatically possible but emphatically excluded by the book's emphasis on YHWH's sovereignty and unique deity, and 'extremely large' requires that the nouns 'city' and 'God' be joined in a construct relationship, which is not the case in the Hebrew text; see Sasson 1990: 228–229, and the explanation offered by Magonet (1976: 32–33).

3. This description of a city's size in terms of the (exaggerated) time required to cross it is without parallel in the Ancient Near East, according to Marcus (1999: 44). Wiseman (1979: 38) suggests that the noun translated 'walk' can also mean 'stay', and that it refers to a typical diplomatic visit consisting of arrival, business and departure.

4. The description of Jonah's ministry in Nineveh is almost as concise as the summary of his message, and each half of the verse consists of seven words in the Hebrew text. Jonah went some distance into the city (*a day's walk*; we may probably infer that he did not make an effort to cover all its territory) and announced, *Yet forty days and Nineveh will be overturned!* Despite his obvious disinclination to his calling, several considerations make it quite likely that Jonah said a bit more: the population understood this message in relation to *God* (3:5), the king realized that the city's guilt was linked to its *evil* and *violence* (3:8), and this would not be the first time that the author did not record all that Jonah said (recall the summary of his confession that he fled from God in 1:10). More importantly, the emphasis on the divine origin of Jonah's message (3:2) and YHWH's unwavering commitment to have Jonah bring that message to Nineveh prevent the reader from suspecting that Jonah said less than, or something different from, what YHWH 'told him' to say.

Despite our tendency to read biblical prophetic warnings as unconditional, there is no doubt that the warning's opening words, *Yet forty days*, reveal that God *might* relent.[4] It is highly unlikely that Jonah would have waited to see what would happen to the city after delivering his message (4:5) if he had understood that message as an unchangeable divine promise of destruction. Similarly, without presuming upon a favourable outcome, Nineveh's king was able to contemplate (in his admittedly different theological calculus) the possibility that God would relent. Still more importantly, Jeremiah 18:7–8 shows that God retains the right to rescind judgment when those threatened by it repent. Finally, the verb used for *overturned* (*hāpak*) is used in radically different ways in the Old Testament, and can refer to a city's being 'turned upside down' in destruction (Gen. 19:21, 25, 29, Qal), to the 'turning' of a curse into a blessing (Deut. 23:5, Qal; cf. Esth. 9:1, 22), to being 'transformed' temporarily into a prophet (1 Sam. 10:6), to 'changing' the sea into dry ground (Ps. 66:6), to changing one's heart (Exod. 14:5), or to producing spiritual transformation in someone (Zeph. 3:9). The ambiguity of the verb

---

4. On the phenomenon in Scripture, see Möller 2001.

suggests that very different outcomes attend Nineveh's possible responses to God's threat of judgment.[5]

5. The immensely important outcome of Jonah's message is presented from two points of view which are arranged in reverse chronological order. First, 3:5 recounts the response of the population in general (upon which 3:10a elaborates). Although the Ninevites knew the God whose judgment loomed over them only as *God* and not as YHWH (as did the sailors), they believed his message transmitted through Jonah and assumed that he had the power to bring about the punishment he threatened (*they believed God*). This Hebrew phrase denotes a wide variety of faith responses, and does not necessarily refer to belief in God that radically transforms the person.[6] The best gauge of the phrase's meaning here is what the Ninevites did in the light of that belief, summarized in the rest of the verse as *fasting and wearing sackcloth* (common in biblical descriptions of repentance in Israel; e.g. 1 Kgs 21:27; Neh. 9:1; Esth. 4:3; Ps. 35:13; Isa. 58:5; Dan. 9:3) and in 3:10 as *repenting from their evil behaviour.*

6. The other perspective from which Nineveh's reaction is presented focuses on the king and his proclamation (3:6–9). Since Nineveh did not become Assyria's capital city until 705, it is very unlikely that the *king* mentioned here is the Assyrian monarch.[7] Recalling the partial fragmentation of the Assyrian Empire in the first half of the eighth century, it is much more likely that this man was one of the magnates who ruled over a swathe of territory that

---

5. See the longer argument in favour of this conclusion in Youngblood 2019: 139–140.

6. See Timmer 2011: 101 for more details. It can refer to Israel's 'belief' in God following miracles (Exod. 14:31), Judah's belief of a prophetic promise of victory in battle (2 Chr. 20:20), or Abraham's paradigmatic faith in YHWH's saving promise (Gen. 15:6).

7. The parallel use of the Assyrian term for 'governor' (*šakin*) and the Aramaic term for 'king' (*mlk*) in the Tell Fekheriyeh inscription suggests that the Hebrew term (*melek*) can be used for someone other than the king of a nation. See Abou-Assaf, Millard and Bordreuil 1982: 137–138.

included or was near Nineveh.[8] The presence of various visiting religious specialists in the royal court makes it possible that Jonah was viewed in the same way in Nineveh's regional context, and the striking response of Nineveh's ruler to Jonah's message leaves no doubt that it was taken seriously.[9]

The ruler's personal response involves two contrasting movements. He arises from his throne, replaces his royal robes with sackcloth, and then sits *down in ashes/dust*.[10] This puts him on the same level as the general population and visibly demonstrates his humility before God's warning. Further, as the representative of Nineveh, he symbolizes the humiliation of the city before God.

7–8a. The administrative or governmental response is no less robust. An edict issued *by the king and his nobles* calls for radical fasting (3:7; the prohibition against drinking is perhaps hyperbolic) and the wearing of sackcloth (3:8a). As odd as the inclusion of animals in both these commands may seem, mentioning them here anticipates the fact that they benefit from God's mercy towards Nineveh no less than its human inhabitants (4:11) (Sasson 1990: 255). Furthermore, their involvement would not be without precedent in Neo-Assyria or in later cultures, although the possibility remains that this text, like the Neo-Assyrian one from roughly a century later, is simply hyperbolic.[11]

---

8. The closest analogy would be a regional governor appointed by the king, on which see Radner 2011: 359, who describes them as 'all-powerful on the local level'. See Timmer 2011: 92–93 for several possible candidates, and Grayson 1993: 33–39 for many more.

9. Wiseman (1979: 43) explores this possibility.

10. The king's leaving the throne may also have involved a substitute king ritual, in which a person considered expendable was placed on the throne for a limited time in the hope that a recognized threat would fall on him. If the substitute did not die during this time, he would be killed in the hope that this would remove the threat. See the summary of the ritual in Timmer 2011: 109–111, which draws on Parpola (1983: xxiv–xxv).

11. Several examples from the Neo-Assyrian period are reviewed by Schaumberger (1934), one of which includes the household's 'cattle, sheep, and donkeys' (p. 133, my translation).

8b–9. The edict then focuses on prayer (3:8b) and repentance (3:8c). This last element is notable for its focus on behaviour, which is captured by the quintessential term for repentance, *turn*. Specifically, the ruler urges the population to turn from evil and violence. *Evil* echoes God's condemnation of Nineveh as *evil* in 1:2, but *violence* adds new specificity (see the same expression in Job 16:17; Ps. 58:2; Isa. 59:6). It is very unlikely that this violence is limited to the city of Nineveh, or that it refers primarily to inner-Assyrian crimes. In the light of Nineveh's religious and political prominence even before it became the capital city in 705, the violence in view is more likely that exercised by the empire as a whole, and thus a reality already known in the northern kingdom of Israel. The king's recognition of guilt thus goes to the heart of the violent imperial project described above in the Introduction. The final statement of the edict recognizes that God may, or may not, respond favourably to the actions of the Ninevites (3:9).

10. God himself states, in 3:10, that the Ninevites *turned from their evil behaviour*, an echo of the edict that confirms that the population put it into practice. In the same way that fasting and wearing sackcloth indicated a degree of belief in God (3:5), the change in behaviour that God saw indicates that their response to Jonah's message was not superficial. At the same time, the very negative portrayal of Assyria in Nahum, and the condemnation and destruction of Nineveh announced there, make the reader wonder just how far this repentance went or how long it lasted. Here it is helpful to contrast the reaction of the Ninevites with that of the sailors in chapter 1, and with the few Old Testament descriptions of genuine conversions to worship of YHWH.

In comparison with the sailors, the most significant difference is the absence of any claim that the Ninevites feared YHWH/God (contrast 1:16). Similarly, there is no indication that they offered the prayer the edict called for (3:8, notably absent from 3:10, and contrast 1:14). In comparison with other non-Israelites who turn to YHWH, other significant differences appear.[12] Rahab (Josh. 2:8–12) was well aware of YHWH's power over the land's inhabitants (2:9),

---

12. Here I follow Walton (1992).

and included herself in those who know that 'YHWH your God is God in the heavens above and on the earth beneath' (2:11).[13] Moreover, her faith led her to join Israel (Josh. 6:25). Ruth similarly shifted her allegiance from her Moabite gods to the God of Israel (Ruth 1:16).[14] The account of Na'aman's healing (2 Kgs 5:15–19) likewise peppers his discourse with references to YHWH, whom he recognized as the only 'God in all the earth', adding that even when he must bow to other gods with his master once back in Aram, this would not indicate a less than exclusive allegiance to YHWH (Aurelius 2003: 157). It is also noteworthy that these three episodes do not involve external rites of repentance or mourning, which suggests that such actions are neither necessary nor sufficient for genuine conversion. These points favour the conclusion that the majority of Nineveh's population underwent a change less significant than that of the sailors in chapter 1. If some Ninevites did turn to the God of Israel, their influence on Nineveh was negligible in the light of the city's subsequent participation in Assyrian imperialism that culminates in Nahum's condemnation of it some hundred years later.

The statement in 3:10 that God *relented* from the threatened destruction upon seeing Nineveh's repentance confirms that the announcement of judgment through Jonah was (implicitly) conditional (Pratt 2000). The element of conditionality distinguishes such situations from those which stress God's unchanging will, purpose and character (e.g. Num. 23:19; 1 Sam. 15:29) (Moberly 1998). God's response to Nineveh's repentance is thus a genuine response, in time and space, to their behaviour in the same paradigm. It is also an unexpected and marvellously merciful gesture towards a city whose past and present did little other than condemn it. Sadly, Jonah's reaction to this plot resolution, a veritable high point in the book, is quite different.

---

13. Butler (2014: 260) draws attention to the links between Rahab's 'monotheistic confession' and Deut. 4:39, which notably leads into a call to faithful obedience in 4:40.

14. Block 1997: 968; similarly, Nielsen 1997: 49–50; LaCoque 2004: 53.

Meaning

The main point of this unit is explicitly summarized by the narrator in 3:10. The Ninevites, from the ruler of the city down to commoners, repented when threatened by divine judgment. In response, God relents and mercifully retracts the threatened judgment. The way that the book presents Nineveh makes this a shocking transformation: a leading city of the Ancient Near East's dominant empire takes God's warning seriously and changes its behaviour in the light of it, even though it does not presume that God will spare it. As surprising as the conversion of the sailors was, the repentance of Nineveh is even more unexpected: its past and present violence, its role in the Assyrian Empire, and its massive size all make its positive response to Jonah's laconic message stunning. This episode, together with that of the sailors in chapter 1, continues to guide the reader towards the book's main theological claim: because grace cannot be merited, those who have received it may not begrudge God's sharing it with others. As chapter 4 reveals, those who cannot bear to see the grace they think they enjoy shared with others reveal that they have not in fact tasted that grace. But in chapter 3, as in chapter 4, God has the last word: he clearly delights to show mercy to non-Israelites, not least because it proves in the clearest way possible that his grace knows no bounds and cannot be deprived of its gloriously indiscriminate nature.

C. Nineveh's deliverance and Jonah's response/prayer (C') (4:1–4)

Context

Chapter 4 presents two responses: Jonah responds to YHWH's deliverance of Nineveh, and YHWH has the last word as he responds, patiently but unrelentingly, to Jonah's response. Our explanation of earlier passages in the book has occasionally jumped forward to 4:2, so one must imagine one is reading the book for the first time in order to fully appreciate the surprise that chapter 4 reveals. Jonah's rejection of God's mercy towards Nineveh, and of the divine character that underlies it, is far more shocking than his simple decision to flee from YHWH. Indeed, as Jonah says, his rejection of God's gracious character gave rise to his decision to attempt flight from YHWH's presence.

The structure of the book also invites the reader to contrast Jonah's ebullient joy at his own deliverance from death in chapter 2, which was not preceded by his repentance, with the scowling, venomous mood of his response (far too mild a term) to YHWH's mercy for Nineveh, whose population did repent. The structure of the unit invites the reader to make one more contrast: between Jonah's second prayer (4:2–3) and YHWH's response to it (4:4b).

Comment

1. The author presents Jonah's reaction to YHWH's mercy to Nineveh in the strongest terms. Incredibly, Jonah considers it to be a *great evil*, something worse in his eyes than was Nineveh's *evil* in God's eyes (1:2)! This statement is so arrogant and blasphemous that it can hardly be understood. Jonah, the Israelite who benefits in countless ways from God's past mercy towards and self-revelation to his people, who shows no awareness of his sin and does not repent even when faced with death (ch. 2), finds a way to condemn the very God who delights to show mercy to the undeserving. In short, Jonah stands in judgment over God, and arrogates to himself the right to decide who 'should' or can fittingly receive divine mercy – he may receive it, and non-Israelites may not. His arrogance is confirmed by his anger with God, probably an ironic subversion of the divine anger over Israel's idolatry at Sinai (Exod. 32:10–11), a passage to which Jonah refers in the next verse.[15]

2. Jonah begins his prayer with the same intensity as the distressed sailors in 1:14 (*O, 'ānnâ*). Incredibly, Jonah is as earnest about his displeasure over God's mercy to Nineveh (which spared many lives) as the sailors were in seeking God's mercy (which would spare their lives). As noted earlier, what Jonah says here clarifies several key points in the book, especially his initial decision to attempt to flee from God's presence, by illuminating the fundamental attitudes, values and commitments that were rooted in his heart before he left Israel.

---

15. See Moberly 2003.

The essence of his problem can be easily stated, even if it seems impossible to explain. Jonah reveals that God's character, which he summarizes here on the basis of Exodus 34:6–7 as *gracious . . . and merciful, slow to anger, abounding in steadfast love, and relenting from disaster*, is the root of his profound angst and irritation. God's revelation of his character in Exodus 34 is the key to understanding why he chose to spare Israel when nearly the entire nation turned away from him and followed other gods while he was still in the process of revealing to Moses the contents of the covenant that Israel had just agreed to (Exod. 24). In other words, the divine mercy, patience and compassion that Jonah finds intolerable were and still are responsible for the survival of the nation of which he is a part, from the time of the exodus until the present (further, 2 Kgs 14:26 makes YHWH's merciful deliverance of the very wayward northern kingdom the driving factor in Jonah's prophetic ministry). Jonah's 'quotation' of the text leaves aside the elements there that affirm God's commitment to justice and selects only those which he thinks are relevant to Nineveh's deliverance. To them he adds one of his own (or cites from Joel 2:13), *relenting from calamity*. Jonah's reuse of earlier Scripture is selective in a way that reflects what he perceives as a completely misdirected exercise of those attributes. But he can't have it both ways: the same divine mercy that spared Israel from the time of the exodus until now, and which has spared his own life, is the same mercy that has most recently spared Nineveh. Here a thread of truth appears in the otherwise erroneous theological tapestry Jonah weaves: he appreciates the fact that the God of Israel has, in a stunning way, shown to non-Israelites the same mercy he has frequently shown to Israel (this is the only passage in the OT that applies Exod. 34:6–7 to non-Israelites).

3. This theological inconsistency brings us to the heart of the problem. Jonah 'knows' God's character to be as described, yet refuses to adjust his beliefs and attitudes accordingly. In addition to refusing to let God be God, Jonah indicts God on the basis of his own self-revelation. This makes Jonah's claim to knowledge 'absurd' (Magonet 1976: 28)! He 'knows' that God is gracious and compassionate only when it is in his or Israel's favour, and cannot tolerate the knowledge that it could be in favour of his and their enemy. Death is better than a life that must accept *that* knowledge![16]

4. YHWH's response in 4:4 is as calm as Jonah's words are irate. God's question to Jonah forces him to consider what is truly *good* (contrast Jonah's judgment that mercy to Nineveh was *evil* in 4:1). *Is it good for you to be angry?* The question is rhetorical, but rather than change his attitude and repent of his self-centredness and pride, Jonah remains mute and unchanged. If God will not grant him relief from his bitter disappointment, Jonah will certainly not abandon his position. In his view, it is better to remain inexpressibly angry and at odds with God in order to remain in his role as God's antagonist than to reject his pseudo-theology, repent of his rebellion and begin to live in submission to God.

Meaning

This passage is without parallel in the Old Testament. A human being, and an Israelite prophet at that, rejects God's display of grace to those whom the prophet deems unworthy. More than that, Jonah somehow imagines once again that he can escape this God, whom he finds intolerable, in death! He has apparently forgotten (or misinterpreted) his earlier deliverance by means of the fish God 'appointed' and believes (at least in part out of sheer desperation) that God might end his life. Not only does this make clear that Jonah had never received and experienced God's grace himself, but it also pushes the reader to the conclusion that those who misunderstand and reject grace cannot enjoy life in relationship with God. The ghastly separation between what Jonah knows to be true (that God is incomprehensibly and wonderfully gracious) and the realities and truths Jonah is willing to accept reveals an unprecedented egoism that sees him put God 'in the dock', so to speak. After these shockingly sinful responses, the unit's last verse provides an equally surprising but radically pleasant turn of events:

---

16. The striking similarity of Jonah's desire to die here to his plan of 'assisted suicide' in chapter 1 confirms the earlier conclusion that his suggestion that the mariners throw him overboard was first and foremost a means of avoiding the call to go to Nineveh.

true to his nature, God gently cross-examines the prophet-turned-accuser. God's patience and mercy truly know no bounds!

D. YHWH contests Jonah's response (D) (4:5–11)

Context
Demonstrating amazing patience towards a recalcitrant prophet, God pursues Jonah when he walks away from him in 4:4 without even responding to his question. After the object lesson of the gourd, four short speeches follow, with the Jonah–God–Jonah–God order giving God the last word.

The absence of a structural parallel for this unit earlier in the book highlights its importance. In some ways the presence of this section is curious, because one can assume that most readers, ancient and contemporary alike, already know by the time they reach 4:4 that Jonah is pitifully and dangerously off course, and see the fittingness of God showing to non-Israelites the same mercy he has so often shown to his people. While these points become still clearer in this last unit, part of its contribution lies elsewhere, in showing God to be a patient pedagogue even as Jonah remains refractory. The author's choice to end his book with a question suggests that he uses this last section to catch the reader in a rhetorical trap of sorts – whether Jonah will repent can never be known, so the reader's response is of primary importance. Will he or she pursue fuller conformity to YHWH's amazing gracious character, and receive grace from him?

Comment
5. In this verse we see Jonah, unable to answer YHWH and unwilling to repent, simply turn his back and walk away. Although Jonah knows that God has decided to spare Nineveh, he may hope that God will change his mind, or that Nineveh's repentance will evaporate as quickly as the gourd will wilt under the rays of the sun. Both possibilities are compatible with his decision to erect a temporary shelter. In any case, what is most telling here is that Jonah, ignoring the gentle divine rebuke in 4:4, cannot walk away from Nineveh without knowing its fate. He yearns to see the city fall – only that could remove the piercing bitterness from his soul.

His hope, in other words, is that the recent demonstration of divine mercy to Nineveh will soon be a thing of the past, overturned by what he considers (tardy) justice against these non-Israelites.

6. God patiently pursues Jonah in 4:6–8 by means of a simple gourd that reveals still further Jonah's petty selfishness. Ironically, this episode almost sees Jonah forget Nineveh and the 'problem' of divine mercy for a moment in the light of his almost overwhelming focus on his own comfort! To bring this final dimension of Jonah's sinful disposition and flawed worldview clearly into view, YHWH Elohim *appoints* a gourd (just as he had *appointed* a fish in 1:17) which serves, in the short term, to shield him from the sun and provide comfort.[17] The use of *evil* (often translated 'discomfort') in 4:6 for Jonah's discomfort is surely sarcastic, but reflects the prophet's ridiculous priorities. While God considers Nineveh's violent behaviour *evil* (1:2), Jonah besmirches divine mercy with the same epithet in 4:1 and now elevates his physical comfort to the same all-consuming level. Just as he had been profoundly troubled by Nineveh's deliverance in 4:1, so he is profoundly happy about the gourd!

7–8. This happiness will not last long! YHWH next *appoints* a worm (presumably almost as happy with the gourd as Jonah) that *attacks* it and makes it wither. As the gourd falls, God next *appoints* a *scorching east wind* that rises with the sun. Wind and heat combine to eliminate Jonah's physical comfort, and he begins to feel weak.[18] Apparently unwilling to seek refuge or refreshment in Nineveh, his egoism and disdain for the gift of life as one created in God's image drive him, for the third time in the book, towards death as his sole source of solace (4:8). The word-for-word correspondence between

---

17. *YHWH Elohim* appears only here in the book of Jonah, and the shift across chapter 4 from *YHWH* (4:2) to *God* later in the chapter may imply that Jonah is gradually distancing himself from God as he has revealed himself to Israel (cf. the similar difference in proximity between the sailors and *YHWH*, on the one hand, and the Ninevites and *God*, on the other). This possibility is explored by Lichtert (2003).

18. In Amos 8:13, the verb used here (*'ālap*) is in parallel with 'thirst', and a similar use is equivalent to exhaustion in Isa. 51:20.

this bitter admission and the last line of 4:3 forces the reader to compare and contrast the two situations. Both reveal the prophet to be God's opposite: absolutely opposed to what God has done to Nineveh and unwilling to tolerate even the least violation of his physical comfort as he waits in vain for the proof of God's mercy to vanish from before his eyes.

9. At this lowest of all the low points in the book of Jonah, God comes to Jonah yet again with the intention of delivering him from his self-caused, sin-riddled angst. God's words here echo his earlier question to Jonah in 4:4: *Is it good for you to be angry about the gourd?* Incredibly, and apparently with more belligerence than in 4:5, when he simply walked away, Jonah not only affirms to God that his anger *is good*, but that it is so intense that it drives him to seek relief from it in death.[19]

YHWH's last response prevents the book from ending with such folly going unanswered. The last exchange between the prophet and YHWH brings the rhetoric of the book to its high point, something Lichtert captures by comparing once more Jonah and the sailors of chapter 1 (Lichtert 2003: 250). The prophet who 'knows' so much more than them of the God of Israel seeks to escape him once more, in death, while the non-Israelite sailors are drawn to trust God entirely even though they know comparatively little of him.

10–11. But the Jonah–mariners contrast is almost insignificant in the face of the contrast YHWH presses upon Jonah in this last address: that between himself (in 4:10) and Jonah (in 4:11). This contrast contains a second one: between Nineveh (for which YHWH cares) and the gourd (for which Jonah cared). Jonah is troubled about the plant, but he did not work for it or cultivate it, and its lifespan is short. Conversely, YHWH *has pity* on Nineveh, which is *great* and contains *120,000 inhabitants* without knowledge of God's historical self-revelation to Israel, as well as a great number of domesticated animals.

The first contrast, between Jonah and God, is fleshed out by the second, between the concern that they have for two things of

---

19. 'Angry enough to die' captures the idea; Jonah cannot end his life simply by being angry, but only when his life ends will his anger end.

radically different value: the gourd, and Nineveh with its inhabitants and livestock. The contrast is intentionally and inherently ridiculous!

While an appropriately minuscule measure of displeasure over the plant's demise would be legitimate, Jonah's all-consuming anger is not only wildly excessive, but tied to *his* well-being rather than to that of the gourd.[20] The well-being of the comparatively astronomically large city of Nineveh is appropriately *great* to God and contains 120,000 human beings who know almost nothing of him, as well as innumerable livestock. One person, even one animal, is of greater worth than the gourd!

The point of the comparison, which takes for granted that reflecting the divine character is an ethical ideal, is that Jonah should be infinitely more concerned about the well-being of Nineveh than about his physical comfort. Jonah's response to YHWH's question should have been to affirm the perfect fittingness of YHWH's pity for the Ninevites and their cattle, praise YHWH for his countless displays of sovereign and unmerited grace, and pursue conformity to his character.

Meaning

Jonah exemplified attitudes and values that were at least real dangers to, if not characteristic of, a sizeable portion of ancient Israel's population, and this brought the book's message home very directly to its original audience. YHWH's election of Israel was for their good, but it was not an end in itself: blessed by YHWH, they were to become a source of blessing to the nations around them (Gen. 12:1–3) by transmitting to them their knowledge of YHWH and modelling for them a lifestyle that revealed his wisdom and goodness as Creator and King (Deut. 4:6). The message is the same for any individual or group, no matter how orthodox in belief, that has tasted God's mercy and grace. With this immense privilege comes the temptation to mistake God's unmerited grace to them

---

20. For this reason, although the same Hebrew expression occurs in both sides of the comparison, it is preferable to translate it as 'be troubled' with respect to Jonah and 'have pity' with respect to YHWH.

as an authorization of their values, plans, and the means they use to achieve them.

Profound gratitude for salvation should leave an indelible imprint on the heart, will, priorities and actions of every believer. The humble disposition and love for others that faith in Jesus Christ produces will, moreover, drive the church to fulfil its mission to the world as it increasingly reflects the gracious character of the God it worships.

MICAH

INTRODUCTION

The book of Micah presents YHWH as the universal king who establishes his kingdom by renewing his people and extending his reign through them and through his messiah. As the King of his people, he will punish the sin of Israel and Judah by exiling them, but will also purify and preserve a remnant of his people who will be defined by their humility and repentance before him, by their trust in his righteousness, and by his deliverance and restoration of them as his people. Some non-Israelites will also turn to YHWH as they see his power and grace in the restoration of the remnant.

1. Authorship and date

As do most of the prophetic books, the book of Micah presents its contents as the word of YHWH that came to Micah (1:1). The link between the God who speaks and the one who transmits his message makes Micah a true prophet (cf. Deut. 18:15–22; Jer. 26:18 states that Micah 'prophesied') even if the same term is used in his book to refer to false or corrupt prophets (3:5, 6, 11). The importance of the connection between the deity and the prophet who speaks on his behalf was recognized across the Ancient Near East, not only in Israel/Judah, so there is all the more reason to attribute the book in its entirety to the prophet (whether or not he put in writing and arranged its content himself) (Hilber 2012).

The reigns of the kings mentioned in 1:1 spanned some sixty years (Jotham, 758–743 BC; Ahaz, 743–714; Hezekiah, 727–698).[1] In the light of the relatively short life expectancy common in the Ancient Near East, Micah's ministry likely did not span this entire period (Bretschneide 2005). It did, however, cover a very significant period in the history of Israel and Judah, during which Israel fell to Assyria and Judah narrowly escaped the same fate. The prediction of Samaria's fall in 1:6–7 requires that some of the book be dated sometime prior to 722, while the superscription requires that some be dated later (as some passages seem to hint; e.g. Sennacherib's siege of Jerusalem or earlier Assyrian campaigns in the Levant may lie behind 1:12).

The book's composition is inseparable from the ministry of the prophet whose name it bears. Neither linguistic nor historical features suggest a date later than the time indicated by the superscription. Efforts to date parts of the book much later than the late eighth or early seventh century, especially oracles that promise salvation, are based on the erroneous assumption that a prophet cannot, even at different times and different phases of his ministry, reconcile the supposedly contradictory messages of judgment and deliverance. The finesse with which the book handles these themes, however, demonstrates that such a radical historical separation of them is unnecessary. This is confirmed by the juxtaposition of these two elements in other Ancient Near Eastern texts.[2]

---

1. Following the chronology proposed by Provan, Long and Longman (2015: 328). The overlap of the reigns of Ahaz and Hezekiah reflects their co-regency, in which Hezekiah's sole reign began only when his father departed the throne; see ibid., p. 367 for discussion.

2. For examples, see Millard 2012. Note also the observation of Cox (2013) that 'hoped-for restoration' is part and parcel of the Sumerian city laments, which focus first on Sumer's destruction.

2. Historical setting

The message of Micah reflects its historical background in several ways. First, the consistent attention that the prophet gives to the northern and southern kingdoms of Israel and Judah makes clear that the united monarchy under David and Solomon remains the ideal and harks back to the time before their division around 930 (cf. 1 Kgs 12). Second, and more immediately, several passages in the book (e.g. Mic. 1:7) seem to reflect recent Assyrian aggression against Judah. What is more, the threat of exile that looms over both north and south can only be understood in relation to Assyria's dominance of the region through most of the period between the division of the kingdom and Micah's ministry.

The biblical presentation of the divided monarchy focuses first on the radical departure from biblical guidelines brought about by Jeroboam's new religious policies and projects in the northern kingdom. Jeroboam I (930–909 BC) attempted to give his new kingdom a distinctive religious identity by having two gold calves built to anchor the cult in Israel rather than in Judah at YHWH's temple (1 Kgs 12:25–33). Other changes included additional infrastructure (1 Kgs 12:31), a new priestly guild without ties to the tribe of Levi, and a new annual festival apparently meant to replace the Feast of Booths that celebrated the exodus (Miller 2000: 93–94).

This religious decline in the north continued apace despite the ministries of Elijah and Elisha, which spanned much of the ninth century. The mixing of Yahwistic religion with Canaanite elements early on gave way to worship of Baal under the influence of Ahab's Phoenician wife Jezebel. In keeping with the promise of covenant discipline for unfaithfulness, these religious deviations were followed by a variety of military and political punishments (presaged by the prophecy of Josiah's destruction of the north's cult infrastructure in 1 Kgs 13:1–5). Almost from the outset, the north was subject to several violent transitions of power, usually accompanied by the massacre of the preceding king's entire family (e.g. 1 Kgs 16:9–13). Yet for over a century, YHWH's mercy towards his wayward people saw these punishments appear only gradually, and Israel thrived politically, if not religiously, under kings such as Omri (1 Kgs 16:24, 27) and his son Ahab (1 Kgs 22:39). Threats arose from time to time, especially from Aram/Syria (1 Kgs 20:1–12) and Assyria. Assyria made Israel one of its vassals during the time of Jehu, whose payment of taxes is recorded and depicted on the Black Obelisk of Shalmaneser III (841).

During the second half of the ninth century, the pace of these covenantal punishments accelerated. Israel repeatedly lost territory to the Aramean kings Hazael and Ben-Hadad (2 Kgs 10:31–33; 13:1–3), and Ahab's dynasty ended violently in Jehu's coup (2 Kgs 9 – 10). Yet when Assyria under Adad-Nerari III conquered Aram and made its king Bar-Hadad his vassal in 796 (Younger 2018: 23), Israel was again able to exert itself. It made the southern kingdom of Judah a vassal for over a decade (2 Kgs 14:8–14),[3] and its economic prosperity returned, albeit at the price of justice, as Amos shows.[4] Jehoash son of Jehoahaz (800–784) was also able to defeat Aram several times (2 Kgs 13:25; 14:28).

During the first 150 years following the division of the nation, the smaller kingdom of Judah followed a similar path, although more slowly. There was an almost constant pressure towards religious decline that began with its first king, Rehoboam, and Judah acted in ways that mimicked the northern kingdom of Israel (1 Kgs 14:22–24). Again, in keeping with the terms of the Sinai covenant, God sent punishments that were meant to bring repentance and reform, including an Egyptian raid only a few years after Rehoboam took the throne (1 Kgs 14:25–28). Unlike in the north,

---

3. Provan, Long and Longman 2015: 360–361. Judah's vassal status could have lasted until the very end of Amaziah's reign, or perhaps beyond, although Judah eventually gained the upper hand, since in 738 Judah, not Israel, was at the head of an anti-Assyrian alliance (Oppenheim 1969: 282–283, Calah slabs). Note the similarity between Israel's subjugation of Judah in 2 Kgs 14:13–14 and Babylon's assault against Jerusalem in 598, 2 Kgs 25:8–17.

4. More than 100 potsherds dated to around 770 BC from Samaria's royal quarter record the delivery of 'old wine', 'bathing oil' and other premium commodities to Israel's capital. Campbell 1998: 409–410.

the decline of Yahwism in the south was occasionally stopped and even partially undone by Davidic kings such as Asa (911–870, 1 Kgs 15:11), Jehoshaphat (870–845, 1 Kgs 22:43), Amaziah (798–769, 2 Kgs 14:3) and Azariah/Uzziah (785–733, 2 Kgs 15:3).[5] As mentioned above, political and administrative instability within the Assyrian Empire during the first half of the eighth century meant that both Judah and Israel were freed from that threat and more or less free to pursue their own designs. During this time Azariah (785–733) regained control of territories to the south of Judah (2 Kgs 14:22).

The resurgence of Neo-Assyria under Tiglath-Pileser III (745–727) coincided with severe and ultimately fatal political instability in Israel, where Zechariah (748–747) and the last five kings that followed him took the throne in rapid succession amid multiple assassinations. Assyria made Menahem (747–737) a vassal (2 Kgs 15:19–20), and after the assassination of Menahem's son Pekahiah it returned around 732 to reassert its control over Israel, taking a good deal of its territory and deporting some of the population (2 Kgs 15:29) (Hays 2016: 47–48). Within a decade, Israel's continuing insubordination incited Assyria to conquer it completely. Its territory became a province of the empire, and much of its population was exiled far away to prevent any further political unrest (Younger 1998).

Micah's ministry began just as Assyria was again making its presence felt in the Levant, during the reign of Jotham in Judah (758–743, Mic. 1:1). Even before Assyria reappeared on the scene, however, God had used Aram/Syria to discipline Judah for its religious lassitude as witnessed by the failure of almost every Judean king to eliminate the high places. Eventually Aram joined the northern kingdom of Israel in a coalition against Assyria, and they threatened Judah with destruction if it did not join them (2 Kgs 16:5). Rather than trusting God (Isa. 7), Ahaz called on Assyria for help, and Tiglath-Pileser destroyed Damascus in 733–732 and struck a telling blow against Israel at the same time.

---

5. Here and throughout this section I follow the chronology proposed by Provan, Long and Longman (2015: 328).

The course of Micah's ministry saw Israel fall to Assyria in 722 and Judah narrowly survive Sennacherib's 701 campaign that destroyed dozens of cities and towns in Judah (notably Lachish) and very nearly take Jerusalem itself before it was ended by divine intervention. While Assyrian influence continued in various ways (Ahlström 1984; Aster 2007) and may even have helped enrich Judah's administrative and economic elite (Dalley 2004), Micah's analysis of the situation in Judah and Israel focuses on social injustice (especially land ownership) and the abuse of power.[6] Archaeology bears consistent (if general) witness to the conditions Micah denounces, and 'socioeconomic stratification was identified in every city or town in Judah' for which sufficient data exists.[7] This social polarization included additional risk for the lower class, which increasingly had to supply the elite with a smaller range of products, especially oil and wine, and thereby reduced the land and labour available for subsistence crops (Chaney 2014: 41–42). We can also infer that a good deal of the (illicit) appropriation of ancestral lands took place as part of bailouts and 'survival loans' that the elite made to farmers whose livelihoods were endangered in times of drought or unrest (Chaney 2014: 42–44). Since Israel's extant Scriptures were the basis for ancestral and inalienable ownership of land, the prophets, priests and king were responsible for preserving this right and the significant financial security and social stability that it ensured.[8] Prophets in particular were to 'stand outside the cultural system' and so to challenge the exercise of social power when it harmed the vulnerable (McNutt 1999: 179). These issues lie near the heart of Micah's ministry, and the contents of his book shed further light on them.

---

6. Coomber (2011: 408) notes the accompanying phenomena of 'rapid population growth, heightened economic activity, the construction of monumental works, and a centralization of administrative power'.

7. Faust (2018: 187), who also observes 'a high level of socioeconomic hierarchy' (p. 188), with 'severe' polarization between the elite and the poor in Judah in particular (p. 192).

8. Davies (1989) helpfully surveys the importance of land in the OT.

3. Genre, structure and unity

a. Genre

The literary genre of the book of Micah itself is not indicated, unlike Nahum, for example, which is identified as an 'oracle' (Nah. 1:1). As is the case with most prophetic books of the Old Testament, Micah consists of a wide variety of literary genres, ranging from expressions of personal grief (Mic. 1:8) to a fictive and fiery dialogue with false prophets (2:6–7) and blunt condemnation (3:12) as well as promises of blessing (4:1–4) and vibrant expressions of praise (7:18–20). The many literary genres that make up the tapestry that is the book of Micah are discussed below, as is their unique contribution to the book's message and rich unity.

b. Structure and unity

The structure of the book of Micah reflects its complex unity. The book presents three cycles of judgment-and-salvation (1:2 – 2:13; 3:1 – 5:15; 6:1 – 7:20). The first and third cycles treat the two themes in two blocks of unequal size (1:2 – 2:11 and 2:12–13; 6:1 – 7:6 and 7:7–20), while the second cycle (3:1 – 5:15) contains a number of smaller units that bring the two themes into closer interrelation. The first cycle focuses primarily on the judgment of Israel and Judah and limits its announcement of deliverance to a very short section (2:12–13). The second cycle gives approximately the same amount of attention to both themes, while the third cycle's slightly longer section announcing condemnation and judgment is rhetorically counterbalanced by the extensive and uninterrupted focus on salvation that begins in 7:7 and runs through to the end of the book. The structures of the individual sections, as well as questions relating to the book's unity, will be dealt with in the exegetical discussions below.

Because the Hebrew text of Micah presents a significant number of challenges in terms of translation and textual criticism, a full translation with notes on the most important issues is included below.

ANALYSIS

1. FIRST CYCLE (1:1 – 2:13)
   A. Introduction (1:1)
   B. Global theophany (1:2–4)
   C. Judgment against Samaria and Jerusalem (1:5–9a)
   D. Lament over the cities of Judah (1:9b–16)
   E. Woe against those who expropriate their fellow citizens' land (2:1–5)
   F. Polemic against false prophets (2:6–11)
   G. Oracle of salvation (2:12–13)

2. SECOND CYCLE (3:1 – 5:15)
   A. First Judgment Speech (against political leaders) (3:1–4)
   B. Second Judgment Speech (against false prophets) (3:5–8)
   C. Third Judgment Speech (against civil and religious leaders) (3:9–12)
   D. YHWH will restore Zion, call the nations and rule over all people (4:1–8)
   E. YHWH will deliver Zion from the nations and from exile in Babylon (4:9–13)
   F. YHWH's ruler will shepherd the flock that YHWH delivers (5:1–6 [Heb. 4:14 – 5:5])

G. The remnant among the nations (5:7–9 [Heb. 6–8])

H. YHWH forms the remnant and punishes disobedient
    nations (5:10–15 [Heb. 9–14])

3. THIRD CYCLE (6:1 – 7:20)

A. Israel's failure to live as YHWH's people (6:1–8)

B. Israel's sin and its punishment (6:9–16)

C. Micah laments the guilt and imminent punishment
    of Judah (7:1–6)

D. Daughter Zion's faith, deliverance and praise (7:7–20)

TRANSLATION

[1:1]The word of YHWH that was to Micah the Moreshite in the days of Jotham, Ahaz and Hezekiah, kings of Judah, which he saw concerning Samaria and Jerusalem.

[2]Hear, all you peoples! / Pay attention, O earth and its fullness! / For the Lord, YHWH, will be a witness against you, / the Lord from his holy temple! / [3]For look! YHWH comes out of his place, / descends and treads upon the earth's high places! / [4]The mountains will melt under him, / the valleys will split, / like wax before fire, / like water poured down a steep slope!

[5]All this because of[1] the rebellion of Jacob / and the sins[2] of the house of Israel. / What is the rebellion of Jacob? / Is it not Samaria? / What are the high places[3] of Judah? / Are they not Jerusalem?

[6]I will turn Samaria into a[4] ruin, / the hillside[5] into a plantation for vineyards; / I will hurl her stones into the valley / and uncover her

---

1. A *beth causa*; van der Merwe, Naudé and Kroeze 2017: 341.
2. The plural is attested in a number of ancient Hebrew witnesses as well as in some later versions; see Gelston 2010: 66.
3. The plural form is most likely original; cf. Gelston 2010: 66.
4. Gelston (2010: 95) proposes that the definite article was present in the *Vorlage* of G and in 1QpMic. Wagenaar (2001: 27) notes the similar grammar and syntax of 1 Sam. 27:5.
5. Hebrew *śādeh* is uncultivated land, whether level or inclined. The hillside vineyard in Isa. 5:1 seems to reflect typical practice, since

foundations. / ⁷All her idols will be crushed, / all her prostitute fees will be burned with fire, / and all her idols I will make a devastation, / for she collected it as a prostitute's fee, / and it will be returned as a prostitute's fee. / ⁸Because of this I will lament and wail, / I will go barefoot and stripped; / I will make a lament like the jackals, / mourning like (the daughter of) an ostrich. / ⁹For her wound is incurable; / surely it has come to Judah, / it has reached the gate of my people, / even to Jerusalem!

¹⁰In Gath do not announce it, / do not weep at all! / In Beth le-Aprah roll yourselves⁶ in the dust! / ¹¹Cross over, inhabitant of Shaphir, in shameful nakedness! / The inhabitant of Za'anan will not escape! / The lamentation of Beth Etsel: / 'He will take from you its support!' / ¹²Surely the inhabitant of Maroth hopes for good, / for calamity has come down from YHWH to the gate of Jerusalem! / ¹³Harness the chariot to the team of horses, inhabitant of Lachish! / She was the beginning of sin for the Daughter of Zion; / indeed, in you were found the rebellious acts of Israel. / ¹⁴Therefore you will give parting gifts for Moresheth-Gath, / the houses of Achzib will become a deception to the kings of Israel. / ¹⁵Moreover I will bring one who takes possession to you, O inhabitant of Mareshah; / as far as Adullam the glory of Israel will go. / ¹⁶Make yourself bald, / shave your hair because of your beloved sons; / enlarge your baldness like the vulture,⁷ / for they will go away from you into exile.

²:¹Woe to those who devise injustice,⁸ / and prepare evil on their beds! / At morning light⁹ they perform it, / for it is in the power of their hand.¹⁰ /

(note 5 *cont.*) 'Valley floors in Israel and the Mediterranean were reserved for grain farming' and slopes offered superior growing conditions for vines, according to Walsh (2000: 32).

6. Note Ketib/Qere.

7. Andersen and Freedman (2000: 238) contend that the Levantine 'griffon-vulture' is in view here.

8. *HALOT* 1.22.

9. Cf. McKane 1998: 59.

10. So Wolff 1990: 67. McKane (1998: 60) unnecessarily hypothesizes that the image 'comes down from a time when a God . . . was believed to energize the blood or a member of the body, when the hand . . . had its own [God], its own source of power'.

²They covet fields and seize them, / and they take households; / they oppress a man and his household, / a man and his inheritance.

³Therefore thus says YHWH, / 'Look! I am devising calamity against this clan from which you will not be able to withdraw your necks! / You will no longer walk proudly, / for it will be a time of calamity.' / ⁴In that day one will lift up a taunt against you / and utter a bitter[11] lament,[12] saying, / 'We are completely ruined! / He has exchanged the allotted territory[13] of my people! / How he removes it from me! / To the unfaithful[14] he allots our fields!' / ⁵Therefore you will have no-one stretching out a measuring line / in the assembly of YHWH!

⁶'Do not prattle!' they prattle. / They do not 'prattle' these things! / He will not turn away reproaches. / ⁷Is it said, O house of Jacob, / 'Is YHWH impatient? / Are these his deeds?' / Do not my words do good for[15] the one who walks uprightly? / ⁸Recently (some of) my people have risen up as an enemy:[16] / you strip the mantle[17] off the garment / from the ones

---

11. Several text-critical issues make the precise sense of 2:4a uncertain; cf. Gelston 2010: 98.

12. *HALOT* 1.675.

13. Cf. *HALOT* 1.323.

14. Waltke (2007: 103) translates this term as 'obstinate' to avoid 'apostate' since that implies that the group in question formerly believed. Dempster (2017: 87) prefers 'captors'.

15. The Hiphil of *yāṭab* is also used with *'im* in Num. 10:32.

16. Contrast the different interpretations proposed by Allen (1976: 292), Wolff (1990: 82), Andersen and Freedman (2000: 316) and Dempster (2017: 90). Here and in 3:3 'my people' is a plural collective distinguished from this (guilty) Israelite/Judean 'enemy', while in 6:3, 5 it is a singular collective identified with Israel (and guilty). Here the group must be distinct from 'the women of my people' in 2:9, and the connection between YHWH's splendour and the children in 2:9 implies the same.

17. Since *'aderet* 'cloak' fits the context well and the absence of the final 't' can be explained via haplography with the following *tapšiṭûn*, I emend *'eder* here. Andersen and Freedman (2000: 317) find the pair of terms redundant and suggest that one or the other be 'omitted as a gloss on the other'. Gelston (2010: 99) proposes that it is 'most probably to be

passing by in security as they return from war! / ⁹The women of my people you evict from their cherished homes! / From her children you take away my splendour for ever! / ¹⁰Arise and go! / For this is no longer the place of rest; / because it is impure it will destroy, / a terrible destruction! / ¹¹If a man who walked according to wind and deception lied, saying, / 'I will prattle to you of wine and liquor', / he would be a prattler for this people!

¹²I will surely gather all of you, O Jacob! / I will surely gather together the remnant of Israel! / I will bring them together like sheep in a fold,¹⁸ / like a flock in the middle of its pasture! / They will be noisy¹⁹ with people! / ¹³The Breaker goes up before them; / they break out, / pass through the gate / and go out by it! / Their king will pass on in front of them, / YHWH at their head!

³:¹And I said,

Hear, O heads of Jacob and you rulers²⁰ of the house of Israel! / Is it not your responsibility to know justice, / ²you who hate good and love evil, / who tear the skin from them / and the flesh off their bones? / ³Who eat the flesh of my people, / and rip their skin from them, / and break their bones into pieces, / and spread them out like flesh²¹ for a pot, / like meat in a cauldron? / ⁴Then they will cry out to YHWH / but he will not answer

---

(note 17 *cont.*) regarded as an alternative to' *'aderet*, which obviates the need to amend the text. The proximity between 'mantle' and 'garment' also suits well the preposition *mimmûl*; cf. its few uses, esp. 2 Sam. 5:23.

18. Wagenaar (2001: 98) and others propose repointing the Hebrew term here and changing the reading from 'Botsrah' (a place) to 'in the fold' (*baṣrâ*), a suggestion I adopt here.

19. McKane (1998: 90) thinks that 'The third person feminine plural is accounted for by assuming a compound subject, a mixture of feminine singular (צרה) and masculine singular (דבר), "fold" and "pasture" being equivalents of "sheep".'

20. It is not clear if this term has a military nuance here. Contrast Smith-Christopher 2015: 109 (for) and Andersen and Freedman 2000: 349–350 (against); and cf. Josh. 10:24; Judg. 11:6, 11; Prov. 6:7; Isa. 22:3; and *HALOT* 2.1122.

21. Following the LXX, and presupposing metathesis of *kišar* yielding MT's *ka'ăšer*; so also Gelston 2010: 101; McKane 1998: 98; and others.

them; / he will hide his face from them at that time, / because they have committed evil acts.

⁵Thus says YHWH concerning the prophets who lead my people astray: / When they have something to bite with their teeth, they proclaim peace, / but against the one who puts nothing in their mouth / they proclaim holy war.²² / ⁶Therefore you will have night without vision, / you will have darkness without divination, / the sun will set on the prophets / and the day will become dark over them. / ⁷The seers will be ashamed, / the diviners will be embarrassed; / all of them will cover their upper lips²³ / because there will be no response from God. / ⁸Contrariwise, I am filled with power – the Spirit of YHWH – and justice and strength / in order to announce to Jacob its rebellion / and to Israel its sin.

⁹Hear this, you heads of the house of Jacob, / and you rulers of the house of Israel! / You who abhor justice, / and who twist all that is upright! / ¹⁰You who build Zion with bloodshed, / and Jerusalem with iniquity! / ¹¹Her leaders render judgment for a bribe, / her priests teach for money, / her prophets practise divination for silver, / yet they lean on YHWH and say, / 'Is not YHWH among us? / Calamity will not come upon us!' / ¹²Therefore on account of you Zion will be like a ploughed field, / and Jerusalem will be a heap of ruins, / and the mount of the temple will be turned into forested heights.²⁴

⁴:¹And it will be in the latter days that / the mountain of YHWH's house will be established at the top of the mountains, / and it will be lifted up above the hills, / so that peoples will flow to it. / ²Many nations will come and say, / 'Let's go up to YHWH's mountain, / to the house of Jacob's God, / so that we may learn of his ways / and walk in his paths.' / For from Zion will go forth teaching, / and the word of YHWH from Jerusalem. / ³He will adjudicate between many peoples, / and will reprove strong nations far and near, / so that they hammer their swords into ploughshares / and their spears into pruning hooks. / Nation will no longer take up the sword

---

22. On this idiom, see *HALOT* 2.1074.

23. This term is rare (Lev. 13:45; Ezek. 24:17, 22), and 'covering the upper lip/moustache' apparently refers to a rite of mourning: Allen 1990: 60–61; Block 1997: 789–790.

24. The MT's plural is attested by 4QXII^g and by Jer. 26:18 as well as in the Vulgate, although all other versions have a singular; Gelston 2010: 102.

against nation, / and they will no longer learn warfare. / ⁴Each one will dwell under his vine and under his fig tree, / and no-one will cause trembling, / for the mouth of YHWH of Hosts has spoken. / ⁵Though all the peoples walk each one in the name of its own god, / we will walk in the name of YHWH our God for ever and ever.

⁶In that day, utterance of YHWH, I will gather the lame, / and those driven out I will gather together, / and those upon whom I have brought calamity.²⁵ / ⁷And I will make of the lame a remnant, / and of the dispersed a mighty nation; / YHWH will rule over them in Mount Zion / from now and for ever. / ⁸As for you, Tower of the flock, Ophel of Daughter Zion, to you it will come, / the former dominion and kingship will come to the Daughter of Jerusalem.

⁹Now: why do you cry out so loudly?²⁶ / Is there no king among you? / Has your counsellor perished? / For agony has seized you like a woman in labour! / ¹⁰Be in agony, and burst forth,²⁷ O Daughter Zion, / like a woman in labour! / For now you will go forth from the city, / and will dwell in the field, / and will go to Babylon. / There you will be delivered! / There YHWH will redeem you from the hand of your enemies!

¹¹And now: many nations are gathered against you, saying, / 'Let her be defiled, / and let our eyes look upon Zion!' / ¹²But they do not understand YHWH's thoughts, / and do not comprehend his plan, / for he has gathered them like sheaves for the threshing floor. / ¹³Arise and thresh, Daughter Zion! / For I will make your horn iron, / and your hooves I will make bronze, / so that you may crush many peoples / and consecrate their unjust gain to YHWH, / and their wealth to the Lord of the whole earth.

⁵:¹ [Heb. 4:14]Now: muster yourselves, Daughter of troops! He has set siege works against us, / with a rod they will strike on the jaw the judge of Israel. / ²[Heb. 5:1 etc.]But you, Bethlehem of Ephrathah, / small among the clans of Judah, / from you will come forth for me / one who will be ruler in Israel. /

---

25. This is probably a refutation of the denial in 3:11 that YHWH would do evil; see the discussion of 'do evil' in Micah in Andersen and Freedman 2000: 434–435.

26. Similarly, Kessler 2000: 205.

27. *HALOT* 1.189; all other uses of the verb involve bursting forth of people or water from an enclosure or source (Judg. 20:33; Job 38:8 [with a womb as the metaphorical enclosure]; 40:23; Ezek. 32:2).

His origins[28] are from long ago, from ancient times. / ³Therefore he will give them up / until the time when the woman in labour will have given birth; / then the remainder of his brothers will return to the sons of Israel.

4[Heb. 5etc.] He will stand / and will shepherd with YHWH's might, / in the majesty of the name of YHWH his God. / They will dwell securely, / for then he will be great to the ends of the earth. / ⁵And this will be peace. / Assyria, when he comes into our land, / and when he treads on our citadels, / we[29] will raise up against him seven shepherds and eight princely men. / ⁶And Assyria they will shepherd with the sword, / and the land of Nimrod with a drawn sword. / He will deliver us from Assyria / when he enters our land / and when he treads upon our borders.

7[Heb. 6etc.] And the remnant of Jacob will be among many peoples / like dew from YHWH, like showers on vegetation / which wait for no-one, / and which tarry for no human. / ⁸The remnant of Jacob will be among the nations, / among many peoples, / like a lion among the beasts of the forest, / like a young lion among flocks of sheep, / who when he passes through tramples and tears, / so there is no survivor. / ⁹May you raise your hand against your foes, / and may all your enemies be cut off!

10[Heb. 9etc.] 'And in that day it will be', says YHWH, / 'that I will eliminate your horses from among you, / and will destroy your chariots. / ¹¹I will eliminate the cities of your land, / and I will throw down all your fortresses. / ¹²I will eliminate sorceries from your hands, / and you will no longer have fortune tellers. / ¹³I will eliminate your carved images / and your sacred pillars from among you / so that you will no longer worship / the work of your hands. / ¹⁴I will uproot your cult poles from among you, / and will destroy your cities.[30] / ¹⁵I will vindicate myself in anger and wrath / against the nations which have not listened.'

6:1 Hear what YHWH says: / 'Arise, bring an indictment before the mountains, / and (let) the hills (hear) your voice.' / ²Hear, O mountains,

---

28. *HALOT* 1.559; hypothetical root.

29. Andersen and Freedman (2000: 478) interpret the verbal suffix as an object suffix, reading 'he will raise up for us'.

30. Some add a Hebrew ṣ before MT's *'āreyka*, yielding 'idols', but this emendation is arbitrary.

YHWH's indictment, / and (hear!) you perennial foundations of the earth, / for YHWH's indictment is against his people, / and with Israel his dispute! / ³'My people! What have I done to you, / how have I wearied you? / Answer me! / ⁴Indeed, I brought you up from the land of Egypt, / and from the house of slavery I redeemed you; / I sent before you Moses, Aaron and Miriam. / ⁵O my people! Remember what Balak king of Moab counselled, / and how Balaam son of Beor answered him, / and (the way) from Shittim to Gilgal, / so that you might know the righteous deeds of YHWH.'

⁶'With what shall I come before YHWH, / or bow before God on high? / Shall I approach him with whole burnt offerings, / with yearling calves? / ⁷Will YHWH be pleased with thousands of rams, / with ten thousand rivers of oil? / Shall I give my firstborn for my rebellion, / the fruit of my body for the sin of my being?' / ⁸Has he not told you, O mortal,³¹ what is good?³² / What does YHWH require of you, / if not to do justice, / to love faithfulness / and to walk humbly³³ with your God?

⁹The voice of YHWH calls to the city – / and sound wisdom feels respect for³⁴ your name – / 'Hear the rod (which strikes) / and (learn) who has appointed it.³⁵ / ¹⁰Are there still (in a) wicked house wicked treasures / and a too-small, accursed ephah? / ¹¹Shall I acquit³⁶ someone with wicked

---

31. See the discussion in Andersen and Freedman (2000: 526–27), and contrast Renaud's suggestion (1987: 130) that it is first of all the typical Israelite addressed in the discourse of 6:1–8.
32. So Dempster 2017: 159.
33. The word occurs only here in the OT, and other suggested senses are 'circumspectly' and 'scrupulously' (Andersen and Freedman 2000: 529).
34. In the absence of textual support for emending 'see' to 'fear', I follow Gelston (2010: 106) in taking the sense of *resh-aleph-he* as 'regard, feel respect for' as in Deut. 33:9 and elsewhere. Some of the senses for *resh-aleph-he* proposed by *HALOT* 2.1157–1160 are not far from what Gelston proposes.
35. Following, with Gelston (2010: 106), the suggestion of Barthélemy (1992: 764). See also the discussions of Waltke 2007: 396–397 and McKane 1998: 193–194.
36. Reading the Piel instead of the Qal; cf. *HALOT* 1.269.

scales / or a bag of false weights? / [12]For[37] her rich men are full of violence, / her residents speak deception, / their tongue is deceitful in their mouth! / [13]I in turn will strike you with weakness, / make you desolate because of your sins. / [14]You will eat but not be satisfied, / filth[38] will be in your midst, / you will divert but not deliver, / and what you deliver I will give to the sword! / [15]You will plant but not harvest, / you will tread olives but not anoint yourself with oil, / and (tread) grapes but you will not drink wine. / [16]One keeps the statutes of Omri, / and all the practices of Ahab's dynasty are observed; / you walk according to their principles. / That is why I will make you a horror,[39] / and her inhabitants an object of scorn, / and you will bear the reproach of my people.'

[7:1]Woe is me! / For I am like the fruit harvesters, / like the grape-gatherers; / there is no cluster to eat, / no first-ripe fig for me to desire! / [2]The faithful person has perished from the land, / there is no upright person among mortals. / All of them lie in wait for bloodshed, / each hunts his brother with a net! / [3]When it comes to evil, both hands are skilled! / The prince asks, the judge too, for a bribe; / the powerful speaks his deepest desire, / and so they conspire. / [4]The best of them is like a thorn bush,[40] / the (most) upright a thorn hedge!

The day of your watchmen, of your punishment, comes; / now their disarray appears! / [5]Do not trust in a neighbour! / Do not have confidence in a friend! / From her who lies in your embrace guard your speech! / [6]For son despises father, / daughter opposes her mother, / daughter-in-law is against her mother-in-law, / a man's enemies are his family!

[7]But as for me, I will watch expectantly for YHWH, / I will wait for the God of my salvation; / my God will hear me! / [8]Do not rejoice over me,

---

37. For the relative particle expressing 'motivation', see van der Merwe, Naudé and Kroeze 2017: 305. *HALOT* 1.99, notes that it sometimes 'becomes a conjunction'. Wolff (1990: 194) sees 6:12 as 'summarizing and then proceeding further'.

38. *HALOT* 1.446, based on an Arabic cognate. Ehrman (1973: 103–104) suggests 'dysentery', while Dempster (2017: 169) prefers 'gnawing hunger'.

39. *HALOT* 2.1554.

40. *HALOT* 1.293.

my enemy; / though[41] I fall, / I will rise; / though I dwell in darkness, / YHWH will be my light. / [9]Because I have sinned against him, / I will bear the fury of YHWH / until he pleads my case / and executes justice for me. / He will bring me out into the light / and I will see his righteousness. / [10]My enemy will see (this) / and shame will cover her who used to say to me, / 'Where is he, YHWH your God?' / My eyes will see (their desire) on her; / then she will be walked over like mud in the streets.

[11]It will be a time for building your walls; / at that time your boundary will be extended. / [12]In that day (people) will come to you / from Assyria and from the cities of Egypt; / from Egypt and from as far as the river Euphrates – / from sea to sea and mountain to mountain. / [13]But the earth will be desolate because of its inhabitants, / because of the fruit of their deeds.

[14]Shepherd your people with your staff, / the flock of your inheritance, / which dwells alone in a woodland, / in the middle of fertile land. / Let them graze in Bashan and Gilead as long ago! / [15]'As in the days when I brought you out of Egypt / I will show him amazing deeds.'

[16]Nations will see / and be ashamed of all their might; / they will put their hand on their mouth, / their ears will grow deaf. / [17]They will lick the dust like a serpent, / like reptiles of the earth. / They will come trembling from their fortresses to YHWH our God;[42] / they will be terrified and fear before you!

[18]Who is a God like you, / pardoning iniquity, / passing over the rebellion of the remnant of his inheritance? / He does not keep his anger indefinitely, / because he delights in faithful love. / [19]He will again[43] show

---

41. *Kî* can be concessive; van der Merwe, Naudé and Kroeze 2017: 433.
42. Although the *'atnaḥ* precedes these last three words, the syntax suggests that this phrase ends here, and that the next two verbs begin a new clause (as did the elided 'come' here).
43. It is possible, and perhaps preferable, to interpret the verbs in 7:19 as jussives ('may he . . .') rather than as simple future forms since they occur at the head of their respective clauses. Table 2 on p. 225 includes the alternative translation of these verbs.

us compassion! / He will subdue our iniquities! / He will throw all our[44] sins into the depths of the sea! / [20]You will show faithfulness to Jacob, / faithful love to Abraham, / as you swore to our forefathers long ago!

---

44. Understanding the third-person masculine plural suffix in MT as misreading –*nw* as –*m*, with Weiss (cf. Andersen and Freedman 2000: 599). Waltke (2007: 447) understands it as cataphoric, i.e. anticipating the plural subjects of 7:20.

COMMENTARY

1. FIRST CYCLE (1:1 – 2:13)

A. Introduction (1:1)

Context

As is typical for most of the prophetic books, Micah commences with a note which situates the prophet in time and geography, providing information necessary for its interpretation. It also identifies the content of Micah's message as YHWH's word.

Comment

The opening line of the book identifies its contents as *the word of YHWH that was to Micah the Moreshite*. As noted above, this establishes the divine authority of what follows, something borne out by the later recollection of Micah as a prophet whose message was true even though parts of it focused on judgment (Jer. 26:18).

The fact that only southern kings are used to situate Micah's ministry historically probably reflects his southern origin in Moresheth (-Gath), a satellite village of Gath, some 20 miles west-south-west of Jerusalem in the hill country of the Shephalah (Luker 1992b).

Although his southern origins are clear, the book's various addresses to the north (Israel) make it virtually certain that Micah prophesied there as well as in the south.[1] As noted in the discussion of the book's historical setting, Micah's ministry largely overlapped the resurgence of Neo-Assyrian efforts to control the territory to its south-west, beginning in the Levant and eventually reaching as far as Egypt. The second half of Micah 1 even sketches what military aggression against Judah might look like.[2]

One of Micah's most important features is its consistent attention to both Israel and Judah. Although the nation of Israel, composed of the twelve tribes together, broke apart into the southern kingdom of Judah and the northern kingdom of Israel around 930 BC, the fact that throughout the book they figure side by side in YHWH's plans for the future demonstrates that YHWH's commitment to his people (whatever renewal, purification, judgment or even redefinition that might entail) is unshakeable.

Meaning

Against any view which might claim these are merely human words, the introduction asserts that this is a divine message in which YHWH has spoken into the world of Judah and Israel at a pivotal time in its history.

B. Global theophany (1:2–4)

Context

This unit (1:2–4) is closely connected to the following (1:5–9a), since the prophet's announcement of YHWH's cataclysmic arrival in 1:2–4 is explained in connection with the sins of the northern and southern kingdoms in 1:5.[3] The sub-unit can be identified as a

---

1. See on this Roberts 2018: 329.

2. Sennacherib's account of his 701 campaign against Judah mentions Jerusalem, the northern Judean city of Timnah and the southern city of Lachish, as well as numerous Philistine sites; cf. Oppenheim 1969: 287–288.

3. On the pragmatic or emotive effect of the section's imperatives, see

judgment speech. Its position and message contrast sharply with
the book's final unit (esp. 7:11–20), which predicts and celebrates
YHWH's deliverance of his people from their sin and the full
realization of his rule over them.

Comment

Despite the focus on Israel and Judah announced in 1:1, the book's
overall perspective is much broader than those two nations.[4] The
first unit (1:2 – 2:13) begins with a call to *all . . . peoples* and to the
earth and its fullness[5] to hear the announcement that YHWH *will be a
witness against you* (cf. Isa. 34:1).[6] The comprehensive extent of the
two addressees makes it certain that YHWH addresses the whole
world here, Israelite and non-Israelite alike. YHWH's function as
a legal *witness* against the defendant is on the same international
stage – he witnesses against humanity as a whole, and his 'zeal to
establish justice is universal'.[7] The book's focus on Judah and Israel

---

Ben Zvi 2000: 26.

4. Wolff (1990: 55) unnecessarily resolves the tension between the
   universal and the local by attributing these two perspectives to
   different redactors; Andersen and Freedman (2000: 157) concisely
   rebut such a suggestion. McKane (1998: 27) agrees that 1:2a is universal
   and suggests the ambivalent 'among you' for YHWH's witness. Ben Zvi
   (1998: 105–109) surveys a wide range of past and present interpretations
   of 1:2.

5. Cf. Deut. 33:16; Jer. 8:16; 47:2 (parallel to 'city and its inhabitants');
   Ezek. 12:10; 19:7.

6. With a person or thing as grammatical subject in apposition with
   'ad (*'ad* is occasionally the subject, as in Num. 5:13), the marking of
   the object with *b* signifies an accusation (Deut. 19:15, 16, 18; 31:19, 26;
   Josh. 24:22; 1 Sam. 12:5; Ps. 27:12; Prov. 24:28; 25:18; Jer. 42:5). The
   other lexical possibilities (e.g. *lĕʿad* 'for ever') noted by Ben Zvi (1998:
   105–106) are excluded by context, as he concludes (p. 105 n. 8). See
   further Chisholm 1997: 337–338.

7. Marrs 1999: 190. McKane (1998: 28) prefers 'among', but Kessler
   (2000: 85) argues that a 'witness' with *b* is always against the accused,
   with reference to Num. 5:13; Deut. 19:16; 1 Sam. 12:5; Prov. 24:28; etc.

is not inconsistent with this global horizon, and simply reflects the prominent role of God's people in redemptive history.

2. YHWH's presence in his celestial temple signifies his universal rule and precludes the possibility that he can be controlled by the religious elite in Jerusalem who served his earthly temple.[8] It also helps the reader understand how the Jerusalem temple could be destroyed (cf. 3:12), since it housed only the earthly manifestation of God's presence. Finally, the *holy* nature of this heavenly abode (the only other use of root *q-d-š* is in 3:5) means that this transcendent event, described as a theophany in 1:3–4, will inevitably change earthly realities in radical ways when YHWH's holy presence collides with human sin (Naudé 1997: 879).

3. The description of YHWH's theophanic arrival begins here. The emphasis on destruction in these verses skips over the accusation and implies that humanity is guilty and merits punishment (cf. esp. Nah. 1:2–8). *His place* emphasizes YHWH's transcendence and majesty. *Yarad, descends,* begins God's entry into the created order for judgment (cf. Isa. 64:1 and a similar descent in Nah. 1:2–8). The activity of treading *on the earth's high places* is a metaphor 'for the imagery of victory and security' (Paul 1991: 156), intimating that YHWH will surely prevail in his punishment of the guilty and in his commitment to establish global righteousness.

4. This verse presents two images of the destructive effects of YHWH's arrival on inanimate creation and unpacks them with two similes. YHWH's descent first brings him into contact with the mountains, which *will melt under him,* and then with the valleys, which *will split* apart. The high and low points (mountains and valleys) represent the earth in its entirety, while melting and splitting emphasize the destructive effects of God's arrival and the

---

(note 7 *cont.*) Kessler also observes (2000: 86; cf. 4:12) that 5:14 (which uses *gôyim* instead of *'ammîm*) reveals that (at least in part) the nations did not understand God's punishment of Israel and Judah. Of course, the divine accusation does not impinge directly on non-human creation in the same way that it concerns human beings; note Mic. 6:2.

8. 'The apparent solidity of geopolitics is seen . . . as insubstantial before the approaching "witness" (1:2)' (Reimer 2013: 213).

speed with which it undoes the created order. As a preface to the condemnation of Israel and Judah that follows in 1:5, this description of YHWH's arrival as judge maintains the largest possible horizon for his intervention, and leaves the reader wondering where he or she is in all this (humans were last mentioned in 1:2a). The far-reaching destruction this event brings with it almost makes it akin to de-creation, and artfully connects YHWH's actions focused on Judah with his global work of judgment and salvation.

Meaning
God's justice knows no boundaries, and his reign will ultimately be realized over the entire creation. His holiness endangers all that is unholy, and his transcendence and majesty exceed what the creation itself can bear. All that follows in Micah, although consistently focused on individual nations, must be seen in this wider context.

C. Judgment against Samaria and Jerusalem (1:5–9a)

Context
Against the backdrop of a global judgment in 1:2–4, the rest of the first section of Micah focuses on particular, local entities. After the condemnation here of both northern (focused on Samaria) and southern kingdoms (focused on Jerusalem) in 1:5, the rest of chapter 1 announces corresponding judgments on Samaria (1:6–9a) and then on Judah (1:9b–16). In 1:6–9a the prophet announces God's punishment of Samaria, which is retribution for its idolatrous practices (1:6–7). Micah's prediction of the total destruction of Samaria causes him deep grief which he describes in detail and for which he cannot be consoled because Samaria's fall is certain (1:8–9a). A longer judgment speech against Judah (1:9b–16) is followed by a woe against despotic land-grabbers and a dispute with false prophets (2:1–11). A short but powerful promise of salvation for the remnant closes this otherwise very negative section on a radically positive note (2:12–13).

Comment

5. Only after the overarching global and theophanic frame of reference is in place does Micah focus on Israel and Judah.[9] The non-Israelite nations will eventually be considered separately, but only after extensive critique of the northern and especially the southern kingdom in chapters 1–3.

Amid the human sin that fills the earth (1:2), YHWH focuses on Jacob's *rebellion* (*pešaʿ*) and Israel's *sins* (*ḥaṭṭāʾôt*). Rebellion against YHWH emphasizes the rejection of his sovereign claims over human beings as their creator and, in the case of Israel and Judah, as their covenant suzerain (Carpenter and Grisanti 1997: 708), while sin refers to behaviour that falls short of God's requirements (Luc 1997: 87–88).

Recalling that some of Israel's elite accumulated wealth by any means necessary, it is not surprising to the contemporary reader that Micah identifies Samaria as a clear example of the northern kingdom's sin. Samaria might evoke condemnation for various reasons: representing a nation that had thrown off Davidic rule, being the royal city of kings who had radically deformed the cult (beginning with Jeroboam I, 1 Kgs 12), or embodying idolatry and trust in other nations rather than in God (Mic. 1:7). The condemnation of Samaria was most likely very surprising to most citizens of the northern kingdom, however. Although other deities and illicit influences had been integrated in the official religion of the northern kingdom, its citizens and elite (e.g. Amos 7) seem to have believed that they were in no danger of divine punishment (Mic. 2:6–7).

The condition of Jerusalem, which Micah acerbically identifies as *the high places of Judah*, is not much better. The consistently negative depiction of 'high places' in the Old Testament (even before the book of Kings; note Lev. 26:30; Num. 22:41; 33:52; Hos. 10:8; Amos 7:9) makes this a very sharp critique of the Jerusalem cult as practised in Micah's day, as does its final position in the list

---

9. 'It is precisely as creator and ruler of the whole world – all the nations – that Yahweh reveals himself in concern for his covenant people' (Andersen and Freedman 2000: 157).

of causes for YHWH's coming judgment (Wendland 2018). Unless the original audience was able to resist the inference that Ahaz's success was a sign of divine blessing (and therefore that his modifications of the temple and its cult were acceptable, cf. 2 Kgs 16), this critique would have struck its audience as implausible. Jerusalem was the place that YHWH chose for the temple and for his fixed presence among his people (2 Sam. 7; Ps. 132), and many in Micah's day wrongly presumed that this commitment could never be interrupted (Mic. 3:11). Yet the existence of 'high places' in Judah shows that deviant religious practices were both widespread and could be attributed to policies and religious practices based in Jerusalem.

It is important to note that in 1:5 (and often throughout the book), 'Israel' refers atypically to the *southern kingdom* and 'Jacob' to the *northern kingdom*, as the following schematic shows:

Rebellion of Jacob (A)	Sins of Israel (B)
Rebellion of Jacob (A)	High places of Judah (D)
Samaria (C)	Jerusalem (E)

Since 'sins of Israel' (B) is parallel with (D) and (E) and cannot be identified with (A) or (C), the two groups are distinct: Jacob = Samaria, and Israel = Judah = Jerusalem. In the same way that Jacob is the population whose sins are manifest in Samaria (place), Israel is the population whose sins are manifest in Judah and Jerusalem (places). These identifications will be assumed in other passages in Micah unless contextual factors dictate otherwise.[10]

6. YHWH's first-person speech here sets off the announcement of judgment from what precedes it and gives it the most solemn tone possible. The destruction announced against Samaria takes account of the city's impressive size and excellent defensive situation. Omri (884–873 BC) had the city built on a scale not yet seen in the northern kingdom, with its acropolis measuring roughly

---

10. Biddle (2000: 151) also argues that 'The Samaria/Jerusalem framework of Mic 1 – 3 employs "Jacob" and "Israel" as references to the North and the South, respectively.'

250 × 550 feet. Ahab further fortified it, and its location atop a steep hill gave it a commanding view over the surrounding countryside (Mazar 1990: 406). The hilltop site was so excellent defensively that the highly trained and well-equipped Assyrian army had to lay siege to the city for three years before it fell (2 Kgs 17:5).

Of course, Micah announces the city's fall *before* this event, and emphasizes that the city will become a heap of ruins, along with surrounding homes and settlements.[11] Formerly a luxurious and elaborate royal domain, the newly cleared hill of Samaria would be an ideal place to plant vineyards, and the fields around the site would presumably be good for other crops. Micah deftly combines the city's impressive stone architecture and elevation in his depiction of the often massive stones that made up its structures rolling into the valley below and its impressive foundations being laid bare. Similarly, the slopes that were essential to its defence are transformed into vineyards. The valley as the place where demolished Samaria's stones come to rest echoes the valleys that YHWH's theophanic judgment splits apart (1:4), and since Samaria's rebuilding is never mentioned by Micah, the whole scene is characterized by finality.

7. This verse details Samaria's/Jacob's sin (cf. 1:5), emphasizing its extensive scope – *all* is used three times. Of all the possible features of the city that could be mentioned in connection with its destruction, Micah focuses on illicit cult paraphernalia and the fees paid for illicit relationships. These two elements are connected by the *for* in the middle of 1:7, so should be understood together. The last term, *'etnan*, refers to a prostitute's fee, but what kind of activity might this presuppose?[12]

---

11. Younger (1999) discusses evidence of Samaria's destruction, most of which is indirect.

12. Andersen and Freedman 2000: 181. McKane's argument (1998: 33) that *'etnā* refers only to a prostitute's fee, while *'etnan* refers to the fee 'which a woman with an insatiable sexual appetite pays to men (Ezek. 16.34, 41)', is not convincing. Note the combination of *'etnan* with *zōnâ* in Deut. 23:18 [Heb. 19]; similarly, Isa. 23:17; Hos. 9:1. *HALOT* 1.103 makes no distinction between the two forms. Allen (1976: 274) and

Two explanations are likely, and do not exclude each other. A first view holds that the 'prostitution' is not literal but refers to diplomatic payments made by Samaria to other nations (e.g. 2 Kgs 15:19). In this case, the idols would probably be literal, having been received as part of the 'political alliances that have morally corrupted Samaria and Judah', and will be 'returned' when Samaria falls and its idols are destroyed or carried away, as is attested by the Nimrud Prism of Sargon II.[13] A second view proposes that Samaria's extensive trade network had generated wealth that some-times took the form of cult images (cf. the idols in Mic. 1:7a) (Waltke 2007: 55). Samaria's trust in other nations for its security (the first option) and the likelihood that both options saw Israel accept and use cult images and statues entail a variety of behaviours that violate the first and second commandments. The primary position of those commandments in the Decalogue and in Deuter-onomy makes these sins even more shocking,[14] and may explain Micah's decision to indict Israel on those grounds here.

8. This subsection shifts away from Samaria and towards the south, eventually focusing on several Judean cities and towns rather than limiting itself to Jerusalem, the destruction of which is announced later (3:12). The brief introduction (1:8) presents this sub-unit as a lament. As a response to the condemnation of Judah and Jerusalem in 1:5 and on the announcement of Samaria's destruction in 1:6–7, the lament presumes the essential unity of God's people regardless of which kingdom they live in (northern or southern).

Following YHWH's speech in 1:6–7, the prophet speaks in the first person in 1:8. His public grief is a reaction driven by the

---

Dempster (2017: 71) suggest that cult prostitutes' pay was melted down and made into idols, which Samaria's foes will in turn use to pay prostitutes, but this seems somewhat forced. Waltke (2007: 59–60) follows this general direction but with less detail.

13. Smith-Christopher 2015: 61. Becking (2002: 160) concludes that 'There is no doubt that the Assyrians took away from Samaria divine images.'

14. Noted by Kessler (2000: 88). For their prominence in Deuteronomy, see Walton 2012: 93–117.

previous section (*because of this*; Wolff 1990: 48) but also anticipates what follows 1:8. The description of his grief invites the reader to have the same reaction to these announcements of divine judgment, and in the framework of the book this reaction includes repentance and trust in YHWH's goodness even through judgment (7:9).[15]

The description of the prophet's grief escalates from simple lament and wailing, through imitation of a population going into exile, to comparisons of the mourning prophet with wild animals. The first term (*lament*) denotes the activity of mourning itself, while the second (*wail*) lays more emphasis on the level and tone of one's cries. Going *barefoot*[16] and *stripped* (of all but the simplest clothing) exchanges the usual attire of the mourner (sackcloth: Gen. 37:34; 2 Sam. 3:31; 1 Kgs 21:27; Isa. 15:3; Amos 8:10; etc.) for the stripped condition of an exile (cf. 2 Chr. 28:15).[17] This adds to the lament the anticipation of exile, an outcome which can hardly be avoided in the light of the destruction described in 1:6–7. The comparisons with wild animals go even further, and show that Micah's 'grief is hysterical'.[18] The prophet's profound sadness shows that he has Samaria's well-being at heart, but on YHWH's terms: rather than rejecting the idea of divine punishment (cf. 2:6–7), he laments its necessity as well as its effects. Yet both before and after the fall of Samaria, his message can bring good to those in the northern kingdom by helping them recognize their sin and repent of it.

---

15. Wolff (1990: 49) is thus wrong when he states that this is a 'thoroughly secular' reaction.

16. Since the verb *šālal* has two possible roots, the form here can mean either barefoot or stripped; *HALOT* 2.1531; cf. Waltke 2007: 65.

17. The examples noted by Smith-Christopher (2015: 65) strongly favour the conclusion that this line evokes images of exile and not of mourning. Kessler (2000: 93) notes that going barefoot (2 Sam. 15:30) can be part of mourning, as can removing one's garments (Isa. 32:11), but neither of those passages collocates going barefoot with removal of clothing.

18. Dempster 2017: 72. Ziese (2000) notes that the jackal's wail explains its Hebrew name ('howlers'). Smith-Christopher (2015: 65) notes that jackals and ostriches occur as a pair in Job 30:29; Isa. 34:13; 43:20; Lam. 4:3.

9a. Ben Zvi is correct to see 1:8–9 as 'Janus verses' that look back to Samaria (1:7) but also forward to Jerusalem (1:9) (Ben Zvi 2000: 33), and Samaria's *wound* here tragically connects Samaria and Jerusalem. The Hebrew term *kî* at the beginning of the verse should probably be translated *for* rather than 'surely', since the certainty of Samaria's fate is already clear. This is emphasized by the statement that its wound, that is, the consequence of its sinful violation of the covenant with YHWH, is *incurable* (*HALOT* 1.70).

Meaning
God's covenant people have by and large shown themselves to be unfaithful and unwilling to submit to him and trust in him. This pattern of sin calls for punishment, and God's wrath against the northern kingdom will bring it to an end. His justice will simultaneously demonstrate the impotence of the false gods that his people served and the futility of trusting in any power beside his.

D. Lament over the cities of Judah (1:9b–16)

Context
This section extends Micah's grief at the coming destruction of Samaria to the southern kingdom of Judah while occasionally elaborating upon the causes for judgment against Judah. In 1:9b–15 the prophet traces an invader's imagined path of destruction through southern Judah, and in 1:16 he foresees that this prefigured destruction will lead to the exile of Judah's population. The first-person speech of the prophet in 1:8 and the strong connection between 1:8 and 1:9, together with other cases in which Micah identifies with his people, favour the conclusion that the prophet is speaking in 1:9 as well (as in 2:8; 3:3, 5), and that *my people* (1:9b) expresses his solidarity with Judah.

Comment
9b. The situation is *not yet* so grave in Judah. *It has come to Judah* might refer to the *wound* (also grammatically feminine, although *reached* is not), or to its direct cause (i.e. the Assyrians) or its indirect cause (i.e. northern or similar influences that affected the south for ill). Indeed, all three options are possible, and a choice of one may

be unnecessary.[19] Whatever the case, Micah's southern hearers will soon find themselves in similarly grave circumstances. The progression from *Judah* to *my people* and finally to *Jerusalem* (using *ʿad* three times) is emphatic and accelerated by the elision of the verb in the last case, which focuses on the city that is home to the Davidic king and YHWH's temple. The reference to the gate is too general[20] to conclude that Micah had Sennacherib's attack of 701 in mind here. *The gate* and *Jerusalem* most likely refer respectively to the part and the whole of the city (note *gate of Jerusalem*, 1:12).

The structure proposed by Suriano (vv. 8–9, 10–12, 13–15, 16) captures a number of features in the text and will be followed here.[21] Verses 10–15 are packed with verbal, aural, grammatical, syntactical and semantic parallels and interconnections, only some of which will be noted below. The echoes of 2 Samuel 1:20 and Israel's defeat by the Philistines in the opening line (*In Gath do not announce it*) and the last location in the list (Adullam) form a Davidic bracket around the ten other sites named in 1:10–15.

10. Verses 10–12 trace a generally southwards movement towards Lachish, moving through the Inner Coastal Plain, while verses 13–15 trace a roughly parallel northwards trajectory 'toward Adullam (and presumably Jerusalem)' (Suriano 2010: 438). Although the location of one or two of these sites remains uncertain, it is likely that all of them lie within about 15 miles of one another.[22] The locations in 1:10–12 would be reasonably close to the coastal

---

19. Smith-Christopher (2015: 66–67) thinks that 'it' refers to the means of punishment, e.g. armies, which connects nicely to the military itinerary that follows in 1:10–15, but also notes that 'either pagan religiosity or economic injustice or both are here said to threaten Jerusalem with infection'. Dempster (2017: 72) concludes similarly.

20. Cf. Obad. 13 and the absence of the term and the setting in 2 Kgs 18 – 19; Isa. 36 – 37.

21. Suriano 2010: 436. There are some similarities between this passage and Isa. 10:27b–32, which describes the Assyrian army's progress through Judah before it stops just short of Jerusalem, but it is unlikely that there is dependence in one direction or the other.

22. Similarly, Kessler 2000: 103.

highway and thus to a route for possible invasion (Smith-Christopher 2015: 78).

The first city named is Gath (1:10), which was in turn under the control of Israel, then Aram in the ninth century, Judah in the eighth, and finally Assyria in 712/711.[23] Since all of the other towns or cities named are presented as Judean (note *your beloved sons* in 1:16), this verse may understand Gath as currently under Judean governance. The command involves a rhyme in Hebrew (*bĕgat 'al-taggîdû bĕkô 'al-tibkû*) and echoes David's lament over the fall of Israel's first king (2 Sam. 1:20), and probably also portends Judah's fall.

Beth le-Aphra, the second town named, is difficult to locate, although one recent attempt identifies it as el-'Areini, a small Judean border fortress roughly 6 miles to the south of Gath that fell to Sennacherib in 701 (Suriano 2010: 442–443). Its name, meaning 'house of dust', connects it with the activity of rolling in the dust (*'āpār*) as an expression of mourning over Judah's coming destruction (cf. Josh. 7:6; Job 2:12; Lam. 2:10; Ezek. 27:30).[24]

The difficulty of locating some of the towns' names and the likelihood that 1:10–12 traces an overall southwards movement

---

23. Saul's and David's victories over the Philistines (1 Sam. 17 – 19; 23:1–5; 27 – 28; 31; 2 Sam. 5; 8; 21:15, 18–22) apparently made Gath a vassal city, since some of David's mercenaries (2 Sam. 15:18–22) and bodyguards (the Cherethites and Pelethites, 2 Sam. 8:18; 15:18; 20:7, 23; etc.) came from there (Katzenstein 1992: 327). It was conquered by Hazael of Damascus in the ninth century (2 Kgs 12:17), then by Uzziah/Azariah in 785–733, who 'breached the walls of Gath' (2 Chr. 26:6) (Provan, Long and Longman 2015: 328). Uzziah's subsequent construction of towns in that area suggests that it came back under Judean control in the mid eighth century, according to Zukerman and Shai (2006: 732), 739; similarly, Japhet (1993: 879). It was then retaken by Assyria in 712/711, as attested in the annals of Sargon II (Oppenheim 1969: 286). Sargon implies that Ashdod had been a vassal prior to his retributive campaign of 711/712, and perhaps the same was true of Gath.

24. Kessler (2000: 105) mentions a Nineteenth-Dynasty Egyptian tomb painting in which mourning women throw dust on themselves.

while 1:13–15 moves northwards make it unlikely that the passage sketches an actual military itinerary.[25] However, there is no doubt that this list envisions military action that focuses on the gates of Judean cities (1:12) and produces widespread grief, shame and disaster at the hands of a conqueror (1:15) who will ultimately exile Judeans (1:16) (Smith-Christopher 2015: 72). It is thus plausible to suggest with Allen that the 'rumours of war' associated with the fall of Samaria in 722 or the campaign of Sargon II against Philistia a few years later underlie the presentation of Judah's precarious situation as reflected here (Allen 1976: 278).

11. Micah continues by commanding the (presumably conquered) inhabitants of Shaphir (probably meaning 'beautiful'[26]) to continue on their way (towards exile) 'in nakedness and shame'. Since the latter phrase shares all but one Hebrew consonant with *inhabitant of Shaphir*, the contrast between the town's beauty and ignominy is ironic.[27] Second, the inhabitants of Za'anan will not *escape*, with the verb (*yāṣā*ʾ) sharing several consonants with *ṣaʾănān* (Za'anan). The verb *escape* seems to be an example of wordplay in which not escaping is equivalent to going out (as conquered exiles), the verb's other possible meaning.[28] For its part, Beth Etsel is explicitly connected with the theme of lamentation because it too will suffer the loss of its peace and well-being at the hand

---

25. Wolff (1990: 49) offers four arguments against seeing the list of towns here as tracing an Assyrian campaign, especially that of Sennacherib in 701: dirges and laments in OT prophetic texts like Mic. 1 anticipate future destruction; Gath came under Assyrian control in 711/712; the sites named here were chosen for their phonetic value as wordplays; and the link between 1:9–16 and 1:2–8 favours seeing the former as prior to 722.

26. Allen 1976: 280. Hebrew *yšbt špr* shares all consonants but one with 'shame of nakedness', *ʿry bšt*.

27. Similarly, Wolff 1990: 60; Waltke 2007: 75.

28. So also Wolff 1990: 60; Smith-Christopher 2015: 73. Allen (1976: 280) and Kessler (2000: 106) suggest contrariwise that Za'anan's inhabitants remain safely within their fortifications and leave nearby towns to their fate.

of the attacker (the last line of 1:11 is the most difficult of the section).[29]

12. Maroth, the sixth town in the list, is mentioned only here in the Old Testament. Its name is based on a Hebrew root meaning 'bitter', and the name of the town reflects the logic of this section that finds the destiny of a place in its name: the town called 'bitter' will wait in vain for good (cf. Job 21:25; Isa. 5:20).[30] Maroth, like the other towns named in this section, will be directly affected by events that bring calamity to Jerusalem, presumably an invading army that sows destruction on its way to the capital city. The second half of the verse frankly states that YHWH is bringing *calamity* against his people (*ra'* can be translated 'evil' in other contexts) and foresees that this calamity will come to Jerusalem's very gates![31] This is ironic in the light of Jerusalem's name, 'city of peace', and terrifying given YHWH's direct involvement in it (Dempster 2015: 73).

13. Especially when compared with the other sites named in 1:10–15, Lachish stands out as more important than all but Jerusalem, since it was the main royal fortress in Judah until its destruction in 701 (Ussishkin 2014: 77). Boasting massive walls and the 'largest, strongest, and most massive city-gate known today in the Land of Israel' (Ussishkin 2014: 77), it was an unparalleled

---

29. Andersen and Freedman (2000: 224) see YHWH as the one who 'takes' away some valuable support, while Dempster (2017: 66) understands 'support' metaphorically and thinks the town's grief and anguish will prevent it from helping neighbour towns to defend themselves. Smith-Christopher (2015: 73–74) suggests cultic connotations for 'near', with the 'support/place' referring to 'loss of possession or territory'. The general sense of loss that will produce lament suits the overall context, and probably presumes military aggression against Beth Etsel, as is the case with the other towns in the passage.

30. The verb translated 'be sick/weary' (presumed root *ḥālâ*) may instead be based on a root (*ḥûl*) that means either 'dance/writhe' or 'hope, expect'. Since the latter sense fits the context, emendation is unnecessary (Gelston 2010: 97).

31. Note the similar movement to Jerusalem in 1:5, and another with the mention of the city's gate in 1:9.

coup for Sennacherib, who decorated his new palace at Nineveh with an extensive series of reliefs, originally about 80 feet long and displayed in a dedicated room, to detail the various stages of its capture by his forces (Ussishkin 2014: 85). For Micah, however, Lachish's importance is religious, and not in a positive sense.[32]

The address to Lachish begins with an imperative, *harness*. The phrase *to the team of horses* (*lārekeš*) sounds like 'Lachish' and probably evokes the city's substantial military importance (2 Chr. 11:9) and possible use as a chariot city (1 Kgs 9:19; 10:26). Sennacherib recounts that he carried away an unspecified number of chariots from Lachish in 701,[33] and slab III of the Lachish reliefs shows the defenders throwing burning chariots down onto the attackers (Ussishkin 1980: 190). Since there were far too few chariots to allow the thousands of people living in and around the city to flee, and because these chariots were almost certainly designed for war rather than for transportation, this command to engage the approaching enemy is sarcastic in the light of the latter's superior strength (Littauer and Crouwel 1992: 891; Jonker 1997: 1110, 1112).

Lachish's importance in the context of YHWH's coming judgment is attributed (now in the third person) to its role as the original or primary (literally 'first'[34]) conduit for the transmission of sin to the Daughter of Zion (Judah's faithful remnant). The speaker then resumes his address to Lachish (in the second person), stating that the *rebellious acts* that characterized Israel were found in Lachish (cf. 1:5) The text offers no details of Lachish's role in this regard, but Lachish's prominence would have given it almost unparalleled influence in Judah.[35]

---

32. Lachish is described in twenty-five words in 1:13–14, roughly twice the number of words used of any other site in the list.

33. The usual tally of items plundered, captives taken, etc., is not available because 'Lachish is not mentioned by name in reports of the third campaign' (Grayson and Novotny 2012: 15 n. 33).

34. The sense of *rē'šît ḥaṭṭā't* is usually understood as 'first/beginning of sin'.

35. Andersen and Freedman (2000: 230) tentatively suggest that Lachish transmitted worship of Samaria's goddess (the *she* in the verse's second

Interestingly, recent excavation of Lachish's eastern gate un-covered a raised two-room chamber whose inner room contained an eight-horned double altar (Ganor and Kreimerman 2019: 218). While one must surmise that this cultic site was perhaps used to resolve disputes at the gate, there is evidence for the intentional desecration of the inner room before Sennacherib's assault in 701. The double altar was broken in two and its horns were broken off, and a used toilet seat was deposited in what had been the holy place, which was subsequently sealed off (Ganor and Kreimerman 2019: 218, 228). The desecration of the shrine (probably associated with Hezekiah's reforms[36]) reveals that its function was thought to violate biblical norms, and the prior use of such a site may have been one way in which Lachish's religious practice led others in Judah astray.[37]

At the same time, the prominence of chariots in the sarcastic command for Lachish to defend itself makes it equally plausible that its chariots and significant fortifications were 'military obsessions that were characteristic of the far more bellicose northern kingdom' (Smith-Christopher 2015: 75), which had contributed '2,000 chariots, (and) 10,000 troops' to an alliance that resisted Assyrian advances into the northern Levant during Ahab's reign.[38] Illicit religious practice and trust in military might rather than in YHWH go hand in hand, and both violate the first commandment (cf. 5:10–14, where only these two sins are mentioned).

---

line). Dempster (2017: 73) plausibly suggests that the sin in question was Lachish's trust in its military might, something Amos had condemned in the north (Amos 6:1).

36. While this particular cause cannot be verified, the dating of the desecration clearly falls during Hezekiah's reign, in the opinion of Ganor and Kreimerman (2019: 231).

37. However, there is nothing uniquely northern about the site or the activities that probably took place there.

38. The citation comes from the Kurkh Monolith of Shalmeneser III, inscribed shortly after the battle of Qarqar (853 BC); see Younger 2003. Even if the number of chariots is exaggerated, Israel's military was clearly well equipped.

As we observed in 1:5, Micah uses the pair 'Jacob . . . Israel' to refer, respectively, to the northern kingdom (traditionally 'Israel') and the southern kingdom (traditionally 'Judah'). We can assume that the same holds true when 'Israel' appears alone, as here, unless contextual factors favour a different referent.[39] The most salient point bearing on this question is that what was *found in* Lachish, that is, the cult infrastructure described above, betrays no links to the northern kingdom. Further, there are no cases in Micah where 'Israel' by itself refers unambiguously to the northern kingdom, but there are cases where 'Israel' alone must refer to the southern kingdom (1:15; 5:1). The logical structure of *In you* [Lachish] *were found the rebellious acts of 'Israel'*, meaning the southern kingdom, is also roughly equivalent (particular – general) to 'What are the high places of Judah [= southern kingdom, general]? Is it not Jerusalem [particular]?' in 1:5. Finally, in the light of 4:8, 10, we may identify *Daughter of Zion* as essentially synonymous with Judah's remnant. This suits well the assertion that some faithful worshippers of YHWH in Judah were led into sin though the example or influence of Lachish.

14. The continuation of the second-person feminine singular grammar and the conjunction *therefore* indicate that the address to Lachish continues in 1:14. The name of the ninth town, Moresheth (-Gath), sounds like 'betrothed' in Biblical Hebrew (*mě'oreśet*), and the use of *parting gifts* (*HALOT* 2.1506) in the same phrase makes it

---

39. The inference that a link between Lachish and Judah (i.e. 'Israel' in 1:13) is more likely than a link between the northern kingdom and Lachish simply because of their closer geographic proximity is discounted by the reference in 1:9a to just such a link: 'Samaria's plague . . . has spread to Judah' (cf. also 6:16; 1 Kgs 16:25–33). The fact that 'rebellion' describes Samaria in the three other cases in which Micah attributes it to a political entity (1:5 [2x]; 3:8) is intriguing but of dubitable exegetical significance. The northern kingdom's more rapid fall into syncretistic worship of YHWH or outright apostasy (e.g. the introduction of Baal worship by Ahab) might make it a more likely source of negative influence (all other things being equal), but that too is hardly determinative.

possible that Micah sees Lachish as 'paying the price' of Moresheth-Gath's capture by Assyria. This transaction is probably a metaphoric depiction of the loss of Moresheth-Gath (a satellite village of Gath; Luker 1992b: 904) as Lachish's loss of yet another ally, since the dowry metaphor can only be understood with difficulty.[40] Since Moresheth-Gath was Micah's home town, this event would have been particularly poignant for the prophet.

The tenth town mentioned, Achzib, can refer to at least two locations, but the one in Judah's territory (Josh. 15:44) is clearly in view here (the other is in Asher's territory, much further north, Josh. 19:29; Judg. 1:31).[41] Like the previous uses of 'Israel' in 1:5 (paired with Jacob = northern kingdom) and 1:13 (alone) that refer to the southern kingdom, *Israel* here most likely refers to the kingdom of Judah. The similarity of the name Achzib (which resembles the Hebrew *'akzāb*, 'deceitful', *HALOT* 1.45) and its location to the name of the town Chezib (i.e. 'Achzib' without its initial vowel) and its location (both towns were located near Adullam in the Judean Shephelah) suggests that the two names referred to the same town (Manor 1992: 903–904). On this basis, we can cautiously infer that the disappointment or deceit referred to involves the failure of Achzib's garment-makers to fulfil orders for Judah's kings (Allen 1976: 282; Waltke 2007: 83), following 1 Chronicles 4:21–23.[42]

15. Mareshah is also mentioned in the territory list of Joshua 15:44 and was fortified by Rehoboam according to 2 Chronicles 11:5–10 (Kloner 1992: 523). YHWH's threat to bring *one who takes*

---

40. Contra Allen 1976: 282 and Dempster 2017: 73, it seems unlikely that Lachish would have consented to Assyria's capture of the small town of Moresheth-Gath, or that Assyria would have accepted such a small compensation in exchange for ending its hostilities.

41. Prausnitz 1992: 57. Sennacherib's account of his Levantine campaign in 701 mentions that the northern Achzib and other towns in Tyre and Sidon 'bowed in submission to my feet' (Oppenheim 1969: 287).

42. Knoppers 2004: 351–352. The 'linen' referred to there is typically used for kings and priests in Chronicles' account of the united monarchy (ibid., p. 351).

possession against this town involves yet another play on words: he will bring *hayyōrēš* against *mārēšā*.

The second half of 1:15 has *the glory of Israel* as its subject, while Adullam, the twelfth and last place named in this lament, is where Mareshah's inhabitants will go.[43] Adullam may evoke David's retreat to this cave during his flight from Saul (1 Sam. 22:1), but David is never called the 'glory of Israel' (Smith-Christopher 2015: 77). Sometimes that title is used for YHWH (1 Sam. 15:29), but it is difficult to imagine how YHWH's glory could enter a cave (in a literal sense of 'go to') or become obscure (metaphorically entering a cave or city).

The flight to Adullam on the part of (northern) Israel's glory (that is, leaders) would be no less problematic, for the only person who fled there in the biblical record was David (1 Sam. 22:1). Further, glory is associated with the house of David in various ways, especially by YHWH's covenantal commitment to exalt his dynasty (Ps. 21:5 [Heb. 6]; Ps. 2).[44] Understanding *Israel* in 1:15 as a reference to Judah makes a dubious reference to the northern kingdom unnecessary while aligning well with the typical association of glory with David and his royal descendants. On this view, Judah's leaders flee the Assyrian onslaught and take refuge in Adullam, which Rehoboam had fortified (2 Chr. 11:7). This Davidic reference at the end of the list of twelve Judean sites forms a neat inclusio around the passage with 'Tell it not in Gath' in 1:10, another link to David by means of his lament for Saul in 2 Samuel 1:20. Finally, the references to Jerusalem itself in 1:9 and 12, and to the various Judean sites named in 1:10–15, strengthen the argument for a southern, Judean referent for *Israel* in 1:15. There is thus good reason to connect *the glory of Israel* with David.

The most likely meaning of 1:15b is thus that the leaders of Judah, and especially its Davidic king, will have to take refuge in

---

43. Adullam was known as a town since at least the time of the conquest (Josh. 12), but here the reference is presumably to the cave nearby rather than to the town proper.

44. The latter is suggested by Collins (1997b: 580). It also refers to the ark of the covenant (1 Sam. 4:21–22).

the town of Adullam (perhaps fortified once again after Rehoboam's reign; Hamilton 1992: 81) or, more plausibly, in a place suitable to the meaning of Adullam, that is, a 'closed-in place' (e.g. Jerusalem during the siege of Sennacherib; a return to the cave of that name near the town seems very unlikely).⁴⁵ The link to David in the first line of the lament (1:10a) also favours seeing here an echo of an inglorious event in David's life that is a harbinger of a similar fate for Judah's Davidic king and his subordinates. The illustrious title *glory of Israel* contrasts all the more sharply with this lacklustre scenario.⁴⁶

16. Corresponding to Micah's initial response of grief at the divine announcement that Israel would be destroyed by YHWH's judgment (1:8), his lament over Judah ends with a command to Daughter Zion to shave her head in mourning.⁴⁷ Since Judah and Jerusalem were both mentioned in 1:9 and all the towns mentioned in 1:10–16 are in Judah, the one who should lament is almost certainly Daughter Zion, that is, Judeans who were faithful to YHWH. This demonstration of grief is called for because her children, her *beloved* or delightful offspring (cf. 4:10; 5:3 [Heb. 2]), will *go away from you into exile*. While 1:6–7 foretold the fall of Samaria and 1:9 hinted that a similar fate might await Judah, the lament over twelve Judean towns and cities culminates in the first explicit affirmation that Judah too will be exiled. The series of commands to *make yourself bald*, to *shave your hair* and to *enlarge your baldness like the vulture* grows in intensity through the verse and expresses the profound grief the 'mother' feels at this news.

---

45. Similarly, Waltke 2007: 85.

46. Kessler 2000: 109. Smith-Christopher (2015: 77) notes that 2 Macc. 12:38 interprets Judas's return to Adullam more positively as regrouping.

47. The inhabitant of Mareshah in 1:15 is the nearest explicit antecedent, but it is difficult to restrict the significance of this closing verse to one town, or to make Mareshah a representative for all Judah. Dempster (2017: 74) thinks Jerusalem is the addressee in 1:16, while Kessler (2000: 109–110) argues that all Judean towns are in view, and that it is unwarranted to restrict the addressee to Jerusalem; Smith-Christopher (2015: 77) and Wolff (1990: 64) agree.

Meaning

The example of the prophet (1:8) and the repeated wordplays associating Judean towns and cities with grief, shame and lamentation (1:10–15) show that the announcement of judgment against Judah should produce profound distress in Micah's audience. Implicit and explicit condemnation of its pride, self-sufficiency and expectation that its sins would not be punished also encourage repentance and humility before God, whose threat of exile implies that these behaviours and beliefs have put in jeopardy his relationship with his chosen people.

E. Woe against those who expropriate their fellow citizens' land (2:1–5)

Context

Chapter 2 leaves behind the lament over Judah's destruction in 1:8–16 and returns to the line of condemnation that was begun in 1:4–7, albeit without focusing exclusively on one or the other of the two kingdoms. The accusations are astonishing, for in ways that parallel the fatal blow that foreign powers will strike against Judah, some of its own citizens are even now perpetrating violence against their fellow citizens by seizing fields and houses and robbing people of their inheritance (2:2–3)! The punishment for these sins (2:4–5) ironically involves the invader taking away these unjust gains and the denial of land ownership to the unjust land-grabbers on the far side of judgment.

The tone of this passage is as sharp as that of 1:6–7, but it provides a more detailed critique of wrongdoing in Israel and Judah. This section's tone and structure are comparable to those of other woe oracles, being 'an intensive outburst of invective directed against wrongdoers, conveying a note of threat, which is then more fully spelled out in the pronouncement that follows' (Clements 1992: 946). The elements follow the normal order for this literary genre: an opening pronouncement of woe (2:1a), an accusation (2:1b–2), and a pronouncement of judgment (2:3–5) introduced by *lakēn* (VanGemeren 1990: 404–405). The rhetorical force of the woe by itself is significant, and since Micah speaks for YHWH (1:1), it is

YHWH himself who ultimately pronounces the judgment that will fall on his disobedient people (2:3), giving it unparalleled force.

Comment

1. The accusation that follows the *Woe* begins where the sins it condemns begin: as desires and plans in the mind. The crimes that are gestating in these people's hearts are described as *injustice* and *evil*, and they will manifest themselves in various ways. Two verbs, *devise* and *prepare*, focus on these sins at this early stage.[48] The fact that these individuals plan and prepare these schemes *on their beds* connects their physical repose with their being morally undisturbed by such evil. Micah adds that they rise at first light, revealing the strength of their desire and the resolve that lies behind their plans: there is no time to be wasted, for they have the power to take the things they so strongly desire.[49] The coveting that lies behind these plans is mentioned in 2:2 and is the root from which the plans grow (Exod. 20:17).

The sequence of planning evil during the night and carrying it out during the day inverts the more common situation in which evil is carried out during the night but those who perform it are punished when YHWH acts in the morning (Zeph. 3:5; Job 38:12–25; Pss 46:6; 90:14; 143:8; Lam. 3:23) (Kessler 2000: 115). This might imply that 'the evildoers put themselves in God's place',[50] and it certainly shows that they are unconcerned by who might see them. Such arrogance and autonomy are inseparable from their elaborate plans to steal their fellow citizens' divinely allocated inheritances.

---

48. Although *pāʿal* normally means 'do', here it should probably be understood in the sense of running through the plan. The appeal by Renaud (1977: 66, cited in Waltke 2007: 93–94) to Semitic anthropology is probably unnecessary.

49. If *kî* is translated as *for*, it cannot be understood as the only reason why these plans are put into action. Rather, the ability to implement their plans means that they do so, but those plans flow out of the desires of their hearts and the plans they have crafted.

50. Kessler 2000: 115; all translations from this work are my own.

2. The plans hatched in 2:1a, b and implemented in general terms in 2:1c are now described in detail. The logically initial sin of coveting is mentioned first, with their neighbours' *fields* as the object. Then follow two transitive verbs that describe the breaking of the eighth commandment as well as others (see below). They *take households* and *oppress* no fewer than four objects: *a man* (*geber*, with connotations of strength, *HALOT* 1.175), *his household*,[51] *a man* (no connotations) and *his inheritance*. The verb translated *seize* also appears in 3:2 as 'rip off' and leaves no doubt that this process is violent (Dempster 2017: 85).

Fields, household, a strong man and a man all overlap with the last term, *inheritance*. *Fields* were the arable portion of each family's inherited property and were typically the primary source of sustenance and revenue. *Households* were constituted of several generations of the family plus its servants and livestock, and this group possessed and worked the land. The *man* probably refers to the patrimonial head of the family through whom the line of transmission normally passed.[52] As the only repeated element, *man* (in his prime) and *man* (i.e. an individual) stress the degree to which the individual Israelite, and the fabric of the society as a whole, depended on these elements (Reimer 2013: 216). As Waltke puts it, '"inheritance" combines the notions of family and property with permanence' (Waltke 2007: 96).

This sinful dispossession of other Israelites is aggravated by the fact that the land of Israel was emphatically YHWH's land. He allotted it to the Israelites through Joshua (Josh. 13 – 19; cf. Mic. 2:5), and only the Levites were without allotted land since they were supported by the nation's tithes and offerings. Since habitation, agriculture and animal husbandry were all connected to the land, possession of one's land was essential for financial independence, social stability and the protection of the vulnerable or unfortunate (all leased or forfeited land was to revert to its original owners at

---

51. The Hebrew term *bayit* can denote either the structure or those who live in it (*HALOT* 1.124–125), but only a household can be oppressed.

52. See Wright 1997: 77–81 for further discussion. Zelophehad's daughters were an exception, Num. 27:1–11; 36.

the Year of Jubilee). It was (at least in theory) therefore impossible to take control of another's land permanently.[53] At most, an indebted Israelite could cede control of his land to another in order to repay a debt, but even this was to be temporary and was far from ideal (Deut. 15:1–6).[54]

These property thieves give no heed to YHWH's many commands to protect the vulnerable (Exod. 23:6; 23:11; Lev. 25:47–55; Deut. 15:7–11), and presumably have no intention of relinquishing control of their ill-gotten land. As explained above, these thefts reject YHWH's will that each tribe and family possess its land inalienably (Lev. 25:13–17; cf. Josh. 13 – 16, etc.; Morrow 2017: 185–187) and ignore the fact that it ultimately belongs to him. Since the land in question is also the rightful owner's *inheritance* (*naḥălâ*), the thieves simultaneously rob their fellow citizen and (if it were possible) YHWH!

3. The pronouncement of judgment (2:3–5) is clearly linked to the sins identified in 2:1–2 by *lakēn, therefore*. YHWH's direct speech leaves no doubt that the sins committed against some of his people are simultaneously against him, and his explanation reuses two words used to describe their sins in 2:1. God 'devises' punishment, using the same verb that describes the rapacious plans of those who expropriate land in 2:1, and the *calamity* (*rā'â*) he plans against them corresponds to the *evil* they prepare (*ra'*).

More striking than these rhetorical details is the fact that YHWH's punishment will strike *this clan*. The term normally refers to the social unit that is smaller than the tribe but larger than the household (e.g. Judg. 21:24; O'Connell 1997: 1140), and to people closely related to one another by blood.[55] On occasion, however,

---

53. Note the prominence of 'inheritance' in Ahab's theft of Naboth's vineyard, 1 Kgs 21:3–4.

54. Smith-Christopher (2015: 83) states, 'Even if the people are allowed to continue to work their land as debt slaves (effectively sharecroppers), this is a violation of the spirit of the Mosaic laws of distributive justice as implied in the legal traditions of the *naḥalā* (tribal allotment).'

55. *HALOT* 1.651. Zobel (1998: 80) concludes that 'A *mišpāḥâ* is therefore defined by kinship structures and includes more than just the nuclear or extended family of the man or woman. It is hard to be more precise.'

the prophets in particular use it to refer to the nation of Judah (Jer. 8:3, 'family') or to the entirety of God's chosen people (north and south; Amos 3:1). It is probable that Micah uses it with the same emphasis as Amos in the light of his consistent inclusion of both north and south (especially with the Jacob–Israel pair, Mic. 1:5; 2:12; 3:1, 8, 9).[56] The familial colouring of the term also highlights the close, compassionate relationship that Israelites should have for their kin but which is flagrantly absent in these situations.

While at first glance this announcement might seem to affirm that YHWH will punish a whole nation for the sins of a few, several considerations suggest that divine punishment is not so blunt. First, those accused (*you*) are distinct from *this clan*, marking the first appearance of the remnant theme in Micah. Second, and more clearly, those most affected by this future calamity will be the proud (2:3), the same persons responsible for the land-grabbing described earlier, and this focus narrows even further to the singular *you* in 2:5.[57] The image of a yoke probably lies behind the warning that *you will not be able to withdraw your necks*, and the shame that divine punishment produces contrasts with this group's present pride and elevated social-political status.[58] A third point that illuminates the mix of particular sins and generalized punishment here is that later in Micah it becomes evident that even the repentant remnant (2:12; 4:7; 5:7 [Heb. 6], 8 [Heb. 7]; 7:9, 18) are not without sin, and so endure God's punishment patiently and

---

56. So also Ben Zvi 1999: 90 and Gignilliat 2019: 108. Kessler's suggestion (2000: 117) that 'this people' distinguishes the group from the rest of Israel/Judah, so that they 'no longer belong to "my people"', makes it necessary to see the oppressed as voicing the lament, an approach that jars with 2:5. The term could also refer to the group of land barons, but in biblical literature those who do wrong are usually referred to in terms that make that characteristic clear.

57. Following Ben Zvi (1999: 88, 94). Dempster (2017: 87) understands the shift from a plural to a singular second-person referent as 'a focus on the individual punishment of each criminal'.

58. So Renaud 1987: 44. Kessler's suggestion (2000: 118) that it is an image of slavery is not very different.

humbly (7:8–9), knowing that his grace will not only sustain them but will renew them and restore them (7:11–12, 18–20).[59] In short, the punishment announced here will affect all those in the northern and southern kingdoms, but is directed especially against those who take others' land by force or by fraud. Not only will they lose the land they took, they will be denied the very possibility of having an *inheritance* in the land. This is tantamount to excluding them from the restored people of God and from the blessings he promises to his people in the land when they are obedient.[60]

4. *In that day* describes the first of two stages in YHWH's response to injustice in Judah and Israel.[61] Ben Zvi suggests that this lament foresees that 'the people of YHWH . . . will lose control over [their] land' (Ben Zvi 1999: 94), but in the logic of chapter 2, that has already happened to the poor and vulnerable. What is new is the loss of land by those who stole it from the poor and vulnerable! The second-person language (whether singular or plural) continues to refer to those who wrongly expropriate land from their fellow Israelites in the sarcastic taunt that follows (cf. Job 27:13–23; Isa. 14:4; Hab. 2:6). In this taunt those who have suffered at the hands of the elite mockingly quote 'their despairing lament'[62] in anticipation of the coming judgment and of their own deliverance (cf. 2:5).[63]

---

59. Waltke (2007: 98) notes that this occurs elsewhere in the OT and at other points in Israel's history, e.g. Dan. 9:5; Neh. 9:33.

60. Renaud (1987: 45) notes the irony that this group removed land from the poor, and that the invader removes their stolen land from them.

61. Kessler (2000: 121) observes that this two-stage structure is fundamental to Micah's perspective on the future.

62. Allen 1976: 290; Waltke 2007: 101. Contrary to Andersen and Freedman (2000: 279), nothing prevents such a lament being directed against the wrongdoers; note Job's speech against his friends in Job 27:1–12 and his use of their speech against them in 27:13–23, and see Seow 2011 for further discussion.

63. The chiasm that switches first-person plural to singular, and then back again, in the last four lines of 2:4 and the absence of first-person grammar elsewhere in the verse are strong arguments for limiting

The total ruin lamented by the undone land barons focuses on their fields and what they thought was the *allotted territory* of YHWH's people. A number of features in their self-focused lament reveal how far removed their views of land ownership and their fellow Israelites are from biblical norms. For example, the phrase *allotted territory of my people* is highly ironic. The *allotted territory* was in fact taken by force or by injustice from those to whom it was allotted by God, yet the words *my people* seem to refer only to the land barons' loss. Similarly, they lament the fact that their (stolen) land is lost to another (probably a foreign invader) but overlook entirely their own role in wresting land from the hands of vulnerable and defenceless Israelites! In other words, these thieves identify themselves with the *clan* mentioned in 2:3 – that is, the northern and southern kingdoms together – assume that the land they took by force is their legitimate inheritance accorded by YHWH, and fail to recognize the distinction that the same verse makes between the *clan* and the *you* with which they are addressed! The only fact that they understand properly is that YHWH is fulfilling his commitment to act in 2:3, yet they call those who take their lands *unfaithful*, apparently referring to the Assyrians or Babylonians with a term that applies equally to themselves. Ironically, although these oppressors think that this loss of land by itself means that they are totally ruined, this is only part of the punishment that YHWH announces against them.

5. The former oppressors are wrong to equate loss of land with total ruin, for 2:5 goes further. In the second future stage of punishment that Micah foresees, those who are not unjust and oppressive

---

(note 63 *cont.*) the lament to these lines, as noted by Kessler (2000: 121). Although elsewhere in the book God, the prophet and Daughter Zion are the only ones who speak in the first-person plural, this does not mean that a sarcastic taunt cannot put that language on the lips of the unjust. The identities of the various persons or groups mentioned in this context are clear enough to justify this view. Mic. 6:7 is debatable, but in 2:9 God clearly distinguishes between 'my people' and the unrighteous in Judah; God or Micah does the same in 3:3, 5.

will receive portions of the land as did Israel in Joshua's time.[64] Stating that the priest will not distribute land to the wicked is tantamount to saying that the wicked will no longer be in the land (and also assumes that the invaders will be driven out, cf. Mic. 5).[65] While Israel in the Pentateuch and later texts is defined as the *assembly of YHWH* to the exclusion of its perennial enemies and (at least in cultic settings) of Israelites with physical imperfections that made proximity to YHWH unsuitable (Deut. 23:1–8; similarly, 1 Chr. 28:8), the same term in the future that Micah predicts is still more clearly defined along ethical–religious lines.[66] The elimination of the unjust from Israel/Judah makes the identity of those two groups open to change, and anticipates the remnant theme that appears more clearly in 2:12–13.

Meaning
Judah and Israel, particularly the more powerful and privileged among them, are characterized by a deeply rooted commitment to self-advancement at the price of the basic well-being of their fellow citizens and by flagrant disregard for YHWH's justice. God will punish their avarice and abuse of power, which focuses on the acquisition of land and material wealth, by expelling them from the land they so ardently laboured to obtain, control and exploit, and even from the people of God.

---

64. This sometimes followed Moses' instructions, Josh. 13:8, 15, 24, 29, 32, and sometimes was done by casting lots, Josh. 14:2 etc.

65. The evidence for reallocation of patrimonial land is very uncertain; see the discussion in Wagenaar 2001: 74.

66. The exclusion of some Israelites and the inclusion of some non-Israelites in Deut. 23:1–8 similarly implies that the 'assembly of YHWH' is fundamentally spiritually determined (hence some non-Israelites can join), but not all the implications of that are worked out there. Isa. 56:1–8 revises this legislation in the light of God's future work of salvation.

F. Polemic against false prophets (2:6–11)

Context

This section presents and responds to a protest against Micah's message of judgment. In the course of his reply the prophet ironically compares the Israelites who oppress their vulnerable and powerless kin to an invading army (2:8), the very threat against which the oppressors had reacted with dismay in the oracle of 2:1–5.

In terms of genre the unit can be classified as a prophetic disputation speech, which counters 'popular opinions' with God's rebuttal through Micah (Floyd 2000: 638). The verb 'prattle/speak ecstatically/prophesy' (*nātap*) forms an inclusio around this sub-unit (2:6, 11).

Comment

6. The shift from second to third person between strophe 1 (*Do not prattle!*) and strophe 2 (*they prattle*) favours seeing Micah's opponents as uttering only the command 'Do not prophesy.'[67] Their prohibition follows directly upon the oracle of 2:1–5, and so can be taken as the outright rejection of Micah's message of judgment. Micah retorts that his opponents[68] [*they*] *do not 'prattle'* about *these things*, that is, judgment.[69] The last phrase, *He* [*YHWH*] *will not turn away reproaches*,[70] is Micah's rejection of their position for the simple reason that their denial of God's anger does not make it go away. YHWH will not overlook the sins of his people.[71]

---

67. Gignilliat (2019: 114) concludes likewise. Micah may be echoing Amos 2:12 here (their verbs are roughly synonymous; see also Amos 7:16).

68. The prohibition is in the plural, although Micah's colleagues are not named; likewise, his opponents are a plurality.

69. Van der Woude (1969: 247) suggests that these 'pseudo-prophet' opponents are members of the 'established religious-political order'.

70. Cf. Gelston 2010: 98–99. Several versions of LXX read the Hebrew verb as a Hiphil. For arguments in favour of retaining the Hebrew text (and the verb 'turn back'), see Waltke 2007: 113.

71. Note the connection between reproach (*kĕlimmâ*) and the consequences or punishment of Israel's sin in Isa. 30:3; Jer. 3:25; Ezek. 16:54, 63.

7. This verse presents and then refutes another protest against Micah's message of judgment, especially as restated in the immediately preceding verse. The people's retort is a blunt misinterpretation of Exodus 34 and other Old Testament texts and traditions. Micah summarizes their flawed beliefs in two questions intended to cast doubt upon his assertion that their consistently sinful behaviour will be met with divine punishment.[72] *Is YHWH impatient? Are these [reproaches] his deeds?* Both questions were probably rhetorical, and Micah's opponents would have responded 'No!'

The first question presumes that God's patience is essentially without end, at least in their case.[73] Divine patience is frequently emphasized in God's relationship with Israel, especially in the catastrophic incident involving worship of the golden calf at Sinai (Exod. 34:6–7). There God punished Israel's sin in a limited way (Exod. 32:25–29, 35) and refrained from destroying the people as a whole in response to Moses' intercession (Exod. 33:12–17). This key text is cited at crucial moments in Israel's later history (Num. 14:18; Neh. 9:17) and informs reflection on the divine character in the Psalms as well (Pss 86:15; 103:8; 145:8; etc.). In the Minor Prophets at least part of Exodus 34:6–7 appears at several points, including Joel 2:12–14; Jonah 4:1–4; Micah 7:18–20; Nahum 1:2b–3a; and Malachi 1:9a.[74] Micah's opponents use the fact that God is

---

The lexeme does not occur elsewhere in the Book of the Twelve. The common English translation 'Disgrace will not overtake us' introduces discord between a third-person masculine singular verb and a plural subject and must supply a direct object in addition to reading the verbal form as *nun-sin-gimel* rather than MT's *samek-gimel*, so it is rather unlikely.

72. Waltke (2007: 113) thinks YHWH is the speaker through 2:7. Wolff (1990: 81–82) proposes the interpretation advanced here.

73. Andersen and Freedman (2000: 311) think the expression refers to divine inability to act.

74. See the explanation of this text and its reuse in Boda 2017: 27–51. For a questionable diachronic or redactional explanation, see Wöhrle 2009. Although the divine impatience mentioned here uses the idea of 'spirit' rather than the phrase from Exod. 34 (a 'long nose'), the question

(often) patient to refute the accusation that his patience with the house of Jacob has come to an end.

The second question also involves a selective, self-serving misinterpretation of God, this time focused on his works. YHWH's *deeds* (*maʿălāl*) in the Old Testament surely include deliverance and are celebrated as such (e.g. Josh. 24:31; Pss 71:16; 77:11 [Heb. 12]; 145:17). However, the point of view expressed in this question ignores the many situations in which the same word (*deeds*) refers to God's discipline, correction and punishment of his sinful people. As a result, the second question misrepresents YHWH as a God who (only) delivers, and that, regardless of the behaviour of those upon whom he has mercy.[75] This theology is wrenched from its biblical contexts and made into a basis for autonomy and immunity to punishment.

The first-person reference to *my words* makes it very likely that this last line is not spoken by the opponents but by the prophet (on behalf of God) (Dempster 2017: 89). Micah's retort at the end of the verse is calculated to correct his detractors' nonchalance towards sin by asserting that, yes, YHWH's words do good, but only to those who walk uprightly! Rather than presuming that God will remain patient with them regardless of their behaviour, Micah's opponents must realize that in the world that YHWH created and governs, and especially in the covenant that he made with Israel, the consequences of one's actions cannot be avoided indefinitely.

8–9. Micah continues his refutation of his opponents' position by confronting them with sins they seem to be ignorant of.[76] To that end he returns to the theme of oppression, explored in

---

(note 74 *cont.*) refers to the same divine attribute. Because 'spirit' is part of the idiom 'short spirit' (*qaṣar rûaḥ*), the question refers to YHWH's patience, not to the patience of YHWH's Spirit. The phrase appears only in Job 21:4 and Prov. 14:29b (in contrast to being 'long of nose' in Prov. 14:29a). Note the similar expressions 'short temper/self' (*qaṣar nepeš*) in Num. 21:4 (Israel); Judg. 10:16 (YHWH); Judg. 16:16 (Samson); and a 'short nose' (*qaṣar ʾap*) in Prov. 14:17.

75. Contrast Ps. 99:8.

76. The Hebrew conjunction *waw* binds 2:8–9 to what precedes it.

connection with the expropriation of hereditary property inheritances in 2:1–5. Here that theme is presented from a new angle and with two additional dimensions of mistreatment of their fellow Israelites. The subsection introduces the subject (the *enemy*), then describes its treatment of YHWH's people in three actions. The description of each action begins with the preposition *from*, emphasizing that this enemy takes away increasingly valuable things: the mantle worn over one's garment, one's home, and finally God's *splendour* from the victims' children.

YHWH's opening words describe the problem in general: a group within Israel/Judah has risen up against the rest of *my people*, who are by inference their unsuspecting, peaceable victims (cf. Isa 63:10, with *hāpak*).[77] The introduction of two different groups within the same nation echoes the 'my people . . . you' distinction made in 2:3, and prepares the reader for the first explicit presentation of the remnant in 2:12–13.

YHWH describes the behaviour of these militant, rapacious persons in three ways. First, they *strip the mantle* from their neighbour's cloak, probably an image of economic power over the less fortunate (cf. the prohibition against taking another's cloak overnight, Exod. 22:26; Deut. 24:13; cf. Amos 2:8) (Kessler 2000: 132). Ironically, these fellow Israelites are returning from war and so consider all hostilities (in that case, with foreign powers) to be a thing of the past.[78] The fact that their fellow citizens accost and deprive them of material goods reveals that conflict is present where peace should reign, and brackets the whole of 2:8 in war-like violence.

---

77. While Micah seems to be the speaker in 1:9 who refers to Judah as *my people*, the reference to *my splendour* in 2:9 makes it more likely that YHWH is the speaker here. It is probably best to see *my people* as protective when uttered by YHWH and by Micah (cf. 1:9; 3:3, 5), with Andersen and Freedman (2000: 316). LXX has a very different reading, presumably misreading the noun and adding a verb (Gelston 2010: 99).

78. *HALOT* 2.1431 proposes several possible senses that all fall within the same semantic field.

Second, they *evict* the *women of my people*[79] (presumably widows,[80] since no husbands are mentioned) from their *cherished homes*. These homes are not necessarily luxurious, but rather represent economic and social security (recall the grave economic consequences of losing one's household and family, and note the children in the phrase).

In doing so, third, they deprive even young children of YHWH's *splendour*.[81] Child slavery may be in view here, since the household has presumably been repossessed for economic reasons. This leads Kessler to propose that the taking away has to do with the children's *splendour* as human beings, with reference to Psalm 8:5, which uses the phrase 'glory and honour' of human beings in general (Kessler 2000: 133). In this case *my splendour* would be that shared by YHWH with his image bearers, but it is difficult to explain how a slave of any kind would not be fully in the divine image.

For this reason, Waltke's suggestion that *my splendour* is 'metonymy for the rich physical benefits that I AM gave his children in the sworn land' is nearer the mark (cf. Ps. 90:16; Ezek. 16:14).[82] In Micah 2:9, the disruption of the social fabric and theological

---

79. The repetition of *my people* ties the victimized groups in 2:8–9 closely together.

80. Allen 1976: 297. Kessler (2000: 132) protests that widows are usually identified as such in the biblical text, but the absence of any males is striking.

81. So Allen 1976: 293. The only other 'glory/splendour' language in Micah is 1:15; cf. Jer. 3:19, and contrast protection of widows and children/ orphans, Exod. 22:22. Wolff (1990: 83) proposes eliminating the first-person singular suffix and revocalizing the noun as 'bedroom', which suits the context but requires emending the text.

82. Waltke 2007: 120. In favour of understanding YHWH's splendour as his work of deliverance, blessing and protection for his people, in Ps. 90:16 the speakers ask YHWH to shown them his 'work' (*pōʻal*) and their children his 'splendour' (*hādār*), while in Ezek. 16:14 YHWH's splendour is his election and blessing of Israel before she wandered from him. Andersen and Freedman (2000: 322) observe that YHWH's glory (a different Hebrew noun) is typically linked to the cult and its infrastructure (e.g. the ark of the covenant).

foundation of Judah and Israel leads to an uncertain and lacklustre future for the youngest citizens, with exile being the most likely explanation. The fact that the powerful have stolen from their own society's most vulnerable and defenceless members shows them to be inhumane and merciless as well as self-authorizing and godless.

Whether or not debt slavery is involved, this lamentable situation is exacerbated by the fact that this condition is apparently permanent (*for ever*; debt slavery involving Israelites was to last only six years, Exod. 21:2–6; Deut. 15:12–18). We can sum up the whole of 2:8–9 as a picture of terribly destructive civil and religious violence in which the powerful and corrupt among the rich oppress, dispossess and violate the rights of the weak in Israel and Judah. This moves their nation away from the covenantally normed society that practises justice and mercy, and towards one in which might makes right.

10. The absence of first-person grammar here suggests that Micah, rather than YHWH, is the speaker who commands the unjust oppressors to leave their land.[83] This outcome parallels that of 2:1–5, where the oppressors are to be punished by expulsion and will own no land in the long term.[84] Although the guilty are expelled from the land never to return, others who are expelled will later return as the remnant that follows YHWH (2:12–13).

The removal in 2:9 of divine blessing from the land due to abuse of the population in general, and especially of families and children, is clarified by the assertion here that the land is no longer *the place of rest*.[85] The land of Israel was to be the resting place for

---

83. So also Jenson 2008: 127. It is also possible that the command is directed to those suffering injustice, in part because the one commanded to leave is not connected to the land's uncleanness. However, the emphasis on judgment that follows in 2:10 is most effective if the rhetorical audience is those whose sins are to be punished in this way.

84. So also Ben Zvi 1999: 96–97.

85. Since both YHWH's place of rest and the Davidic dynasty are linked to Israel's rest (e.g. Ps. 132; the same Hebrew term, *měnûḥâ*, is used in both passages), this particular *place of rest* at the end of the eighth century is centred on Jerusalem.

God's obedient people under his blessing (Num. 10:33; Deut. 12:9; 1 Kgs 8:56), but if the nation was disobedient, the various covenant punishments, and most clearly exile, would inevitably bring that restful existence to an end. Not only is the land without rest, it is *impure*. The promised land could be made impure in various ways, most notably through bloodshed (Num. 35:33–34) and corrupt religious practices (Jer. 2:7–8; Ezek. 23:7–8; 33:26), and both of these sins are mentioned in Micah (see 1:7; 3:2–3, 5, 10, etc.).[86] Since the land is the subject of the verb *destroy*, the wicked and not the land itself will be destroyed (*HALOT* 1.285–286). The emphasis on this destruction as *terrible* implies that even exile is not the ultimate punishment – death will find them (cf. Amos 9:4). This perspective on the oppressors complements the fate of the land barons in 2:5, who will not be part of restored Israel.

11. Micah's closing remark forms a sarcastic inclusio with 2:6, and focuses on one of the root problems among his opponents: their lack of attention to YHWH's speech through his attested and Torah-based prophets (cf. O'Dowd 2009: 69). Micah claims that if someone were to tell them lies, and promise only wine and liquor, that would be enough to qualify him as a 'prattler-prophet' and to satisfy his audience's appetites.[87] Conspicuous by its absence is the critical appraisal of prophets on the basis of the Sinai covenant that forms the foundation of the message of true prophets. This radical misalignment of their beliefs and values with respect to YHWH's revealed will shows Micah's opponents to be totally indisposed to knowing YHWH as he is. They are interested only in what serves their social status, material and financial wealth, and physical satisfaction (Ben Zvi 1999: 97–98). If this remains their defining characteristic, the destruction announced in 2:10 cannot

---

86. See further Averbeck 1997a.

87. Noting the presence of the Hebrew words 'wind' and 'lying' here and in 1 Kgs 22, Dempster (2017: 92–93) sees an allusion to the prophet Micaiah ben-Imlah, who contradicted the rosy predictions of four hundred Israelite pseudo-prophets.

fail to strike them.[88] This radical difference also accounts for their title as *this people* rather than as the prophet's/God's people, as in 2:8.[89]

Meaning

This section is very revealing in terms of practical theology. What makes these people tell Micah not to preach, and deny that judgment is possible? Because they mistakenly believe themselves to be living in accord with YHWH's word and will, the hearer/reader is confronted with the danger of self-deception. Furthermore, this danger is all the greater when one's actions offer access to material wealth and power. The fact that many of these people rejected prophetic warnings serves as a warning against domesticating God, taking sin with only moderate seriousness, and usurping God's importance and authority in our lives. C. S. Lewis captured the significance of these things in his insistence that 'if you have not chosen the Kingdom of God, it will make in the end no difference what you have chosen instead . . . We shall have missed the end for which we are formed and rejected the only thing that satisfies.'[90]

G. Oracle of salvation (2:12–13)

Context

This section is the first in the book to present the theme of deliverance, and it does so in close connection with the clearest description yet of the concept of the remnant. YHWH in his role as shepherd-king will end the anticipated exile of Judah and Israel. The liberation will include the remnants of both nations, who will be led to freedom (and presumably to a restored Jerusalem, 4:1–4) by YHWH.

---

88. Ben Zvi (1999: 98) thinks that 'The conveyed message is . . . that the community should check the validity of a contemporaneous prophet or teacher against the current knowledge imparted by YHWH' (cf. Deut. 18).

89. So also Kessler 2000: 131.

90. Lewis 2001: 190–191, cited in Rigney 2018: 294.

Comment

12. The recipients of YHWH's deliverance and restoration include the remnants of both the northern and southern kingdoms. Not all *Israel* (i.e. the southern kingdom of Judah) will survive judgment and be delivered, and given what has already been said about the northern kingdom (2:4, 10) we can assume that *Jacob* here refers only to the part of the northern kingdom's population that is not characterized by the violence, oppression, coveting and autonomy spelled out earlier in this chapter. The earlier distinctions between the oppressor and the oppressed in 2:1–5 and between those who rob garments and houses and the vulnerable from whom they take them in 2:8–9 have prepared the reader for the concept of the *remnant* (*šĕʾērît*) as a subgroup within a larger group. The concept returns at key points after 2:12–13 as well (cf. *šĕʾērît* in 4:7; 5:7, 8; 7:18; *yeter* in 5:3, in addition to passages that present the concept with other terms).[91]

Interestingly, the creation of the remnant is not described here (see 4:6–7). Rather, its existence subsequent to the destruction and deportation anticipated by 1:10–16 and 2:4, 10 is simply affirmed (Kessler 2000: 139). The gathering of *Jacob* and *the remnant of Israel* presumes that they have been scattered by exile, and entails the reunification of the whole people of God (i.e. the remnants of the northern and southern kingdoms).[92] The use of two cognate infinitive-finite verb pairs for *gather* and *gather together* (the only such pairing in the book; Dempster 2017: 100) emphasizes the certainty of that ideal outcome despite the severe difficulties and threats facing the faithful.

God's role as a shepherd is part of his kingly role which appears explicitly in the next verse.[93] The passage emphasizes the unity (*yaḥad*) of the sheep drawn from the two groups named as well as

---

91. Roberts (2018: 332) suggests that 2:12–13 'may have originally been addressed to the survivors of the Northern Kingdom after the disaster of 734–732 B.C.E. or the later disaster of 725–722 B.C.E.'

92. Dempster (2017: 101) thinks that *remnant of Israel* 'further specifies Jacob'.

93. Wagenaar (2001: 231) observes (with reference to G. Widengren) that the 'gathering of the dispersed . . . played a prominent role in the royal ideology of Ancient Mesopotamia'.

their number (a *noisy* multitude). Against the backdrop of oppression, violence and loss of inheritance earlier in the chapter, this image implies a radically new phase in YHWH's relationship with his purified people.[94] YHWH's actions here have strong parallels with his deliverance of Israel at the time of the exodus (Ps. 78:52–55), the second exodus in Isaiah (40:11), the apparently exilic prayer for restoration directed to YHWH as 'shepherd of Israel, you who lead Joseph like a flock' (Ps. 80:1; also Jer. 23:3), and the prayer of Micah 7:14.

13. This verse looks more closely at how the gathering and reunification of the remnants of Jacob and Israel will take place. It focuses not on historical details, but on the driving force (person) behind it and on the radical liberation that such a gathering entails.

The *Breaker*, identified later in the verse as YHWH, goes in front of the people of his flock (cf. Exod. 23:23; Num. 14:14). *Breaker* implies freedom from captivity or exile, and the image of YHWH breaking through the walls (most likely not literal) that hold his remnant people captive and prevent their return to the land is enriched especially by the use of the same term in 2 Samuel 5:20, when YHWH gave David victory over the Philistines. The image of breaking through opposition or obstacles does not jar with the more quotidian image of passing through gates, and neither image should be taken literally.

The last verb is the only one not associated with the gate, so the movement described begins behind the walls and gates (*break out* and *pass through* are the only perfect verbs), *goes out* of them, and finally moves away from them.[95] The movement thus anticipates

---

94. The fact that this oracle foresees a post-exilic reality is no reason to date its composition to that period.

95. Contrast the suggestion of Kessler (2000: 142) that the broken walls are the point of departure for the freed exiles, and that the gate marks their destination. Ben Zvi (2000: 66) finds in the middle of 2:13 'a staged, sequential set of ellipses that involve almost all the key words' in which 'gate' is the only explicit object and four verbs (one twice) are used to highlight the liberation and movement into freedom: they break through (the gate), (they pass through) the gate, they go out through it, they pass by (with) their king before them; YHWH is at their head.

later passages in Micah in which the remnant returns to Jerusalem (note 4:10; 7:9–12). In this case, the restoration of Israel and Judah is inseparable from the purified land (2:5) and from the multiplication of its population (2:12). YHWH is the main actor in this passage, and his roles are those typically associated with images for royalty. As the one who liberates his people, God is the Breaker; as the one who gathers them, he is their Shepherd; and as the one who rules over his reconstituted people in his royal city, he is their King.[96]

Meaning

The radical change described in 2:12–13 can hardly be overstated. Judah and Israel as described earlier in the first section of the book (1:2 – 2:13) are guilty of sin, worthy of divine punishment, oppressed without hope of deliverance, and threatened by Assyria. The future paradigm foreseen here presumes the removal of the sin and guilt that exposed Judah/Israel to judgment and contaminated the land; explicitly excludes sinners from the restoration of Israel and Judah (2:5); involves a limited punishment that does not prevent God's liberation of his people; promises an end to exile, liberation to the oppressed and the reunification of the dispersed people of God; predicts that the numerous (2:12) remnant will return to a purified land (2:5); and affirms that the remnant will enjoy liberty, security and provision under YHWH's reign (2:12–13).[97]

---

96. Goswell (2019) helpfully explores the significance of the general absence of a Davidic king from Micah. Note the similar divine roles in Exod. 15.

97. The strong concentration of positive images and beneficent divine involvement makes very unlikely the suggestion by Smith-Christopher (2015: 104) and others that 2:12–13 may be a warning of destruction or an unreliable oracle from Micah's opponents. Allen's suggestion (1976: 302–303) that the movement in view here refers to the return home of Judahites who took refuge from Sennacherib once YHWH had destroyed the Assyrian army fails to take account of the reunification of the southern and northern kingdoms and of YHWH's predominance as King, as well as the context's emphasis on a purified land and the removal of evildoers from Israel/Judah.

2. SECOND CYCLE (3:1 – 5:15)

The beginning of a new section is evident from Micah's only use of the introductory phrase *And I said* (3:1). This verse also uses the imperative *Hear* that appears in 1:2 and 6:1 at the head of other major sections. The book's second judgment–hope cycle begins with an indictment of Israel's elite in 3:1–3, which is followed by an announcement of judgment against them in 3:4. An indictment of false prophets follows in 3:5, an announcement of judgment against them in 3:6–7, and a contrasting reaffirmation of Micah's divine commission in 3:8. In 3:9–12 the indictment is broadened to include all in religious or civil leadership in Judah/Israel. The corresponding announcement of judgment against Jerusalem (3:12) is the most far-reaching of the chapter.

Chapters 4–5 shift to almost entirely positive predictions of restored Zion's future after its judgment and the spiritual transformation of its new population. The components and results of this future change are explored in several different ways: the nations appear for the first time in a positive role, coming to restored Jerusalem and finding peace under YHWH's reign (4:1–4);

the remnant is delivered from exile and danger by the Ruler from Bethlehem (4:9 – 5:6); and the nations' varying responses to the remnant and their God are sketched (esp. 5:7–8). The section closes with a presentation of the purification of the remnant alongside the destruction of the nations that do not heed YHWH's word (5:10–15), complementing the opening scene of 4:1–5.

A. First Judgment Speech (against political leaders) (3:1–4)

Context
Chapter 3 presents three judgment speeches, each addressing the guilty party, then presenting an accusation and an announcement of judgment.[1] Each sub-unit is introduced by a call to listen (excepting 3:5, which introduces a new speech unit), followed by the accusation and the announcement of judgment (3:8 exceptionally contrasts Micah with pseudo-prophets).[2]

In sharp contrast to the short but powerful description of the *future* return and restoration of the remnant of God's reunited people under YHWH as shepherd-king (2:12–13), Micah 3 paints the *present* sins of the leaders of both nations in shocking colours. In doing so, it offers the clearest identification yet of those responsible for oppression and injustice in Judah and Israel, highlighting again the distinction between just and unjust *within each nation*.[3] Furthermore, the theme of the elimination of the unjust from Israel/Judah, introduced in 2:1–3, 5, 10, is developed extensively in chapter 3. This judgment is focused on corrupt rulers and religious leaders (3:4, 6–7), but in its final stage will affect all of Judah (as was the

---

1. Wolff 1990: 92. See the more detailed analysis of the unit's structure in Ben Zvi 2000: 70–71.

2. Ben Zvi (2000: 71) observes that 'a ubiquitous network of repeated vocabulary and of puns extends over the entire text' and strengthens its cohesion. See also the observations of Dempster 2017: 109.

3. Given the great significance of Israelite kings reigning justly, it is notable that no king is mentioned here, even accepting the prophetic habit of sometimes not mentioning the king, on which see Ben Zvi 2000: 86–87.

case with Israel, 1:6–7) when the temple is destroyed and the southern kingdom falls (3:12). Even that, however, is primarily 'on
account of' the corrupt leaders (3:12a).

Comment

1. *And I said* is an editorial remark from Micah that reaffirms his
authorial link to the book in its entirety while also introducing his
reaction to continuing sin among his people. The command *Hear*
introduces not only 3:1–4 but the entire second section of the book
(cf. 1:2; 6:1).[4] As in 1:5 and 2:12, the pair *Jacob . . . Israel* designates
the northern and southern kingdoms, respectively, as the audience
of this judgment speech.[5] It focuses on the egregious injustices
perpetrated or permitted by the rulers and authorities in both north
and south (the kings of the two nations are presumably included).[6]
Micah presumes that they are to *know*, that is, be intimately
acquainted with, *justice (mišpāṭ)*. As the only positive attribute he
mentions, this should be the defining characteristic of rulers in
both kingdoms.

Mišpāṭ is a judicial term that, like 'justice' in English, can refer to
justice abstractly or concretely.[7] God is the source of justice in the
Old Testament (Seifrid 2000). The laws he reveals in Exodus 21 – 23
are 'judgments' *(mišpāṭîm)*, and the example of Solomon asking for
wisdom to judge justly (1 Kgs 3) makes clear the king's obligation
to heed and promote God's will rather than his own. Judges too are
warned against partiality (Deut. 1:16–18; 16:18–20) with a view

---

4. 3:1 makes clear that the prophet is the speaker in 3:1–4; contrast 3:5–7
   (but note Micah's first-person speech again in 3:8). Waltke (2007: 149)
   argues that YHWH accuses in 3:3.

5. Contra Renaud 1987: 59, who thinks that they refer only to Judah.

6. Andersen and Freedman (2000: 349) suggest that 'heads' in 3:1
   contrasts with YHWH 'at the head' of his restored people in 2:12.

7. The definite article may emphasize the distinctive nature of the justice
   YHWH demands, over against a very different definition that suited the
   corrupt schemes of the elite; cf. van der Merwe, Naudé and Kroeze
   2017: 219 on the article's designation of 'a class of persons or things
   that are definite in themselves'.

towards 'righteous judgment' (Miller 2011: 143). It is assumed that the leaders not only have a far-reaching responsibility to establish justice in particular legal cases, but that as a rule they are to protect and promote what is good while opposing what is evil (3:2). The sense of *mišpāṭ* thus is close to 'what is right and proper, righteousness' (Johnson 1998: 92), or 'the good' (Carroll R. 2007: 105). But even though the judiciary is a relevant context for *justice*, it is not the only one in ancient Israel, and Micah's accusation ultimately has to do with the rejection of 'the requirements of the covenant' by the two nations in a variety of settings.[8]

2–3. Micah makes two shocking assertions in 3:2–3. First, although justice should be the defining characteristic of a leader in Israel/Judah, he alleges that these leaders *hate good* (which is very closely related to *justice* in 6:8) and *love evil* (the same word as *calamity*/'evil' in 2:3). This identifies them as the opposites, and even enemies, of yhwh, who loves justice and hates evil (Ps. 45:7 [Heb. 8])! It also depicts them as disobeying an earlier prophet's command to 'hate evil and love good' (Amos 5:15) (Schart 1998: 185). Accepting Micah's critique at face value, one can only conclude that the social and religious fabric of society is severely damaged and cannot last much longer. It also implies that these leaders are either self-deceived (they believe that their 'good' is God's 'good') or willingly oppose God and his will (Pak 2018). Their surprise at Micah's condemnation of them reveals their very 'different understanding of the nature and practice of justice' (Carroll R. 2007: 106).

The second assertion is more shocking still. Micah uses the imagery of cannibalism to describe these rulers' 'robbery and economic exploitation of the populace'.[9] The extensive description, which includes seven elements, reflects both the widespread nature of such economic oppression in Judah and its morally outrageous nature:[10]

---

8. Dempster 2017: 111, with reference to Mic. 6:8.

9. Smith-Christopher 2015: 110. His suggestion (p. 111) that literal cannibalism during a siege may also be in view is improbable.

10. As Kessler notes (2000: 149), the description of this wrongdoing in metaphorical terms presupposes that the acts themselves are well known to the audience.

(1) *tear the skin from them* (2) *and* [*tear*] *the flesh off their bones,* (3) *eat the flesh of my people,* (4) *and rip their skin from them,* (5) *and break their bones into pieces,* (6) *and spread them out like flesh for a pot,* (7) [*spread them*] *like meat in a cauldron!*[11] The variety of the anatomical elements and the repetition of several of them strengthen the image further, as does the focus on the whole person in the last two lines: skin, bones, flesh, skin, bones, them (people), them (people).[12]

While this imagery is not without biblical precedent,[13] Micah's extensive development of the motif is without parallel (Kessler 2000: 149). The shocking metaphor of cannibalism highlights the invasive, predatory, depersonalizing nature of these acts. The first five lines of the sub-unit explicitly preserve the personal identity of these violated persons with possessive suffixes, pronominal suffixes or other means (v. 2: 'their skin', *their bones,* plus *from them*; v. 3: *of my people, their skin from them, their bones*). The final two lines stress, contrariwise, what such treatment makes the victims resemble (Heb. *k*), and only here are neither they nor part of their bodies grammatically present. The point is clear: the leaders sustain their economic and social lives by savagely preying on the vulnerable and defenceless, essentially robbing them of their lives in the process.[14]

---

11. The only other use of *cauldron* (*qalāḥat*) appears in a cultic context, but this is not reason enough to assume a cultic setting here, contra Andersen and Freedman (2000: 354).

12. The last verb (*pāraś*) in 3:3 has no explicit object and is elided in the last clause of the verse.

13. See esp. Prov. 30:14; for oppression in general, Ps. 27:2; for cannibalism in general, Lev. 26:29; Deut. 28:53, 55; Jer. 19:9; Ezek. 39:18; Zech. 11:9; for metaphorical consumption of the vulnerable by corrupt rulers and judges, Zeph. 3:3.

14. As McKane (1998: 101) puts it, 'Micah lays the blame for the failures of government in that sphere [internal social structures] at the door of administrators whose motives are malevolent and whose methods are cruel, who seek to maximize their own gain at the expense of the well-being of the community for which they are responsible.'

4. *Then* refers obliquely to an unspecified time of judgment or retribution[15] when the tables are turned and the oppressors are in danger (Exod. 14:10; Num. 11:2; Judg. 3:9; frequently in the Psalms). *They* refers to the authorities addressed in the second person in 3:1–3 who consumed the general population and non-elites by unconscionable economic and social injustices. Because the context is not eschatological, at least an initial horizon of punishment would be the Assyrian Empire's military activity in the Levant towards the end of the eighth century. The first divine response leaves the oppressors to their fate, which is bad enough, while the second removes divine favour from them (*hide his face*).

The divine response to their call for help once this punishment falls upon them is silence. In theological terms, this is a refusal to deliver those who refuse to repent of their violent abuse of their fellow citizens. This is made clear by the statement at the end of the verse that they *committed evil acts*, a comparatively benign summary of the metaphorical cannibalism that was their consistent and premeditated pattern of behaviour.[16] Micah also asserts that YHWH *will hide his face from them at that time*, meaning he will deny them his presence, beneficent attention, help, deliverance and peace (cf. Num. 6:24–26).[17] The collage of covenantal terms that expresses what YHWH's face symbolizes makes this punishment equivalent to the denial of covenant-based residence and rest in Israel (2:5, 9) and the threat of destruction (2:10) announced against the oppressors in Micah 2. The sharp separation between this group

---

15. Similarly, Wagenaar 2001: 245.

16. The Hebrew causative verbal stem (Hiphil) underlines their intent, *HALOT* 2.1270; cf. Andersen and Freedman 2000: 356. Ben Zvi (2000: 83) argues that throughout Mic. 3 the speaker 'repeatedly characterizes the leaders as those who willfully pervert the messages and basic lore whose source is in YHWH, that is, the contents of "divine, authoritative communication or instruction".'

17. Wolff 1990: 101. Waltke (2007: 152) defines it as 'a very concrete act of his [God's] anger and wrath'.

and the rest of the covenant community is notable and continues the remnant theme.[18]

Meaning

This section offers a brutally direct critique of the abuse of power by religious leaders in particular. Charged with the responsibility of promoting justice and what is good, many leaders in Micah's day had elevated their own appetites and aspirations over these God-given values. Their self-centred worldview drove them to violence of all kinds against those whom they were supposed to protect, instruct and guide in God's will and ways. YHWH rejects their usurpation of his centrality and condemns their violence, promising to punish it in the worst way imaginable by refusing to deliver them from the inevitable consequences of their sin.

B. Second Judgment Speech (against false prophets) (3:5–8)

Context

The second judgment speech in this unit focuses on one category of religious leaders: the prophets. As in the preceding unit, the condemnation (3:5) is followed by an announcement of punishment (3:6–7), this one longer than the previous unit's. Its special relevance to Micah's diametrically opposed ministry is underlined by the contrast he draws between them and himself in 3:8.

Comment

5. True prophets lead YHWH's people in his ways,[19] but those identified here instead *lead* them *astray*. Specifically, these prophets *proclaim peace* to those who pay them to do so, contradicting Micah's message of coming judgment. The peace they promise, *šālôm*, is shorthand for the Sinai covenant's blessings, and significantly is the

---

18. Waltke (2007: 155) concludes that 'Its leaders are members of God's outward kingdom, "my people", but they are not part of its inward spiritual kingdom.'

19. *My people*, if a divine utterance, is used differently here from 'his people' in 6:2, where it is negative; cf. Andersen and Freedman 2000: 368–369.

final element in the high-priestly benediction of Numbers 6:24–26. Ironically, when they are not paid to deliver the message of peace that their audience wants, they attack their kin in ways they say foreigners won't and *proclaim holy war*, equating their enemies with God's![20]

6–7. The condemnation of individuals who had at least some legitimate roles (e.g. prophets) raises the question whether these were true prophets who corrupted the divine messages they received, or false ones who received influences or intuitions from demonic sources. The following points strongly favour the latter option.[21] First, not all of these activities were legitimate on biblical grounds, at least if not practised by authorized persons. The most common one is that of a prophet, who could receive either visions (Nah. 1:1; Obad. 1) or, presumably in another way, the 'word of YHWH' (Mic. 1:1 and frequently elsewhere). However, the possibility that there might be false prophets was recognized from the very beginning (Deut. 13; 18), and Israel's later history bears witness to this recurrent problem.[22] Since these prophets were speaking for gain and led *my people astray*, their pronouncements were inevitably not from YHWH (3:5). The same holds for their attacks on those who refuse to pay them. *Seers* (*haḥōzîm*, 3:7) fall into the same category, since the terms are roughly synonymous (cf. 1 Sam. 9:9; Amos 7:12–15; also the similar terms in Mic. 5:12).[23]

Divination (from the root *qāsam*), the other activity the passage mentions, is routinely presented as illegitimate in the Old Testament (note esp. Deut. 18:10, 14, where it is contrasted with true

---

20. Dempster (2017: 112) suggests that 'In addition to slandering reputations, humiliating people, and spiritually abusing people, this also meant cursing them.'

21. *Pace*, for example, Wessels 2009: 39, and Waltke 2007: 163, although the latter terms them 'false prophets', as do most interpreters. Dempster (2017: 112) adopts a position similar to mine.

22. In rare cases, YHWH may speak truth through an (otherwise) false prophet, e.g. Balaam (Num. 22 – 24), or send a 'lying spirit' to a false prophet (1 Kgs 22).

23. Verhoof 1997: 1069, 1071; Romerowski 2004: 1334.

prophecy; 1 Sam. 15:23; 2 Kgs 17:17; Jer. 14:14; 27:9; 29:8; Ezek. 13:6, 9, 23; Zech. 10:2).[24] While the levitical priests could divine (in a more general sense) by means of the Urim and Thummim and the high priest's breastplate (Exod. 28:30; 1 Sam. 28:6; Ezra 2:63 // Neh. 7:65), the phenomenon here involves neither authorized persons nor legitimate means.[25] The essential difference, in short, is that YHWH did not associate himself with or involve himself in them.[26]

This leads to a second consideration that argues against seeing Micah's opponents as true prophets: there is no affirmation that these *prophets, seers* and *diviners* were ever authorized or sent by YHWH. The only possible implication that YHWH might have been the source of their messages is the fact that he does not (any longer?) respond to them (3:7). However, the similarity of 3:7 (*there will be no response from God*) to 3:4 ('YHWH will not *answer* them' when they 'cry out to YHWH') makes it more likely that he ignores their call for help, not their request to give (more) revelation, which in any case they emphatically reject when it comes through Micah (e.g. 2:6, 11).[27] YHWH's refusal to deliver them is thus added to his making them unable to practise divination. God will interrupt the *illegitimate* means of revelation they typically use and will not respond to their calls for help once they are unable to (falsely) prophesy as

---

24. The only quasi-exception is the nominal form in Prov. 16:10, which compares a royal exercise of judgment with a *qesem*, presumably 'by means of an oracle', *HALOT* 2.1116.

25. Kessler (2000: 156) draws attention to the parallel prophecy-divination in 3:6.

26. Horsnell 1997b: 946, 948. O'Dowd (2009: 69) argues that 'True prophecy . . . affirms the great commandment (Deut 6:4–9) by hermeneutically applying the first commandment (Deut 5:6–7) to the future world of international religious discourse.'

27. Andersen and Freedman (2000: 375) reason similarly that the verb means '"reply" not revelation'. It is also possible that *ʾĕlōhîm* here should be translated as 'gods', highlighting the non-Yahwistic source of their visions and oracles.

before.[28] As a result, 'they are disgraced as they are exposed in their lies and are ashamed' (Smith-Christopher 2015: 117).

Finally, Micah is clearly identified as the *only* one who speaks for YHWH, at least in the social-religious context of this particular accusation (1:1; 3:7). As such he fiercely opposes the false prophets, seers and diviners who do not speak for YHWH (cf. Jer. 14:14). His speech also contrasts sharply with the silence that God will impose upon them. In short, the two groups seem to share only the function of speaking publicly while having diametrically opposed messages and thus incompatible positions with regard to God's revealed will.[29]

The punishment announced against these pseudo-prophets is elaborate, and it spans most of 3:6–7. The first part announces the end of all visions, divination and sources of prophecy using terms

---

28. If, contrariwise, YHWH revealed his will to these false prophets and they ignored it, very little changes in terms of their actual pronouncements. However, the idea of YHWH speaking to a prophet who fails to transmit his message seems to remove any reason to refer to that person as a prophet (of YHWH). Wolff (1990: 103) and, similarly, Kessler (2000: 156) may be correct to note that a transition from legitimate to illegitimate prophet was possible: 'Whoever speaks falsely in behalf of Yahweh will have the word taken from him', although Deut. 13:1–5; 18:20 obviate this divine interruption of revelation by calling for the prophet to be executed. Ben Zvi (2000: 82–83) sees a very weak connection (if any) between what these prophets were saying and YHWH's revealed truth, as do Kessler (2000: 156) and Andersen and Freedman (2000: 375–376). Contrast Wolff's view (1990: 101) of them as normally orthodox, and unorthodox only in this particular setting; similarly, Allen (1976: 312), who speaks of the 'abuse of prophetic gifts'.

29. The decision to accept or reject a given prophet's message on the basis of Deut. 18:9–22 requires the hearer's reflection and evaluation on the basis of preceding revelation, most fundamentally the Mosaic *tôrâ*. As a result, in the case of a yet-unproven prophet, 'Israel and the prophet will be tested: the prophet by Israel and as a result, Israel's heart by Yahweh' (O'Dowd 2009: 67).

for darkness or imagery of daylight ending (3:6). The result is 'silent darkness' (Smith-Christopher 2015: 117) or 'visionless visionaries and speechless preachers' (Marrs 1999: 197). The last part describes the shame, humiliation and even sadness (symbolized by covering one's lip) that will come upon these prophets when they are no longer heeded by the population and no longer able to make a profit from false prophecy. Their false predictions will not be realized, and whatever sources of insight or information they formerly used will no longer be available. The lack of any *response* from God at the end of 3:7 most likely refers not to his refusal to reveal his word for his people to these pseudo-prophets (see the discussion above), but to a divine refusal to answer them when they cry out for help.

8. The importance of distinguishing between Micah and his message and the false prophets and theirs is underlined by the explicit first-person contrast (*'ûlām, contariwise*, 'however', plus the first-person pronoun *I*) that Micah appends to this judgment speech. The primary difference is that Micah's speech derives directly from *the Spirit of YHWH*,[30] while theirs does not. This gives him and his message power and might and ensures that it is *justice*, while the pseudo-prophets and their message lacked these essential characteristics.[31] Rather than prophesying what coincides with the wishes of paying customers and cursing those who refuse to pay (3:5), Micah (surely a minority voice) announces God's message concerning the *rebellion* of *Jacob* and the *sin* of *Israel*.

Meaning
Micah condemns the abuse or usurpation of a prophetic role or gift in very strong terms. Not only did his opponents mislead God's

---

30. Among other reasons for translating *rûaḥ* as *Spirit* (i.e. a personal entity) is the direct link between YHWH's Spirit and Micah's speech – the Spirit communicates. Block (2011: 206) uses the term 'divine agent' and cites A. R. Johnson's description of it as 'an "extension of YHWH's personality".' Wessels (2009: 41) notes that Hos. 9:7–8 also associates the prophets with 'the Spirit' (with the definite article).

31. Similarly, Wessels (2009: 42), who also notes that the leaders critiqued in 3:1–7 exercised power without any connection to justice (p. 46).

people by promoting untruth and wrong instead of truth and right, they invoked divine anger against those who refused to compensate them for their services. Just as with the leaders who abused their power in the preceding speech, God will leave these prophets to their own devices when their grasp on power and influence fails. Despite their veneer of orthodox Yahwism, Micah demonstrates that they are without God's Spirit, and so without power to withstand divine judgment.

C. Third Judgment Speech (against civil and religious leaders) (3:9–12)

Context

The third and final judgment speech includes the groups mentioned in the two preceding ones (rulers, prophets) as well as others, notably priests. The condemnation section (3:9b–11) is the longest of the three, and its wider scope corresponds to its extensive announcement of punishment, which is nothing less than the destruction of Jerusalem (and, by implication, of Judah). This low point, however, is not the end, and chapter 4 presents a stunning transformation of Zion that will see it radically changed by YHWH's presence and rule.

Comment

9. Verses 9–11 identify the audience and then present a lengthy accusation. The leaders and rulers of both northern and southern kingdoms (cf. 1:5; 2:12; 3:1) are addressed at the outset, but this third speech quickly focuses on sins in Zion and Jerusalem (3:10–12; Samaria has already been condemned to destruction in 1:5–7).[32]

---

32. Roberts (2018: 330) thinks *Jacob . . . Israel* in 3:9 is 'inclusive' and refers only to the southern kingdom in the light of the quick shift in 3:10 to Jerusalem and Zion, but the use of the same phrase in 3:1 for an unspecified audience and the clearly distinct referents for Jacob and Israel in 1:5 and 2:12 favour keeping that distinction here. The presence or absence of 'house' (*bayit*) before the proper noun does not affect the referent; cf. 1:5. See also the discussion of Ben Zvi 2000: 79.

Their hearts *abhor justice*, and this manifests itself in various ways. Their intolerance of all that is *upright* or just (3:9d) spills over into all spheres of society and produces a terrible result (3:10): Zion/Jerusalem is built through *bloodshed* (the plural *dāmîm* always refers to illicit violence; Andersen and Freedman 2000: 383) and *iniquity* (*'awlâ*).

10. It is impossible and unnecessary to decide if the building referred to here is literal (i.e. construction) or not (i.e. advancement, consolidation of political or social power, etc.).[33] To some extent the two are inseparable if, as here, the builders are the elite or in positions of authority, as the context of chapters 2–3 (and especially 3:11) strongly suggests. Through various means, those who could advance themselves or their causes while ignoring YHWH's will and the well-being of their fellow citizens sought to *build* a city that reflected those twisted values. The mention of *bloodshed* leaves no doubt that these policies were pursued with abandon, and that not even human life was considered as important as these corrupt leaders' projects and aspirations.

11. Verse 11 shifts to the third person but continues the condemnation of the *leaders* of the south by accusing them of corrupting the exercise of justice for financial gain. Micah then charges that this same pursuit of material wealth has corrupted the *priests* and the *prophets* (already condemned in the previous section). The inclusion of all three groups here makes the condemnation of the south complete and reveals a shocking inversion of values in which God's will and word, and the well-being of their fellow citizens, are worth less than the payments they receive from their corrupt supporters.[34]

Most shocking of all is the blithe contentment of these corrupt leaders with this terrible status quo, an attitude that Micah highlights by presenting it as their own words. The rhetorical question presumes that YHWH is (inevitably) *among* them, and they are certain

---

33. Kessler (2000: 163) thinks that the building is literal and so sees the king as the object of critique, since only he could conscript a workforce.

34. Although priests had a judicial function using the breastplate (Exod. 28:15–30), Micah focuses on their teaching role (2 Chr. 15:3).

that nothing bad could happen to them. Far from thinking of YHWH as the Holy One who is committed to justice and cannot tolerate sin, they seem to think that their safety is guaranteed by his presence among them despite their egregious sins.[35] This twisted view is sometimes called Zion theology, a mixture of expectations and presumption based on Jerusalem as the site of YHWH's temple, Zion as his chosen mountain at the centre of the world, and the coming of the nations to Jerusalem to submit themselves to him and his Davidic king (cf. Pss 122; 125; 129; 132:8–18) (Walker 2000: 589). While these blessings and promises were indeed granted to Israel, none was unconditional, yet many Israelites were apparently willing to overlook this in order to convince themselves that God would never punish them.

This explains the prophetic critiques of absolute trust in the temple, in the king and in Israel's privileged status, rather than in YHWH's promises to bless obedience (e.g. Deut. 28:1–14). Micah and faithful prophets before and after him asserted that YHWH could and would punish his people for their disobedience, could remove the blessings of the Davidic covenant from a disobedient monarch, and could turn Jerusalem into a heap of rubble. Micah's announcement of destruction focused on Jerusalem (3:10) and its temple (3:12) would thus have been a direct contradiction of beliefs of the nations' leaders, and would have made him terribly unpopular, if not intolerable, among them. The root issue is again theological: what attitudes and types of behaviour reflect YHWH's character and will, and what does YHWH do (if anything) when his chosen people disregard his will?

12. Micah makes absolutely clear that YHWH's character and will are radically holy, and that because many Judeans' behaviour is diametrically opposed to him, Judah will be destroyed. This condemnation is not indiscriminate: *on account of you* ties the punishment to the radical disobedience of the nation's leaders and elite in particular.[36] The solidarity of God's people, however, means that

---

35. Renaud (1987: 70) offers a perceptive interpretation of these people making a god in their own image.

36. So also Kessler 2000: 167.

all will suffer (in varying degrees) the consequences of the sin most evident in only some members of their society. Still, those who submit to YHWH's kingship, even when it involves collective punishment, are also the ones who will be delivered – at least in the ultimate and most important sense, as 4:1–4 shows. A rebuilt Zion under its divine King is the ideal abode, and the removal of sin (7:9, 18–20) ensures that these people will not remain under God's judgment. If *my people* is YHWH's expression of ownership in 3:3, 5 (cf. also 2:8, 9), this series of judgment speeches includes a hint that YHWH never confuses the just and the unjust (or, in the light of 7:9, the penitent and the impenitent). The fall of Jerusalem is not the end of God's people but rather a strong rebuke of behaviours and values that are inconsistent with life in covenant with him.

The description of Jerusalem's destruction is given three parallel descriptions. The first two grammatical subjects are *Zion* and *Jerusalem*, while *the temple*, the place of God's presence and the focal point of his judgment, is last. Each clause presents an image that contrasts sharply with the Jerusalem of Micah's day.

The first image is metaphorical: *Zion will be like a ploughed field*. In the same way that ploughing removes all growth from the ground and renders it barren until it is planted, the destruction of Zion will (hyperbolically) leave nothing standing. The second image is literal and less hyperbolic: *Jerusalem will* become *a heap of ruins*.[37] The third image presents Mount Zion not as without vegetation (not the point of the metaphor in 3:12 in any case), but as without the temple. Ironically, Mount Zion is referred to as *the mount of the temple*, which it was in Micah's day, but that same place will be *without* the temple after judgment. The only description of the mountain in that context is that it will be *forested* or wooded, something possible only

---

37. The Babylonian destruction of Jerusalem was widespread, and very little of its population remained there afterwards; cf. Lipschits 2003: 328. The plural ending in *n* rather than *m* is not problematic (the singular appears in 1:6); see *HALOT* 1.816 and Wagenaar 2001: 123–124. The witness of the Greek textual tradition is variable but probably does not presuppose a different Hebrew *Vorlage*; see Glenny 2015: 87–88.

in the absence of a structure as large as the temple. Several elements of this description echo the description of Samaria earlier in the book, especially *ruin[s]* and the destruction of buildings (1:6), and the empty space where each city stood being filled with wild growth (vines in 1:6; trees in 3:12) (Biddle 2000: 150).

Meaning

The now-familiar condemnation of religious leaders focuses on a misplaced confidence due to misinterpretation of God's forbearance and patience. Religious infrastructure and these leaders' history, coupled with autonomy and self-importance, lead them to conclude that God is on their side regardless of what they do. This self-deception, which pushes away warnings of 'disaster' (3:11), is so far advanced that radical judgment is inevitable. The God upon whom they presumed and whose holiness they ignored will destroy Jerusalem and its temple, undoing the external manifestations of his relationship with his people in the light of their widespread sin. Only radical spiritual change such as that announced in 2:12–13, chapters 4–5 and 7:7–20 can ensure that God's people will permanently enjoy his presence and blessing.

D. YHWH will restore Zion, call the nations and rule over all people (4:1–8)

Context

Micah 4:1 marks a turning point in this section of the book (3:1 – 5:15). The order of 4:1 – 5:15 is also rather unusual, and contrasts as sharply as possible with the visions of judgment in chapter 3. It begins at a high point in the distant future, focusing on a radically transformed Zion to which the nations flow and where YHWH's reign is fully established over Israelites and non-Israelites alike. But that initial perspective is in fact the end point, the final phase of YHWH's plan to restore his people and establish his kingdom in its fullness. Between that goal and the Zion of the present, sketched in stark colours in chapter 3, lies a difficult and sometimes counter-intuitive way forward. In 4:9–10 the spectre of exile in Babylon is introduced, and other hardships and purifying trials lie along the way. A radical purification of Zion in 5:10–14 and the destruction of the nations that will not submit to YHWH in 5:15 remove the final obstacles to the realization of the initial vision in 4:1–8, and so the unit ends almost where it began.

The structure of this section is the subject of continuing disagreement.[38] The unit's contours are generally clear, but the precise boundaries of each sub-unit are sometimes difficult to determine.[39] Furthermore, multiple structures can be discerned in the text, and it is likely that the author did not write with only one structure in mind. As a result, the structures proposed below are not exclusive of others, and we will give attention to their possible interrelation rather than juxtaposing them as exclusive alternatives. In terms of its literary genre, Micah 4:1–8 can simply be termed an oracle of salvation with two complementary parts, 4:1–5 and 4:6–8.

Comment

1. A generally future setting is established by the verb that begins 4:1, while the following phrase *in the latter days* establishes an explicitly eschatological setting.[40] The nature of the circumstances and events presented here is an even stronger indication of the passage's eschatological nature, for they are highly discontinuous with the present (cf. ch. 3).[41] Further, nearly every facet of the image presented in 4:1–4 cannot be improved upon, such that

---

38. See Richelle 2012; Cuffey 2015.

39. For example, Richelle (2012: 238) identifies 4:1–7 as a unit on the basis of the inclusio 'mountain of the temple of YHWH' in 4:1 and 'YHWH will judge them on Mount Zion' in 4:7. This is certainly an inclusio, but the focus on Mount Zion continues in 4:8, where the announcement of salvation depends on what has gone before (4:1–7), and is thematically difficult to join to 4:9 (although 4:8 does introduce second-person feminine grammar that 4:9 continues).

40. A nearly identical oracle appears in Isa. 2:2–4. For detailed discussion of the relation between Isa. 2:2–4 and Mic. 4:1–5, see Waltke 2007: 213–220.

41. Peterson (1992: 575) defines eschatological circumstances as those so discontinuous with the present that 'one can speak of an entirely new state of reality'.

the exalted Zion under YHWH's worldwide rule is quite simply the goal towards which all divine covenants, promises and actions push.

After the mountain of YHWH's house is made like a forest hill in fulfilment of 3:12, it will (almost incredibly) be made superior to all other mountains. The elevation of YHWH's house and mountain (as in 3:12, the two elements are essentially coextensive) above every other mountain signifies his exaltation above all other gods, who were often thought to reside on mountains or other elevated sites (Walton 2018: 87). The international significance of YHWH's exaltation is confirmed by the following statement that *peoples* [non-Israelites] *will flow to it*. Whether or not they learn of YHWH's supremacy by his *teaching* coming to them (see the end of 4:2), the horizon of this passage is as broad as the one found at the very beginning of the book (1:2–3), but presents salvation and restoration rather than judgment and destruction.

2. *Many nations* further describes the group of non-Israelites first introduced as *peoples* in 4:1. The reason given for their coming to the newly exalted Zion is their desire to *learn* from YHWH in order to obey him. This intention excludes their fidelity to other gods and includes the conviction that YHWH alone is God, since the elevation of YHWH's temple above all others demonstrates that other so-called deities are radically inferior to him.

Rather unusually in the Old Testament, this verse foresees the nations coming to Zion as the result of (*for*) YHWH's *word* coming to them, even if the agent that brings that word to them is not identified.[42] This word inevitably includes the truth of his unique deity, but need not be limited to that. In any case, many non-Israelites come to Zion to learn from and obey YHWH as the direct result of the elevation of YHWH's *house*, that is, the demonstration of his sovereignty. In contrast to the Zion of chapter 3, whose reputation and actions were antithetical to YHWH's character and will, Zion is now a perfect reflection of its God and a faithful representative of him to the world around.

---

42. See the discussion of centripetal and centrifugal mission in Timmer 2011: 30–37.

3. YHWH's restoration of Zion simultaneously brings good to the nations as he adjudicates between and reproves them. The peace that characterizes the establishment of YHWH's rule (contrast the false peace offered by the pseudo-prophets, ch. 2) comes about only as YHWH transforms them from bellicose empires that seek their own wealth and glory to reconciled members of a humanity submitted to him and enjoying his blessing and provision.[43] The element of correction (*adjudicate*) means that this is more than a political reconciliation of enemies; it is first and foremost a divine work that puts these nations in a proper relation to YHWH, and consequently to one another. The result is a complete elimination of war and even of threats, for the nations' weapons are transformed into agricultural tools, which are used in the context of abundant agricultural yields. This promise of worldwide peace would be especially powerful for Judeans living amid the tides of empire that ebbed and flowed almost continuously through the Levant (cf. 4:9). Theologically, descendants of Abraham who longed to see themselves blessed so as to be a source of blessing to others (Gen. 12:1–3) would readily understand the eschatological weight and glory of this prophecy.

4. The final element of this depiction of global shalom develops the images of agricultural abundance and peace by echoing the peace and prosperity that were realized during the reign of Solomon (1 Kgs 4:25 [Heb. 5:5])[44] and the absence of fear which was the sign of covenant blessing (Lev. 26:6; cf. Jer. 30:10; 46:27; etc.; contrast the punishments of Mic. 6:14–15). Notably, each person's contentment with his or her own crops assumes that the

---

43. 'Judging between' (*šāpaṭ*) parties is eschatological only here, in Ezek. 34:17, 20, 22 and in the parallel text in Isa. 2:4, but always has in view a contention in which (at least) one party is in the wrong. The parallel term 'judge/adjudicate' (*yākaḥ* with *l*; cf. Gen. 24:14, 44; Job 32:12; Prov. 9:7, 8; 15:12; 19:25; Isa. 2:4; 11:4) when used in contexts of dispute means to correct or rebuke, either positively (e.g. Isa. 11:4) or, more often, negatively.

44. Zech. 3:10 is also predictive and connects these idyllic conditions to the removal of the land's iniquity.

expropriation and property theft that Micah condemned earlier are also things of the past among Israelites and non-Israelites alike (4:6–7) (Brueggemann 1981: 194). Further, ownership of one's own land and of what grows upon it hints that renewed Zion is larger than Jerusalem/Judah and that its blessings reach far and wide. The creation of this marvellous new world is certain because YHWH has foretold it. His fidelity and power guarantee the prophecy's fulfilment.

5. This commitment on the part of Micah, speaking on behalf of a group, is a response to the vision of 4:1–4, and includes those in Israel/Judah who share his unconditional commitment to following YHWH (*we*).[45] For that reason it is best seen as occurring during his ministry, a change in setting made possible by the fact that the nations in this verse are still following their own gods and thus hardly in the radically different circumstances foreseen in 4:1–4. The response shows that this group knows that it must be faithful to YHWH in order to be a source of blessing to the nations (cf. the remnant theme). It is also a response of gratitude and amazement at YHWH's commitment to perfect and deliver them from the judgment promised against Jerusalem in 3:12.

6. Verses 6–8 complement or provide background for the material in 4:1–5, and are linked to it by the phrase *In that day*, which refers back to the eschatological period introduced in 4:1 and closes the brief flashback to Micah's present in 4:5. The two sections also share a focus on Mount Zion and YHWH's transforming, restorative work. Although set in the same period, the events described here are logically prior to the static, ideal Zion presented in 4:1–4, and describe how God will bring his people to that eschatological end point: he will form a remnant from the Israel/Judah that has come through judgment. Both terms for *gather* were also used to describe the restoration of Israel/Judah in

---

45. Interestingly, non-Israelites were the subject of the most recent use of first-person pronouns prior to 4:5, and that response was also driven by the word of salvation that drew them to YHWH as subjects and worshippers rather than as enemies.

2:12, and here too they emphasize YHWH's unique role and the unity of the groups that he gathers.

Those whom YHWH will deliver are identified as the lame, those driven away and those he has afflicted. The *lame* are mentioned here for the first time in Micah, and are not mentioned again after 4:7.[46] Their metaphorical disability implies their inability to transform themselves into the people YHWH has called them to be, and may recall the identity of the restored community as sheep in 2:12–13.[47] The rarity of *lame* (elsewhere only in Gen. 32:32; Zeph. 3:19) makes an allusion to Jacob's struggle at Peniel possible (Gen. 32:32), and would strengthen the overtones of spiritual transformation in this passage (Renaud 1987: 82).

Those driven out occurs only here in Micah, but the theme of exile is not uncommon in the book. It first appears in 1:16, and is implied in 2:4, 10, while a return to the land is at the centre of the restoration predicted in 2:12–13. Exile could also be inferred from the destruction of Jerusalem in 3:12, and the gathering here probably undoes that tragic event while going far beyond it, since not all Judeans returned from exile and the return did not issue in the establishment of YHWH's kingdom as foreseen here. The nature of this group as *driven out* presumes that until delivered, they are under the control of a foreign power that they cannot overcome. This applies to the literal sense of exile as well as to the larger salvific domain that the image often includes in Micah.

Finally, the identification of this group as those upon whom YHWH has *brought calamity* reveals that YHWH's restoration of his people does not bypass his justice or leave unpunished the sins so amply detailed in chapters 1–3.[48] But the judgment here does not spell the destruction of this group, who will now be fully delivered, and this process gives rise to the remnant.

---

46. See the discussion in Fiorello 2014: 163–166.

47. So also, Waltke 2007: 221; Kessler 2000: 194. Andersen and Freedman (2000: 433) prefer a military connotation for 'gather'.

48. Ironically, the only other use of the Hiphil of *rʿʿ* in Micah appears in 3:4, where it describes the 'evil deeds' of the leaders of the northern and southern kingdoms.

7. YHWH's gathering of the groups mentioned in 4:6 leads to their unification as a new (single) group, described first as *a remnant*. While in earlier appearances of this theme the remnant was distinct from those who were (most) guilty or did not survive the judgment, here it is distinguished from those who did survive but were not gathered, that is, those who are not 'lame' or 'gathered'. As in other cases, the remnant is part of, but not identical to, the larger Israel/Judah group from which it is drawn (cf. the remnants in Gen. 45:7; 2 Sam. 14:7; Jer. 44:12), and its later appearances in Micah presume the identity presented here.

The *dispersed*, another description of those whom YHWH delivers in this passage, are to become a mighty nation (*HALOT* 1.868). The remnant *is* the new nation, in continuity with but not identical to the Israel/Judah of Micah's day. This group will be changed from one subjugated to a malevolent power to one which, although subject to YHWH (cf. 4:5), is not for that reason without strength. On the contrary, as his people, his strength is theirs (cf. Num. 14:12). Here again, the fulfilment of this prophecy cannot be limited to the return from exile but looks forward to the consummation of God's kingdom on earth.

Verse 7 ends with the assertion that YHWH will reign for ever over this group in Zion. This is one of only two times that Micah uses the root 'king/rule' (*mlk*) to speak of YHWH's *rule* over his restored people (cf. 2:13), but the theme of royalty is much more common, and appears both in the gathering of the remnant in 4:6 and in the temple-mountain scene of 4:1–4. The exclusive attribution of royal prerogatives and roles to YHWH in these eschatological passages reinforces the impression that even YHWH's Davidic king is only a deputy or vice-regent, and that all power belongs to YHWH. The various elements of 4:6–8 (centred on YHWH's reign at Jerusalem) fulfil the foundational pattern for YHWH as Israel's deliverer (Exod. 15:17–18) and parallel Isaiah's development of the second exodus theme (Kessler 2000: 195).

8. This verse develops further the idea of the remnant as a nation. Although the Masoretic Text includes a paragraph marker after 4:7 (but not after 4:8), it is best to see 4:8 as a 'Janus verse', one that looks both backwards to 4:7 and forwards to 4:9. That being

said, its future perspective suggests that it is more closely linked to
4:6–7, so it is discussed here.[49]

As in the first restoration passage (see 2:12), God speaks directly
to his restored people. Kessler notes the artistic and chiastic structure of this verse: 8a consists of a double address followed by a
verb, while 8b includes one verb followed by a double subject
(Kessler 2000: 199). This chiastic structure, and the gapping of the
subject in 8a, allows us to treat both halves of the verse together.
In 4:8a, restored Jerusalem is referred to as *Tower of the flock* and
Ophel of Daughter Zion, and as the *Daughter of Jerusalem* in 8b. All these
terms are equivalent to the *remnant* in 4:7. The first title (*Tower of the
flock*) may be a play on Isaiah's prediction of Jerusalem's destruction
in Isaiah 32:9–14. The second (*Ophel*) refers to Zion's citadel
originally captured by David (2 Sam. 5:7) or the temple mound/
mount and has connotations 'of stability . . . of fixedness'.[50] The
third (*Daughter of Jerusalem*) is probably chosen because of the
exclusive link between Jerusalem and royalty in the Old Testament,
or to evoke the purity of Daughter Zion/Jerusalem.

The only subject of the verse is also repeated: *the former dominion*
and *kingship*. One might wonder why the text seems to look back (to
David or Solomon) when the whole passage looks forward to YHWH's
rule. This is best explained by looking further back than David, who
in any case served under, and did not displace, YHWH's rule over
Israel. In other words, *the former dominion* refers to YHWH's original,
direct rule over his people which was later exercised by David as
vice-regent (cf. Exod. 15:18; 1 Sam. 8:7; Ps. 149:2). This line of
thought seems to be present elsewhere in Micah as well. Kessler
draws attention to the very modest expectations with respect to
the Davidic line in 1:14 (to which 1:15 should be added) and to the
ancient origins (*from long ago, from ancient times*) of the coming messianic ruler (5:2 [Heb. 1]) (Kessler 2000: 200; Goswell 2019).

---

49. The tone of despair and present suffering that begins in 4:9 strongly
    argues against joining it to 4:6–8. Further, 4:9, 11 and 5:1 [Heb. 4:14]
    all begin with Hebrew 'attâ, suggesting that a new unit begins at 4:9.
50. Follis 1987: 178, cited in Waltke 2007: 235. Andersen and Freedman
    (2000: 439) favour the temple mount.

The reign foreseen in 4:1–4, in any case, cannot be exercised by a mere human being. Andersen and Freedman thus prefer to speak of 'Yahweh as King and David as Ruler' (cf. 4:8 and 5:2 [Heb. 1]), respectively.[51] This arrangement also appears in Psalm 2, and the precedence of YHWH's reign even in Jerusalem (cf. 2 Sam. 6) further suggests that this is probably the best way to understand 4:8 in the context of the rest of the book.[52]

Meaning

God's response to the sin that corrupted many within ancient Israel and Judah begins with judgment that focuses on Judah (3:12) but goes much further. While the transformation of Zion is breathtaking, perhaps the most striking element in this passage is the inclusion of non-Israelites among those whom YHWH brings to a radically transformed and exalted Zion. This fulfils his original intention to bless 'all the clans of the world' through Abraham and his descendants, meaning that Israel's remnant (under the leadership of its messianic king, as ch. 5 will show) will bring news of YHWH's salvation to 'the nations'. The ultimate horizon of this passage is nothing less than the new heavens and new earth 'in which righteousness dwells' (2 Pet. 3:13). The fundamental unity of all believers is evident in the way that the creation of the *remnant*

---

51. Andersen and Freedman 2000: 439. Similarly, Ben Zvi (2000: 112), and Renaud (1987: 87), who stresses the proximity of 4:7 (YHWH's rule) and 4:8 (messianic, Davidic rule).

52. In support of this, note Smith-Christopher's observation (2015: 151) that *memšālâ* refers 'only occasionally to the rule of Israelite kings (1 Kgs 9:19), but appears in Psalms to refer to the "rule" or "dominion" of God (Pss 103:22; 114:2; 145:13)'. Firth (2009: 374) notes that in 2 Sam. 6 and context 'David recognizes Yahweh's authority over him as king' and notes further that YHWH's ark came to Jerusalem before David's coronation in that context. Mettinger (1982) notes the link between the ark and royal rule. Contrariwise, Wolff (1990: 119, 125) argues for an 'earthly, royal rule in Jerusalem' in 4:8, while McKane (1998: 129–30) unnecessarily thinks there is 'incompatibility' between 'kingship of Yahweh and Davidic kingship'.

in 4:6–8 parallels God's transforming work among the nations in 4:1–4 by bringing them under his rule in Zion. The believing response to this grand vision inevitably includes a wholehearted commitment to following YHWH (4:5).

E. YHWH will deliver Zion from the nations and from exile in Babylon (4:9–13)

Context
This section leaves behind the eschatological focus on Jerusalem's restoration and transformation and returns to Judah's present or near-future dilemma. It announces that the ultimate consequence of Judah's sins will be exile, yet also reveals that exile will not be the end of God's people as such. For reasons which Micah explains especially in 7:18–20, YHWH will deliver Daughter Zion from exile and extend his sovereign rule over the nations.

Although the structure of this section is hotly debated, the following observations provide us with solid footing. Especially helpful is Renaud's observation that each *'atah* in 4:9 – 5:1 [Heb. 4:9–14] introduces a stage in Zion's fall: pain (4:9), the nations gathered against her (4:11), and siege and humiliation of her judge (5:1 [Heb. 4:14]), and that each announcement of judgment or woe (4:9–10a, 11; 5:1 [Heb. 4:14]) is followed by a promise of deliverance (4:10b, 12–13; 5:2–6 [Heb. 5:1–5]).[53] The ruler theme ties 5:1 to 5:2,

---

53. Renaud 1987: 87. Goswell (2019: 155) also argues that 4:9 – 5:3 are three subsections, each demarcated by an introductory *'attâ*. Thus, the *'attâ* in 5:1 (Heb. 4:14) should be taken with the same weight as in 4:9, 11, as suggested by Wendland (2018). Renaud (1987: 88) further notes that 'Each time the movement from distress to promise is made with two imperatives with a feminine y-suffix, followed by the conjunction *kî*, "for".' In a similar vein, Waltke (1993: 693) observes that 'Each of these three sections is addressed with a vocative, "daughter Zion" (vv. 10, 13) and "trooplike daughter" (v. 14 [Eng. 5:1]), followed by an imperative.' Richelle (2012: 244) proposes an alternative structure for 4:1 – 5:14 (Heb.) in which each element begins with a significant promise: 4:1–7, Jerusalem (temple, worship); 4:8–14, Jerusalem (palace, ruler); 5:1–14, Bethlehem.

while this section (4:9–13) is tied to the following (5:1–6) by the twin themes of danger/trial and deliverance.

On this basis, the passage reflects the following structure, and is connected to 5:1–6, which is introduced with the third and final 'now'.

4:9–10   Daughter Zion's exile and deliverance
4:11–13   Daughter Zion delivered from the hatred
            of nations

Comment

9. Although the Hebrew word ('*attâ*) that begins 4:9 does not inevitably indicate time (i.e. 'now, at this moment'), the time frame of this verse is clearly not that of the ideal future foreseen in 4:1–4, 6–8 (*in the latter days, in that day*). Rather, the setting of 4:9 – 5:1 [Heb. 4:14] is one in which Judah is in grave distress due to its sin, crying out for help (4:9) and surrounded by menacing nations (4:11). The *now* that begins 4:9 is thus not a chronological indicator, but a conjunctive adverb marking a transition in the discourse (van der Merwe, Naudé and Kroeze 2017: 452).

Although most uses of *cry out* appear in contexts of victory or jubilation, the verb can also express fear (Judg. 7:21; Isa. 15:4; Joel 2:1), as it does here. To this the last line of 4:9 adds agony comparable to that of childbirth, indicating a severe crisis in Judah. Because 4:10 indicates that the exile of Judah to Babylon is imminent,[54] the answer to the rhetorical question is 'No'.[55] Whether or not Micah foresees the flight of Zedekiah from Jerusalem in the days leading up to the city's destruction (2 Kgs 25:3–12) or the end of the monarchy as an independent political power after it became Egypt's and then Babylon's vassal, there is no effective

---

54. Andersen and Freedman (2000: 442) argue that 'the moment of utterance' is 'the time when Jerusalem is in her last convulsions'.
55. So also Dempster 2017: 135, and similarly, Jeremias 2007: 180.
    Ben Zvi (2000: 115) reasons that even if there was a literal king on Judah's throne, his kingly role was of no consequence since exile is imminent.

leadership, and especially no hope for deliverance, in Judah's last kings.[56]

10. The double commands to *be in agony* and *burst forth*[57] confirm that the interrogative *why . . . ?* in 4:9a is answered by the two rhetorical questions: 'Why do you cry out? Because you have no king, because your counsellor has perished! So be in agony!' Micah names Babylon as the political entity that will bring about Judah's downfall, even though Babylon's covert diplomacy (e.g. sending its envoys to develop a relationship with Hezekiah, Isa. 39) was no clear indication that about a century later it would successfully revolt against, and then assume control over, the Assyrian Empire of which it was currently only a prominent province.[58]

The shift to deliverance comes into view only at the end of 4:10, following the prediction that *Daughter Zion* (clearly a group rather than a literal city, which she will leave[59]) will leave Jerusalem and eventually arrive in Babylon. *There* introduces the promises that YHWH will *deliver* and *redeem* her, even though she will then be in exile. As the following contexts show, this deliverance is not merely from Babylonian exile, but from sin's consequences.

11. The second half of the passage develops further, and arguably in a more eschatological direction, the critically important

---

56. Kessler (2000: 205) argues that *king* and *counsellor* cannot refer to YHWH here, since YHWH is never a grammatically undetermined 'king' but always 'the King' or 'your King'. In context, this establishes a nice contrast with YHWH as deliverer (cf. also 5:6) and the one who has his own 'counsel' in 4:12. The two terms (*king* and *counsellor*) likely refer to the same person, in part because they are in parallel, and in part because the two activities of ruling and planning are both attributed to YHWH in 4:12 (similarly, Waltke 2007: 238–239).

57. *Be in agony* in 4:10 has the same root as *agony* at the end of 4:9 and ties the rhetorical question to a phrase which makes clear how it should be answered.

58. Waltke (1993: 695) notes that 'This prophecy is among the earliest references to the Babylonian captivity in prophetic literature.'

59. Andersen and Freedman (2000: 446) deny that this distinction is possible, but their proposal that 'the city' is Babylon is implausible.

fact that the exile of Judah is not God's final word, and that he will deliver Daughter Zion even from that extreme trial. This development is put in bold relief by the recognition that the *many nations gathered against* Judah have deeply malicious intent and hope to defile Zion and satisfy their desire for her subjugation.[60] The expression of this desire in their own words, as it were, captures well their lust for power and glory.[61] The cultic denotation of *defiled* suggests that this desire focused on the temple as the city's most sacred place (Waltke 1993: 696).

12. This verse states twice that a divine plan is guiding the events predicted in this and the surrounding units, but that YHWH's designs are unknown to the nations who fulfil them. Thinking that they amass spoil, gain territory, and glorify themselves and their gods, the nations are in fact serving God's purposes.[62] Further, although they will destroy Jerusalem, YHWH will hold them accountable for their actions, and the image of *sheaves* on *the threshing floor* portends their violent and complete end (cf. Amos 1:3). The exile and deliverance of Daughter Zion are thus a series of events played out on the national stage but whose importance is fundamentally theological (cf. 5:15). YHWH's plans and actions will deliver Daughter Zion and destroy those who threaten her.[63]

13. After making clear that he will orchestrate the fall of Zion's enemies, YHWH calls her to participate in their destruction. As

---

60. Edom participated in the downfall of Jerusalem alongside the Babylonians (Obad.; Ps. 137; Ezek. 35:5, 11–13). Andersen and Freedman (2000: 456–57) argue that 4:11–13 may refer to a more ultimate conflict. In favour of this, note *Babylon* in 4:9–10 versus *many peoples* in 4:11–13, and the language of ultimate destruction here versus simple liberation from Babylon in 4:9–10.

61. See Smith-Christopher 2015: 157–159, who explores the imperial facet of this 'gaze'.

62. Kessler (2000: 212) argues on the basis of 1:2 and 5:15 that the nations' ignorance involves guilt: they should have known better.

63. Andersen and Freedman (2000: 453–454) offer valuable theological reflections on God's control of history and his ability to use sinful human schemes for his own good purposes.

before, two imperatives mark the transition from woe to weal. God then announces that he will equip Daughter Zion for that task, again with two images: an iron *horn* and bronze *hooves* (cf. Mal. 4:3 [Heb. 3:21]). God's empowered people can then *crush* or pulverize many *peoples* (cf. 2 Sam. 22:43), an image for complete defeat. As was the case in Israel's conquest of Canaan, the spoils are consecrated to YHWH rather than enriching Zion. The despoiling of the peoples is also a *lex talionis* punishment, taking *unjust gain* from those who oppose and denigrate YHWH and giving it to him.[64] This elimination of his enemies falls within YHWH's purview as the *Lord of the whole earth*, and will put the lie to the claims of the various empires and forces that attempted to overcome his people and frustrate his plans.[65]

---

64. The language used for this conflict echoes that of the conquest (*ḥērem*), but the object of the verb is *unjust gain*, not a population. *Unjust gain* (*beṣaʿ*) is not used elsewhere in Micah. The noun is always negative in Isaiah but is associated with individuals (Isa. 33:15; 56:11; 57:17), while Hab. 2:9 uses it of Babylon with a cognate verb. Whether God comes to possess the nations' spoil, so to speak, or whether it is 'his' by being destroyed is debatable. Biblically speaking, both happen with *ḥērem*, as in the conquest (people destroyed, material goods consecrated). Thus, when Waltke (1993: 699) notes that in the Mesha Inscription the idea of 'devote by destroying' is present and so applies to the nations, he seems at least to miss the focus of 4:13 on material goods, which would have been consecrated. In fact, both kinds of 'devotion' are present in the Mesha Inscription: the population is killed, and the temple vessels are taken away to Kemosh's temple (lines 14–18a).

65. Assyrian, Babylonian and Persian monarchs called themselves 'king of the four corners [of the earth]', and the claims of Rome's emperors were comparable. See Dempster's helpful reflection (2017: 152–153) on the significance of 4:11–13 in the time between Christ's first and second comings. This characterization of these 'peoples' addresses, in part, Jeremias's impression (2007: 183) that 4:11–13 is incompatible with 4:1–4, although the 'peoples' there are characterized in very different ways and so should be distinguished from those here.

Meaning

Although the promises of God's faithfulness to his people and his rebuke of their despair refer first of all to the tumultuous future that awaited the faithful remnant in Judah, the same promises ensure the security and ultimate victory of his people in all ages over sin and their spiritual enemies. Especially when evil seems to have the upper hand, believers must remember that God's plans and wisdom take account even of opposition to him (Acts 2:23) and that their enemies will not ultimately triumph. In response to their prayers and in fulfilment of his commitment to fully establish his reign over all things, his kingdom will come in its fullness. His people are called to persist in 'holiness and godliness' and so to 'hasten the coming of the day of God' (2 Pet. 3:11–12, ESV).

F. YHWH's ruler will shepherd the flock that YHWH delivers (5:1–6 [Heb. 4:14 – 5:5])

Context

This section presents the same overall structure and sequence as 4:9–10, 11–13. After announcing future woe or judgment (5:1 [Heb. 4:14]), it adds a long section detailing the deliverance and future flourishing of God's people.[66] Waltke sees this oracle, as well as 4:11–13, as coming during Sennacherib's siege (Waltke 2007: 296, 298), when the Davidic monarch was unable to rescue himself from the Assyrian threat. This is plausible given the references to Assyria in the passage, but dating individual sections is usually, as here, tentative at best.

This unit adds to the earlier descriptions of Zion's deliverance in 4:10–13 a human 'ruler' not currently on the scene. This person apparently assumes the role formerly held by the humiliated ruler of 5:1 [Heb. 4:14] and complements the destruction of enemy nations (4:13) with the establishment of his worldwide kingdom

---

66. Richelle (2012: 242–243) argues concerning 5:1–15 that 'and you' sets off what follows just as it does in 4:8, and, on the other hand, 'therefore' in 5:2 connects it to 5:1, while the repetition of *wĕhāyâ* through the rest of 5:5–9 brings all of 5:1–9 into unity.

(5:4). However, this ruler also opposes and neutralizes the threat posed by the Assyrians in particular (5:5–6).

The substructure of the unit is as follows:[67]

5:1–5:2 [4:14 – 5:1]	Old and new rulers
5:3–5a	From present distress to future peace under the Ruler
5:5b–6	The Ruler delivers from the Assyrians

Comment

1 [Heb. 4:14]. The third *now* in 4:9 – 5:6 again presents Zion (*Daughter of troops*) in a situation of dire need. The speaker, presumably the prophet, identifies himself with Judah under attack. The single imperative calls for her to muster her soldiers, for an anonymous enemy has already laid siege against Jerusalem (most likely Assyria, from whom the ruler introduced in 5:2 will deliver Daughter Zion in 5:4–6). The use of siege works, probably including portable shelters for attackers attempting to breach a city's walls, indicates that the siege is in its later stages.[68] Indeed, the humiliation of Jerusalem's *judge*, that is, king, by a metaphorical slap on the cheek is inevitable.[69] The title *judge* (*šōpēt*) for Judah's king is probably used in part to create an 'alliterative wordplay' with the *rod* (*šēbeṭ*) that will strike his cheek, partly to stress the royal role of establishing and maintaining justice (something the Judean king has failed to do in Micah), and partly to maintain Micah's insistence that only YHWH is his people's King.[70]

2 [Heb. 1]. The shift from danger and shame to deliverance is abruptly introduced by a change of addressee from Jerusalem to Bethlehem of Ephrathah. The contrast between Jerusalem, Judah's largest and most important city, and Bethlehem, so small that

---

67. Following Wendland 2018.

68. See Christensen 2009: 282, whose illustration of a mantlet is based on Yadin (1963: 295).

69. The same idiom with the same sense appears in 1 Kgs 22:24; Job 16:10; Lam. 3:30.

70. Following Goswell 2019: 156.

'it was not felt worthy of inclusion in the list of towns in Joshua',[71] leads to the paradoxical elevation of the *ruler* from there over the judge of Jerusalem.[72] This contrast is sharpened even more when the reader realizes that the 'I' who speaks to Bethlehem is none other than YHWH. The use of *Israel* elsewhere in Micah suggests that the term here refers to the (restored) southern kingdom, but the Davidic element introduces a perspective prior to the division of the kingdom and so probably foresees a reunification of the two kingdoms under this one ruler (note David as a king who shepherds and rules Israel in 2 Sam. 5:2, and *sons of Israel* used in Micah only in 5:3). It is thus preferable to understand *Israel* here as a reference to the (re)united kingdom over which he will rule. As a ruler *for* YHWH, this person must be a descendant of David. Among other reasons,[73] the ancient *origins* of this ruler most probably refers to the Davidic covenant established long ago (2 Sam. 7:1–16, but note also Gen. 49:8–12; cf. Ps. 89:19 [Heb. 20]; Amos 9:11; Neh. 12:46) which remains intact despite the problems foreseen in 5:1 [Heb. 4:14].[74]

---

71. Jenson 1995: 210. The list appears in Josh. 15:20–63.

72. Luker 1992a. The 'to be' of the Hebrew text in this phrase is unnecessary and should probably be omitted as a copyist's error duplicating the same term later in the verse; so Renaud 1987: 98.

73. Note especially the parallel elements in Ps. 89 in vv. 19 [Heb. 20] ('long ago'), 22 [Heb. 23] ('the wicked will not humble him'), 25 [Heb. 26] (global reign), 27 [Heb. 28] (highest of all kings), and the focus on the present (i.e. exilic) humiliation of Judah and its king later in the psalm. Note also 'come forth' in 2 Sam. 7:12.

74. Waltke (1993: 705) argues that when *'ōlām* is qualified by 'days' or similar terms, the phrase always refers 'to a definite time' rather than to eternity, with reference to Deut. 32:7; Ps. 77:5; Isa. 51:9; 63:9, 11; Amos 9:11; Mic. 7:14; Mal. 3:4. Goswell (2019: 157) observes that 'Like Isaiah 9 and 11, Micah 5 does not designate the coming ruler under the title "king", even though all three passages clearly indicate that he is a Davidide . . . In each case, the human ruler is subordinated to the Divine King.'

3 [Heb. 2]. The conjunction *therefore* connects this verse to the preceding, but, as Waltke suggests, it indicates an implication rather than chronological consequence: 'the foregoing being the case, therefore' (Waltke 2007: 277). This verse sheds some light on the period of Judah's humiliation that begins in 5:1 [Heb. 4:14] and lasts until 5:2 [Heb. 1].[75] The speaker is again the prophet, who refers to YHWH and the ruler in the third person throughout 5:3–6. Accordingly, the subject of the verb *give them up*[76] is probably YHWH, who spoke in 5:2 and whose plan to exile, and then deliver, his people (*them*) has already been announced in 4:10.

The reprise in 5:3 of the image of the woman in labour is unexpected insofar as no birth followed the labour-like pain and alarm that the image expressed in 4:9–10, but the link between the two is both lexical (the same participle is used in all three verses) and semantic. Zion in 5:3 *is* (not 'is like', as in 4:9–10) a *woman in labour* who will give birth, and (merging Zion's role with Bethlehem as the ruler's village of origin) her child will be YHWH's ruler.

The rest of the verse unpacks some of what will happen when that moment arrives. First, the birth of the new Davidic ruler coincides with the *return* of the *remainder of his brothers* to the *sons of Israel*, of which Judah has been (until now) the locus. The unified nation of Israel under David evoked in 5:2, and the reunification of north (Jacob) and south (Israel) predicted in 2:12, strongly suggest that this return refers to the same reunification of all the ruler's brothers. The focus on the ruler that began in 5:2 makes him the most likely referent of the possessive pronoun *his*. He is also the most recent person introduced in the preceding clause by being born to the woman in labour. The Davidic ruler's relation to his brothers, that is, the tribes other than Judah, is based on their common ancestry, and this unity is echoed at key points in the nation's history that involve David (note esp. 2 Sam. 5:1; 1 Kgs 12:24). The rest of the descendants of Jacob thus rejoin Israel, that

---

75. Ben Zvi (2000: 125) calls 5:3 a 'motive clause characterizing the period prior to the reign of the new David'.

76. Renaud (1987: 102) notes the same conjunction and verb in Isa. 7:14.

is, Judah, but their primary identifying feature is their brotherhood with the Davidic king, not simply with the tribe of Judah.[77]

4–5a [Heb. 3–4a]. This verse predicts what the new Davidic ruler will do using the metaphor of shepherding, which was tied to YHWH's gathering, protecting and ruling of the remnant earlier in Micah. His flock is the *sons of Israel* mentioned in 5:3, now augmented by the return of those exiled (especially the northern tribes). The verb *stand* carries connotations of permanence and stability here (cf. the same collocation in Isa. 61:5).[78]

This ruler-shepherd wields YHWH's *might* (in fulfilment of 1 Sam. 2:10[79]) and does so *in* (or with) YHWH's *majesty*.[80] These adverbial phrases describe a very close relationship between YHWH and his ruler while preserving a personal distinction between them. This divinely enabled and authorized rule allows his flock to *dwell securely*.

Although the subject of *he will be great* (*gādal*) could be YHWH, there is no need for a sudden change in subject driven by the fact that greatness is best predicated of YHWH. The ruler's greatness is the result of God's empowerment, and so does not stand in tension with his uniqueness.[81] The implications of his worldwide rule, mentioned in passing at the end of 5:4, will be unpacked in 5:5–6 (cf. Ps. 2:8; 72:8; 96 – 99; Isa. 11:4, 6, 9; etc.). The final result of the new Davidic ruler's actions appears in the first line of 5:5: *This will be peace.*[82] This *peace*

---

77. Schibler (1989: 109) sees Hezekiah's efforts at reunification as an initial fulfilment of this oracle. The fact that *sons of Israel* appears only here in Micah leads Waltke (2007: 281) to understand the ultimate fulfilment of this event as follows: 'When the Messiah appears and restores Israel's fortunes there will no longer be a remnant within Israel, but all Israel will know *I AM*, as Jeremiah foresaw (Jer 31:31–34).'

78. *HALOT* 1.840. Wolff (1990: 146) connects it to the ruler's accession to the throne, as does Kessler (2000: 227).

79. I owe this reference to Kessler (2000: 227).

80. *Gāʾôn*, the only use in Micah; cf. Isa. 2:10, 19, 21.

81. E.g. Goswell 2019: 160–161. Goswell's appeal to the Psalms is inconclusive because it does not take account of the different contexts there.

82. If translated 'This one will be peace', the phrase refers to the ruler of 5:4, and the meaning is essentially the same.

signals the end of Judah's humiliation and exile at the hands of non-Israelite nations, and the rest of this section develops this idea (5:5b–6).

5b–6 [Heb. 4b–5]. Beginning here, the passage presents a new scenario in the context of the Davidic ruler's YHWH-authorized reign that will bring peace, after the restoration of the *sons of Israel* and not in Micah's own day.[83] Speaking as part of the *sons of Israel* in the first-person plural, Micah projects the threat that Assyria and Nimrod (i.e. Babylon) pose into the distant future.[84] Notably, their aggression does not reach Jerusalem, but only the citadels, that is, fortified cities meant to impede such an invasion. In the event of their (or similar) aggression against YHWH's ruler and his people, the Davidide, still the ideal shepherd and ruler, shares some of his responsibilities with others. They are referred to as *seven shepherds and eight princely men* raised up by the people who will *shepherd Assyria with the sword*, meaning 'establish control over it by force'.[85] Yet 5:6 states that *he* will accomplish this deliverance, and this underlines the superiority of the Davidic ruler (the only masculine singular actor in the context) over these figures.[86] The answer to the

---

83. Ben Zvi (2000: 128) sees here 'a symbolic world in which both Assyria and "the land of Nimrod" (i.e. Babylon; see Gen. 10:6–10) may function as representative of the foes of the kingdoms of Judah and Israel'. The events foreseen follow the general trajectory of 4:11–13, although here (in contrast to the seventh- and sixth-century invasions of Judah) the enemy is soundly defeated. It is highly unlikely that this passage is an incantation, as suggested first by K. Cathcart and more recently by Wagenaar (2001: 294), not least because the parallel with CTU 1.119 falters due to the lack of any volitional forms in Micah.

84. As Dempster (2017: 140) notes, this typological understanding of these two empires fits well with Micah's use of *Nimrod* for Babylon (cf. Gen. 10:8–10).

85. Jeremias (2007: 187) sees these as references to 'a large group of military leaders' (my translation).

86. There is no need to oppose the 'popular leaders' of the preceding verse with the one here (*pace* Goswell 2019: 163). Note, on the contrary, Renaud's argument (1987: 107) that 'The Messiah covers the initiative of

question of the ideal king raised in 4:9 is thus that YHWH is Israel's absolute king and the new Davidide is his designated ruler over renewed Israel and the world.[87]

Meaning

The focus on YHWH as Israel's only saviour is modified by the inclusion of a messianic figure here. As is often the case, God accomplishes his plan through very unremarkable avenues, including the birth of his messianic ruler in Bethlehem. Under YHWH's blessing and in fulfilment of his mandate, this ruler will establish a worldwide kingdom characterized by peace no less than by the defeat of evil. This eschatological hope is no less important in the early third millennium than it was in ancient Judah, especially because it helps God's people resist the temptation to advance God's cause through human means rather than through the message and by the power of their King.

G. The remnant among the nations (5:7–9 [Heb. 6–8])

Context

This short section focuses on the *remnant of Jacob* (cf. *Jacob . . . remnant of Israel* in 2:12). In the light of the reunification of the northern and southern kingdoms' remnants as described in 5:1–6 [Heb. 4:14 – 5:5], especially 5:3 [Heb. 2], and the illicit nature of the north's original separation from Davidic rule, *Jacob* here probably includes the faithful from both kingdoms. This passage explores

---

(note 86 *cont.*) Israel's anonymous collective with his high authority . . . He assumes, in short, their projects' (my translation). Note also the consistent use of 'we/us/our' in 5:5–6, on which see Kessler 2000: 234. See also the detailed discussion in Andersen and Freedman 2000: 477–478, who note possible emendations (cf. *BHS*).

87. There can be no question of Hezekiah filling this role, either in Micah (cf. 5:2) or in Isa. 36 – 39. I am therefore inclined to see *Assyria* and *Nimrod* as representing *faithful Israel's* enemies. Similarly, 'He will be *our* peace' is the sentiment of Micah and those who trust in YHWH's messianic shepherd-ruler for deliverance.

two diametrically opposed roles that the same remnant can have among the nations, which presupposes that the nations are a diverse group among which some will react positively to the remnant (cf. the word of YHWH coming to receptive nations in 4:2) while others will oppose them.[88] The fate of each subset of the nations is determined by these two possible reactions.[89]

Like 5:5 [Heb. 4] and 5:10 [Heb. 9], this section is introduced with *and* it *will be* (*wĕhāyâ*). Although Richelle is correct that this element unites many parts of chapter 5, its structural importance varies. In 5:4 [Heb. 3] it appears within the unit 5:1–6, and in 5:8 [Heb. 7] it appears within the unit 5:7–9. Contrariwise, the uses in 5:7 [Heb. 6] and 5:10 [Heb. 9] introduce new units with distinct themes (Richelle 2012: 242–243). The unit clearly ends after 5:9 [Heb. 8], which is followed by a paragraph marker in the Hebrew text.

Comment

7 [Heb. 6]. As noted above, the reunification of the northern and southern kingdoms' remnants as described especially in 5:3 [Heb. 2] favours understanding *remnant of Jacob* as inclusive of the faithful from both Israelite kingdoms. The book of Micah has already presented the non-Israelite nations, on the other hand, as being sometimes bellicose and predatory and sometimes conciliatory and even ready to worship YHWH. That diversity is at the centre of the binary effects that the same remnant has on the diverse group of *the nations . . . many peoples* (5:8).

In the first case, the remnant will be *like dew from YHWH, like showers* that fall *on vegetation* at a time not of human choosing. The divinely determined timing is reminiscent of the assertion that God's ways with his people follow a plan that only he knows (4:12). The

---

88. See the discussion in Timmer 2015: 99–101, 103–106, on which I draw here.

89. Timmer 2015: 99–100, 103–104. There is little reason to accept interpretations which presume that *the nations* is a homogeneous group, and that therefore the two 'remnant' verses are ideologically incompatible, e.g. Anbar (1994). The short discussion in Biddle (2000: 161–162) is more helpful.

significance of this first half of the diptych, however, flows from its effect on the vegetation on which it falls. The Old Testament consistently presents the effects of dew as beneficial (Gen 27:28, 39; Deut. 33:13–14, 28; 2 Sam. 1:21; Ps. 72:6; Prov. 19:12; Hag. 1:10; Zech. 8:12), and the effect of the remnant on (some of) the nations here should be seen in the same way.[90] The transmission of divine teaching, which apparently takes place in Micah 4:2 and is well received by non-Israelites, is a plausible means to this end (cf. Deut. 32:2).

8 [Heb. 7]. The other half of the diptych that presents the dual roles of the remnant likens it to a lion or young lion among other animals. Among both wild and domesticated animals, the lion or young lion *passes through* and *tramples and tears (in pieces)*, leaving only death and carnage behind. Since the lion is the apex predator, no other animal can deliver its prey. Self-serving commitment to one's own advancement above all else and the consequent decision to treat Israel/Judah as a means to an end, as some nations do in Micah 4:11, exemplifies how the remnant can be an indirect cause of these aggressors' loss and destruction.

9 [Heb. 8]. This verse reflects on the second, negative role that the remnant has among the nations in 5:8. The placement of the imperfective verb at the head of the phrase gives it a volitional force, so that it expresses either a wish regarding the remnant mentioned in 5:8 or a prayer that YHWH would overcome his enemies through the remnant's negative role in 5:8. While it is possible that the singular *your* refers to the remnant as a collective (the first option), several considerations favour seeing this verse as a prayer to YHWH.[91] First, earlier in Micah, it is YHWH who delivers Daughter Zion from her enemies (4:10), so his involvement is always of primary importance. Second, in the same way, it is YHWH's designated ruler, introduced in 5:4, who establishes his

---

90. The interpretation proposed here for 5:7–8 [Heb. 6–7] is confirmed by Prov. 19:12, which contrasts the danger of a king's wrath (compared to a lion's roar) with his favour (compared to dew on the grass). Gignilliat (2019: 187) observes that in Hosea, God is like a lion in judging his people (Hos. 5:14) but like dew in restoring them (Hos. 14:5).

91. As do Renaud (1987: 111), Wolff (1990: 157) and others.

global kingdom with God's strength. Third, when a hand is raised against God's or Israel's enemies elsewhere in the Old Testament, it is especially God's hand (Ps. 89:13 [Heb. 14], notably in a psalm focused on the Davidic monarchy; Isa. 26:11).[92] Fourth, when the remnant speaks of its opposition to its enemies in 5:5–6, deliverance is again attributed to leaders (5:5) and to YHWH (*he*, 5:6), not to the remnant itself. Fifth, YHWH is the agent of the same verb (*kārat*) in its other uses in Micah, all of which immediately follow in 5:10–13. Finally, in 5:15 YHWH states explicitly that he will destroy 'the nations that do not obey', which is precisely the situation envisaged in 5:8. In the same section, moreover, God commits to destroying both the remnant's sin (5:12–14) and the weaponry and power structures on which it focuses (5:10–11), rendering its military action impossible. It is thus most likely that the *you* addressed in 5:9 is YHWH or his ruler, and that the speaker is the remnant itself, which prays for God's judgment of the nations to be accomplished through his use of the remnant.[93]

Meaning

The remnant of God's people, scattered among the nations, transmit and live out his message of judgment and salvation. This reality lies behind Paul's statement that he and the other apostles are 'a fragrance from death to death' to those who are perishing but a 'fragrance from life to life' to those who are being saved (2 Cor. 2:15–16, ESV). His self-evident insufficiency for that task is more than compensated for by Christ's already and not-yet victory and the grace he supplies (2 Cor. 2:14), something anticipated in the prayer in Micah 5:9 that YHWH's adversaries would be vanquished and his cause triumph.

---

92. Waltke (2007: 313–314) and Kessler (2000: 243–244) offer further considerations that favour the position I take here.

93. Waltke (2007: 319) summarizes this line of thought well: 'The remnant of Jacob's decisive role in history depends entirely upon *I AM*'s initiative: he chose them; he disciplined them; he gathered them; he led them forth; he raised up their Messiah; he converted them; and he sends them forth.'

H. YHWH forms the remnant and punishes disobedient nations (5:10–15 [Heb. 9–14])

Context

This section further defines the remnant and correlates its role among the nations with YHWH's actions in the same domain (5:15 [Heb. 14]). All but the last verse focus on sins that characterized the remnant before its creation – that is, that characterized those who will be transformed (cf. 4:6–7) and whose hope and trust will be redirected from military power or false gods to YHWH. The passage resembles other biblical descriptions of ritual reforms or legislation but betrays no dependence upon a particular passage (Ben Zvi 2000: 137, 140).

Interestingly, the sins mentioned here are not the forms of social injustice that figure so prominently earlier in the book, but rather internal dispositions and commitments that led this group to place their trust in military equipment and infrastructure (5:10–11 [Heb. 9–10]) or in false gods and false revelation (5:12–14 [Heb. 11–13]; cf. the false prophets in Mic. 2 – 3). The result of these uses of things both licit and illicit was that they essentially worshipped themselves.

The passage is introduced by the same *it will be* that begins 5:7 [Heb. 6]. The chronological setting is thus quite vague, and the relation of this unit to the others is better understood in terms of its relation to other aspects of the remnant's formation and function in chapters 4–5. This section is one of the clearest descriptions of the changes that lead to the appearance of the remnant of Israel/Judah, referred to here in second-person singular language. This unit consists of seven bicola (pairs of parallel lines), all of which are presented as YHWH's direct speech. Six are focused on the creation of the remnant (the subject of the preceding unit), while the last one is focused on the nations.

Comment

10 [Heb. 9]. *Horses* (or steeds) and *chariots* are mentioned only one other time in Micah, in 1:13, where they are clearly of military significance. The same holds true here: in the light of YHWH's omnipotence exercised through his new Davidic ruler as described earlier in chapter 5, these horses and chariots represent military power in which Judah placed its trust.[94] The focus on military equipment here also corresponds to that in 4:1–5, so that the two passages form a conceptual bracket around the salvation-material in 4:1 – 5:15 [Heb. 14] (Kessler 2000: 174).

11 [Heb. 10]. At first glance this verse goes even further than the destruction of sinful Samaria (ch. 1) and Jerusalem (ch. 3), although the national defeat implied in both those cases is not less extensive. But the focus here is not simply on cities as centres of population, but (note the pair *cities . . . fortresses*) on infrastructure that embodies military power and so represents misplaced hope for peace or an unsuitable means for subduing the remnant's enemies.[95]

12 [Heb. 11]. The plural *sorceries* probably emphasizes as much the severity of the problem as the variety or number of practices. Sorcery involved either predicting or attempting to control the future, and thus was in opposition to Yahwistic prophecy in the case of prediction. In the case of protective spells, it ignored YHWH's control of history and the use of the cultic practices he ordained (e.g. repentance and sacrifices) to deal with the consequences of sinful behaviour. Sorcerers within Israel were therefore to be executed (Exod. 22:18 [Heb. 17]).[96]

Fortune tellers are more directly involved in prediction, as the term suggests, and so were directly opposed to the prophetic channel of revelation that YHWH made the norm for Israel (Deut. 18:14). This practice too was relatively common outside Israel (cf. Isa. 2:6 [Philistines]) and within Judah in Micah's day and later

---

94. Andersen and Freedman (2000: 491) suggest that they are illicit cult features like those that Josiah took away which 'were given to the sun' (2 Kgs 23:11), but the military focus of 5:10–11 [Heb. 9–10] is clearly distinct from the focus on cult in 5:12–14 [Heb. 11–13].

95. This verse and its context echo the dual critique of Lachish that is presented very briefly in 1:13.

96. For the practice of the larger category of 'divination' in Neo-Assyria (thus including Babylonia in Micah's day), see Verderame 2014. More broadly, see Snell 2011: 28–29 and Bottéro 2001: 170–185. The semantic field of *kešep* is not very specific, and the word appears only a few times in the OT; cf. *HALOT* 1.503.

(Jer. 27:9) (Horsnell 1997a). Like sorcerers, these occult magicians were to be eliminated from Israel (Exod. 22:18 [Heb. 17]; Lev. 19:26), something that God commits to doing himself here.

13 [Heb. 12]. YHWH turns next to the activity of worship, specifically the use of cult statues. Despite the insistence of the then-extant parts of the Old Testament that worship of YHWH was not to involve images, the problem of idolatry was recurrent throughout much of Israel's history, from the patriarchs onwards (Gen. 31:19; 35:2; Num. 25:2; Josh. 24:23; Judg. 10:11–14; 1 Kgs 11:4). *Carved images* were part of Canaanite religious practice (Deut. 7:5, 25), yet the author of Kings (2 Kgs 17:41) attests to their use, separately or as part of YHWH worship, in Israel and Judah. Micah mentions them here in relation to the remnant, and YHWH singled them out in his condemnation of Samaria in Micah 1:7. It is striking in that connection that the Assyrian king Sargon II claimed that during the plundering of Samaria in 722 he carried away the cult statues of the temple in Samaria (Becking 2002).

Sacred pillars or stones were also common in ancient Mesopotamian religion, and Israel was to remove those erected by the Canaanites once in the land (Exod. 23:24; Deut. 7:5). This directive was often not followed (e.g. Hos. 10:1–2), and several royal reforms in Judah therefore pursued their destruction (2 Kgs 3:2; 18:4; 23:14). These images were at best syncretistic, and perhaps outright non-Yahwistic.[97] Their most common location was either within a town or at a city's gates, which explains their inclusion in this list (Hess 2007: 200, 302–306).

These are perhaps the most serious infractions slated for destruction in this section, since both a heart attitude (also present in trust in military might) and an illicit piece of cultic equipment are involved. The result of YHWH's destruction of these items goes further than the physical realm, however. A change of heart is necessary for an idolater to turn from worship of something created to worship of the Creator, and YHWH's purification of the remnant therefore includes a subjective, internal aspect as well as the external one the text focuses on.

---

97. Cf. Smith-Christopher 2015: 183–184.

14 [Heb. 13]. The list of illicit cult equipment continues with *cult poles* (*ʾăšērîm*), often wooden poles set up 'in worship contexts'.[98] These poles apparently symbolized the goddess without being crafted as representations of her, as were cult statues properly speaking (Day 1992: 486). The reading *cities* is doubted by some since it is the only item that appears twice in the list of things God will destroy in verses 10–14, but there is little doubt that the Masoretic Text preserves the original reading (Gelston 2010: 77, 105). However, in the light of the strong parallelism evident throughout the passage and the fact that no other term is repeated, Wagenaar's proposal that the MT consonantal text be kept and the term be read as a plural of the hypothetical root *ʾar*, 'tree', based on Aramaic and Arabic analogues, is a valid alternative.[99]

15 [Heb. 14]. We must understand *šāmaʿ* as *listen* or 'obey' rather than simply 'hear' since Micah consistently links judgment to a preceding sin – the sin in this case being a failure to respond properly to YHWH's word, which presumably came to them much as it came to nations which responded quite differently in 4:2–3. The appearance of *the nations which have not listened* is not surprising given the global scope of YHWH's work of judgment (1:2–4) and the complementary perspectives on the nations presented in chapters 4–5. Those who submit to YHWH's will and word are welcome in restored Zion (4:1–4) and flourish by virtue of the remnant (5:7 [Heb. 6]), while those who oppose his will and plans find themselves crushed under his remnant (4:13; 5:8 [Heb. 7]) and subdued under his Messiah (5:4–6 [Heb. 3–5]).[100]

---

98. McConville 2002: 288. The singular 'Asherah' in the OT sometimes refers to the goddess known from Ugarit; cf. Day 1992: 485.

99. So Wagenaar 2001: 200, following an extensive survey of less probable (consonantal) emendations that lack textual support. If *cities* is retained, one must understand a link between cities and idolatry, defended by Jeppesen (1984).

100. Especially in the context of Jonah and Nahum, the books on either side of Micah, it is clear that a nation's reaction to truth about YHWH determines its fate.

The section 4:1–4 thus complements the section 5:10–15 [Heb. 9–14]. The fate of the nations in 5:15 is the inverse of that in 4:1–4, and the reason is clear. In the earlier passage the nations who submit to YHWH are reconciled to him and to one another, while here those who do not obey YHWH find that their efforts to establish peace on their terms bring about their ruin instead. In the same way, the purification and ultimate well-being of the Israelite remnant in 5:10–14 corresponds to the 'programme of eschatological disarmament'[101] predicted for the non-Israelite nations in 4:1–4. The double role of the remnant in 5:7–8 and the binary fates of the nations there confirm the prominence of divisions within the nations (un/receptive to YHWH, i.e. transformed, or not) and Israel/Judah (remnant/nations, i.e. transformed, or not).[102]

The second unit of the book of Micah thus closes after having developed a number of points present in the first two chapters: the identity of the remnant and the means by which it comes to be; the positive and negative roles that the remnant plays among the nations; and, perhaps most surprisingly, the insistence that 'many' non-Israelites will enter a new, reconciled relationship with YHWH 'in the last days'. Those within Israel/Judah who are not similarly transformed will not experience the transformation, restoration and blessing that characterize life in the Zion that YHWH will rebuild and exalt for all to see.

Meaning

There is no such thing as half-hearted worship or incomplete consecration of oneself to God. YHWH's zeal for eliminating his people's trust in other helpers, their penchant for sources of security other than the absolute protection he alone offers, and their hankering after authoritative guidance above and beyond what he has already given show that he will leave no stone unturned and no sin unopposed in his work of sanctification. His transformation of his people will often even include pain, at least in the sense

---

101. Renaud 1987: 115; all translations from this work are my own.
102. Gignilliat (2019: 65) notes this in relation to the divine character as expressed in Exod. 34:6–7.

of giving up pet sins and crutches which hamper spiritual growth. But such 'growing pains' are an inevitable part of the process of dying and rising with Christ. His perfection of his people after this life will complete this work and see them made ready and suitable for sinless life in his presence.

3. THIRD CYCLE (6:1 – 7:20)

The third and last section of the book of Micah begins, as did the first two, with the call to *Hear*. Dempster observes that this section 'amplifies and intensifies the previous two sections while stressing a call to repentance and renewal', moving in the direction of internalizing YHWH's holiness in concert with the temple's exaltation (Dempster 2017: 153). It also follows the pattern in which condemnation and correction (6:1 – 7:7) are followed by announcements of salvation for those who hear (7:8–20). This last section is notable for its personification of the Daughter of Zion, who speaks of herself (7:8–10), and for its address to YHWH on the part of Micah and/or Daughter Zion (7:14–20).

The unit begins with a modified covenantal lawsuit against all Israel (north and south) in 6:1–8. This is followed by a judgment speech in response to a variety of open and covert sins in 6:9–16. The final element in the section dealing with sin and its consequences is a sort of lament over the disappearance of faithful people from the land/earth (7:1–6). The section that predicts deliverance begins with Daughter Zion's expression of faith in 7:7–10, then announces the expansion of Zion (7:11–13), and closes with a prayer for YHWH to complete his work of deliverance (7:14–17) and a hymn of praise that celebrates his utterly unique character as Saviour (7:18–20).

A. Israel's failure to live as YHWH's people (6:1–8)

Context
The structure of the passage, especially of the opening verses, depends on how one identifies the speaker(s). The passage's genre is loosely related to the prophetic lawsuit (*rîb*), which typically includes the following elements:

1 An introduction calling the audience to hear and often appealing to heavens and earth as witnesses;
2 Questioning of witnesses and statement of the accusation;
3 The prosecuting attorney's address to the court contrasting the people's sins with God's saving acts;
4 Description of the inability of cultic ritual to atone for such wrong acts;
5 A warning and a call to turn back to God and obey him.[1]

Taking account of the way that the unit adapts the covenant lawsuit and integrates other elements, the following structure appears:

1–5 YHWH's defence against Israel's rejection of his will and faithful character (incomplete and adapted covenant lawsuit) (1a: call to all to listen; 1b: call to Micah to convoke the confrontation; 2: Micah convokes Israel; 3–5: YHWH demonstrates his innocence).
6–7 The Israelites' protest that their sacrificial cult is already an appropriate response to YHWH's grace.
8 YHWH's expectations of Israel: faithful covenant life with him and one another.

---

1. Butler 1995: 163. Andersen and Freedman (2000: 509) propose that the same elements constitute the 'formal, analogical' parallel to the covenant lawsuit as found here and in Ps. 50.

Insofar as Micah adapts the covenant lawsuit for the purposes of this speech, it is significant that the elements of condemnation are replaced by a call to conversion (Renaud 1987: 129). The setting of the passage is impossible to specify, but its literary features presuppose its relevance to both northern and southern kingdoms.[2]

Comment

1. YHWH's initial invitation calls all people (as in 1:2) to give attention to what he is saying.[3] Micah is then commanded to convoke the mountains and hills as witnesses for the trial-confrontation between YHWH and his people.[4] The mountains and hills have 'gazed as silent observers since time immemorial' on all that has transpired in YHWH's relationship with Israel, so the veracity of what follows is sure.[5]

2. In response to YHWH's command, Micah calls the mountains and earth's very foundations, which existed long before YHWH's relationship with Israel began, as witnesses to his confrontation with his

---

2. Joosten (2013) argues that the passage's echoes of 1 Sam. 12 involve the motif of 'leaving Israel', with YHWH doing now, with respect to the northern kingdom, what Samuel did vis-à-vis the whole nation long before. Apart from the problems raised by judging this passage an 'oratorical fiction' by an anonymous prophet speaking after the fall of the north, there is no indication in 6:1–8 that YHWH is abandoning his people or the northern kingdom, although both ideas are present elsewhere in Micah.

3. As a minimum, the reader/hearer is included, as Kessler (2000: 261) prefers.

4. As Joosten (2013: 449 n. 3) observes, 'the prophetic speech must have been preceded by a divine mandate'. For a concise presentation of other ways of identifying the speakers and addressees, see Ben Zvi 2000: 143–144 and Andersen and Freedman 2000: 513. Wolff's proposal (1990: 173) that the mountains and hills represent the nations is implausible.

5. This felicitous phrase is from Allen (1976: 365).

people.[6] God's intention is to bring suit (*rîb*) *against his people* and to *dispute* (*yākaḥ* Hithpael) with *Israel*. The first term puts his covenant relationship with Israel in the foreground, and both terms suggest a covenant prosecution leading to a pronouncement of guilt and punishment. Unlike most forms of the covenant lawsuit, however, this one is adapted (see above), so serves a different purpose.[7]

3. The second-person singular grammar treats the whole nation, whose origins are traced back to the exodus, as a collective throughout this *dispute*. YHWH first implies that Israel is acting as if he had acted against it or had wearied it by acting inappropriately or unsuitably.[8] As Renaud notes, 'The rhetorical questions of v 3 have every appearance of a speech for the defence that picks up the very words of the adversary.'[9] YHWH's use of the possessive *my* to identify Israel as (still) his people underlines how deeply he cares for them despite their wearying him.[10] His demand for a response goes unanswered, however. The absence of any indictment against YHWH here is a very important argument from silence for his eminently just and gracious treatment of Israel/Judah. In the light of God's saving deeds mentioned in 6:4, the idea contemplated here that he would mistreat or weary Israel/Judah is preposterous. Rather than 'trying the patience' of his people, he has treated them far better than they might have reasonably expected.[11]

---

6. Smith-Christopher (2015: 189) argues from the claim that Micah is a 'lowlander' that the *mountains* represent Jerusalem, but this seems to force the image (Zion is not a hill and is singular).

7. As Ben Zvi (2000: 150) observes, 'the text clearly contradicts the expectations raised by a lawsuit simile'.

8. This idea is so absurd that it appears only here in the OT.

9. Renaud 1987: 120. In 7:9 faithful Zion knows that YHWH will plead her case against her enemies. As the only other uses of *rîb* in Micah, 7:9 implies that the audience addressed here is far from ideal.

10. Renaud (1987: 124) observes that this possessive pronoun by itself contains 'more or less all of the argumentation that follows' in 6:3–8 (all translations from this work are my own).

11. Thompson (1997: 748) suggests 'to try the patience of' for the more relational uses of the verb.

4–5. YHWH then lists five divine demonstrations of his provision and grace to disprove the unstated accusation that he had harmed or mistreated Israel. The first two involve the exodus, the Old Testament's example par excellence of his saving grace and power: he *brought up* Israel *from Egypt* and *redeemed* it from *slavery*.[12] The third involves providing them with leaders, presumably representing the spheres of law, cult and prophecy.[13] The fourth episode is YHWH's inversion of Balak's intention to curse Israel so that it is blessed instead (Num. 22 – 24). Finally, his protection after that, even though it began at the ignominious Shittim and Israel's partial apostasy there, lasted all the way to Gilgal, where the wilderness generation was circumcised and Israel's entry in the land was marked by the cessation of the daily manna (Josh. 5).

YHWH did all this so that Israel would *know* his *righteous deeds* (cf. 1 Sam. 12:7), but contrary to expectation Israel has misinterpreted YHWH's past and present treatment of it as harmful and wearying. This implies a deeply flawed view of what God wants Israel to be: God's people by and large seem to be chafing against the implications of their election.[14] The logic of YHWH's indictment is very similar to Deuteronomy's argument that YHWH's love,

---

12. Marrs (1999: 200 n. 52) and Renaud (1987: 119) see a play on words in the similar sounds of 'weary you' (*helʾetikā*) and 'brought you up' (*heʾelitikā*)

13. Marrs (1999: 201 n. 54) notes that Targumic tradition holds that 'Moses taught tradition and law; Aaron brought reconciliation to the people; Miriam instructed the women.' Similarly, Dempster (2017: 157) and Kessler (2000: 264) take the three as representative of political/legal, priestly and prophetic leadership. Renaud (1987: 125) sees them more generally as 'guides in the desert and thus as concrete signs of his [God's] divine care and protection', much like Waltke (2007: 352) and Andersen and Freedman (2000: 522), both of whom refer to 'leadership' more abstractly. The three are mentioned together elsewhere only in the genealogy of 1 Chr. 6:3.

14. 'Narratives not only can ground identity, they also clarify accountability,' notes Carroll R. (2007: 111).

shown in his saving actions on Israel's behalf (e.g. Deut. 4:37–39; 7:8–10; 10:20–22), should produce a response of love in Israel that drives obedience (cf. Deut. 4:40; 7:11; 11:1–2).¹⁵ God's saving deeds for Israel oblige it to revere and love him as expressed through obedience to his will and conformity to his character. Indeed, his character as shown in Israel's history is not only holy and righteous, but also gracious, self-giving and compassionate.

6. In verses 6–7 Micah puts in Israel's mouth the words of a characteristic response to YHWH's reminder of his salvific, patient, gracious shepherding of Israel.¹⁶ Interestingly, rather than recognize YHWH's impeccable and superlatively righteous behaviour towards his flawed covenant partner, Israel's response intimates that whatever he expects in response is too much, even wildly excessive. This attitude reveals Israel's complete misunderstanding of its relationship with YHWH, and tellingly focuses mainly on cultic actions performed at the temple (*come before*, *bow*, offer sacrifices) that one can perform superficially, without the corresponding heart attitude and patterns of behaviour that are essential to a healthy relationship with YHWH.

Indeed, the questions seem to imply that Israel is already doing enough (i.e. that anything more than is already being done would be excessive; cf. *wearied* in 6:3). The questions do not reveal an Israel that is ignorant of God's covenant expectations and therefore genuinely seeking guidance. Rather, it mistakenly believes that it knows God and his will, and that the status quo is entirely acceptable. This means mixing religious performance and mistaken beliefs (3:11, *Is not YHWH among us?*) with sins, many of which are evident to an objective observer. The fact that Israel does not mention repentance or any change in non-cultic behaviour

---

15. This Deuteronomic theme is capably explored by McConville (1984: 32, 120).

16. The first-person speaker in 6:6–7 is distinct from the divine/prophetic voice in 6:8, and can hardly be Micah's self-representation, so can only be Israel's response to YHWH's indictment. See further Renaud's explanation (1987: 129) of this 'person' as a 'type' of the people's 'latent tendencies'.

confirms that the people in general have understood a relationship with YHWH in radically superficial terms.[17]

Israel's sarcastic response to YHWH's recitation of his unchanging commitment to do it good begins in verse 6 by limiting its purview to the cult (*come before*). The second question is roughly equivalent, but uses a unique divine title, *God on high*, instead of YHWH.[18] While the name YHWH should remind Israel of God's saving, paternal self-revelation to them in the exodus (Exod. 3; 6), and *God on high* should remind them of his infinite majesty (cf. Ps. 92:8; Isa. 57:15), neither seems to have held any meaning for them! This diminishing of God's glory is part and parcel of Israel's radically inflated self-importance (or, conversely, of its pitifully low idea of what YHWH deserves from them). Perhaps most strikingly, there is no awareness that what YHWH has done for them was unmerited, and that profuse gratitude therefore should be their natural response.

The sarcasm continues as Israel proposes several ways, each more radical than the last, by which it might approach its God. The first means of approach is normal. A *whole burnt offering* could serve as a gift, votive offering, to make atonement, or most often to accompany a sin offering when used by individuals (Averbeck 1997b: 1020–1021).

The second way is normal but of unusual value. *Yearling calves* are mentioned only here in prophetic literature (cf. Lev. 23:18–19; Num. 7; 28:3, 9, 19; Smith-Christopher 2015: 194), and could be used for some offerings (Lev. 22:27). The fact that this apparently happened only rarely (cf. Lev. 9:3) suggests their elevated value when compared with other sacrifices, and thus reveals a sharpening of Israel's tone as the response continues.

---

17. The typical nature of this characterization argues against seeing it as a response *in extremis* to Assyrian aggression against Judah, *pace* Waltke 2007: 370, who follows Willis.

18. The verb *kāpap* without the preposition / describes being 'bowed' under oppression (Pss 57:6; 145:14; 146:8; Isa. 58:5); cf. Fretheim 1997. The context makes it likely that there is a connotation of oppression in its use here despite the distinctive syntax of the formulation compared to the four other uses (noted in *HALOT* 1.493).

7. The tone sharpens even more rapidly in the next three sarcastic proposals for how Israel thinks it must approach God.[19] Rams are used in guilt offerings (Lev. 5:15) as well as in other offerings, albeit one at a time (the exception proves the rule; note 1 Chr. 29:21 and cf. 1 Kgs 8:63; 2 Chr. 29:32). The proposal of *thousands of rams* is the first use of excessive intensification, and leads into even more extreme intensification. *Oil* was used in daily life for lighting, incense and anointing, and in the cult as part of grain offerings and some sacrifices, typically in modest quantities (e.g. at most ½ hin, *c.*2 litres, Num. 15:4; 28:14) in a recipe (Lev. 2:7), spread over a grain offering (Lev. 2:1) or smeared on wafers (Lev. 2:4). *Ten thousand rivers of oil* replaces one measure with *ten thousand*, and the usual quantity of a few litres with *rivers*, to create a wildly excessive amount, with the clear implication that YHWH's demands are similarly incredibly excessive.

The third element escalates far beyond any permitted or commanded sacrifice by proposing the sacrifice of one's *firstborn* to atone for one's *rebellion* and *sin*.[20] While every firstborn belonged to YHWH (Num. 3:13), the Levites were his instead (Num. 3:12; 8:16–18), and any child sacrifice is roundly condemned in the Old Testament. Micah surely intends to do more with this element of Israel's response than simply show that YHWH never asked for so much. The irony of this ridiculously exaggerated suggestion is twofold. First, the Israelites *already* belong to YHWH just as really as whole burnt offerings represented their complete commitment offered to him. The title *My people* (6:3, 5) is based on YHWH's fatherly relationship with Israel, his 'son' (cf. Exod. 4:22; 19:5–6 among many possible references for the all-inclusive nature of this relationship). This relationship was established by his election of

---

19. Dempster (2017: 155) sees the questions in 6:7 as 'escalating'.

20. *Rebellion* (*pešaʿ*) is the first term for sin used in Micah (1:5), and *sin* (*ḥaṭṭāʾt*) the second (1:5) (the same collocation in 1:13; 3:8; 7:18 uses *ʿāwōn*). *Pace* Smith-Christopher 2015: 195; the quasi-offering of Isaac was not a cultic event. Dempster (2017: 159) points to Ahaz's sacrifice of his son when he became king (2 Kgs 16:3) as an example of child sacrifice for political and magical rather than cultic ends.

Abraham and his redemption of his descendants from slavery in Egypt. Second, a holistic self-dedication is precisely what YHWH seeks (and deserves) in response to his unmerited and innumerable deeds on Israel's behalf (Pss 40:6–8; 119; etc.).

8. The prophet's response goes in precisely the direction of self-sacrifice out of gratitude. Without denying that part of a proper relationship with God involves sacrifices to atone for one's sins, Micah focuses on behaviours and dispositions that are not limited to the sphere of the cult. Since these things are already known to Israel, he implies that Israel has failed to understand their importance and their place in the covenant relationship. All these behaviours and values are *good*.

The only directly comparable use of *ṭôb* in Micah is in 3:2, where it is contrasted with evil (which Judah's leaders love) and is very close to the holistic *justice* to which YHWH calls his people.[21] Although the speech itself is directed to Israelites, the *O mortal* hints that the obligation for a God-honouring life is not limited to them. This is corroborated by Micah's treatment of the non-Israelite nations, which contrasts the behaviours and fates of the nations (4:1 – 5:1 [Heb. 4:14]) with those who 'refuse to listen' (5:15 [Heb. 14]).[22]

The rest of 6:8 draws on Deuteronomy 10:12–13 for several of its formal features, and on the book of Deuteronomy more generally for its overall message (see Table 1 on p. 201; shared vocabulary is underlined). The opening lines of each passage share several non-verbal elements and syntax, and use similar verbs.[23] Several shared

---

21. Kessler (2000: 269) notes a number of uses outside Micah that point in the same direction while clarifying the breadth of the concept (e.g. Gen. 2) of the 'good' as that which 'is good for one's relationship with God and others'.

22. Dempster 2017: 159; contrast Waltke 2007: 362–363.

23. Dempster 2017: 160. Micah's 'seek' (*dāraš*) is neither stronger nor weaker than Deuteronomy's 'ask' (*šā'al*). The former verb is in the semantic field of 'seeking' what is not currently seen, known or possessed, while 'ask' is a 'request' for what is not currently possessed or enjoyed. The only use of *dāraš* in Deuteronomy that has YHWH as

Table 1 Shared vocabulary and concepts in Micah 6:8
and Deuteronomy 10:12–13

Deuteronomy 10:12–13	Micah 6:8 (a, b, c, e, d, a)
And now, Israel,	Has he not told you, O mortal,
What does YHWH your God ask of you	What does YHWH require of you,
if not to revere YHWH your God	if not to do justice,
to walk in all his ways	and to walk humbly with your God?
and to love him	to love faithfulness,
and to serve YHWH your God with all your heart and all your being,	
to keep all the commandments of YHWH and his statutes which I am commanding you, for your good?	what is good?

verbs also appear in the hortatory sections ('love', 'walk'; Deuteronomy's 'fear' roughly parallels 'serve' here), and both passages
stress that obedience is for Israel's 'good'.

It is worth reflecting upon how Micah defines the essence of
a right relationship with YHWH and others. It involves, first,
observing an ideal divine norm (*do justice*) that, as readers of Micah
already know, involves dealing with others in a way that accords
with YHWH's will and protects them from exploitation and
mistreatment. To *love ḥesed*[24] presumes that one will practise this
faithful, loving, divinely modelled care for others, but it also calls
God's people to cherish the virtue and thus the God who is its

---

subject and a sacrifice as object is Deut. 23:21, where God will surely
'require' (infinite/finite verbs) what has been vowed (one other use has
land as object, Deut. 11:12). There is clearly some proximity of Micah
to Deuteronomy, so it is notable that the only use of *dāraš* in Micah
with YHWH as subject states that he desires a certain pattern of
heart-and-life, not cultic actions. Here I draw on the semantic fields
delineated in *NIDOTTE* 5.158, 169.

24. This expression in unique in the OT (Andersen and Freedman 2000: 528).

source at the deepest level of their being.[25] Finally, *to walk humbly with your God* means to live in relation to God in a way that recognizes the enormous disparity between God and the human being in every category and makes his will, character and glory paramount. The vertical element that the expression captures is thus inseparable from the horizontal element involving other human beings.[26] In Deuteronomy as in Micah, humility is an inescapable consequence of Israel's utter dependence upon YHWH's grace (Deut. 8:3).[27] The last grammatical element in the exhortation, *your God*, encourages Israel to respond to YHWH being fully aware that just as they are his (6:3), he is theirs by covenant.

Meaning

The lifestyle to which Micah calls his audience is how YHWH has always wanted Israel to act – even how he defines (ideal) Israel.[28] It is essentially *imitatio Dei*, something that Deuteronomy draws upon repeatedly (Deut. 5:15; 10:18; 14:1; 15:15; 24:19)[29] and that binds together the two moral dimensions of 'definite actions on behalf

---

25. Dempster (2017: 161) notes that while 'doing justice' is something that one does, 'loving faithfulness' is 'something that one is'.

26. Van der Merwe, Naudé and Kroeze (2017: 376–377) note that *'im* expresses the religious 'devotion' of an inferior for a superior here.

27. In Deuteronomy, some of the elements in Micah's exhortation are deployed differently, even though that book's overall message is consonant with Micah's distillation of Yahwism here. In Deuteronomy, love is typically directed to 'YHWH your God' and expresses itself in obedience (as does reverence), while 'walk' is often connected to the 'way' traced by YHWH's just commandments as developed extensively in Deuteronomy's exposition of the Decalogue (e.g. Deut. 5:33; 8:6; 10:12).

28. Andersen and Freedman (2000: 527) state, 'the implication is that this has always been the essential requirement. Compare Deut 10:12–13.'

29. McConville (1984: 18) observes that 'Israel's holiness not only carries implications for their behavior but is also related to the idea of sonship of YHWH, suggesting that the holiness of Israel is actually a reflection of [YHWH's] own character.'

of others, as well as inner dispositions before God and the community' (Carroll R. 2007: 112). In the context of Micah, this passage calls Micah's audience to a radical change of behaviour, and demands much more than bare cultic worship.[30] As Marrs puts it, 'moving from where the people are to where God intends them to be will involve a dramatic transformation of their understanding of the cult and socio-ethical implications of the divine–human relationship' (Marrs 1999: 199). It is, at bottom, a call to see God as he is, not as the domesticated, harmless deity they imagined (3:11), and to live accordingly.[31]

B. Israel's sin and its punishment (6:9–16)

Context
The reader may infer from the strong emphasis on condemnation and punishment in this passage that the indirect, measured call to radical change in 6:1–8 was not successful. Following the non-condemnatory exhortation to all of historical Israel (i.e. north and south) in 6:1–8, this unit likely focuses on Judah. Not only does Micah, a southerner, lament the absence of any just persons from his context (i.e. the south) in 7:1–6, but it would be unnecessary to inform a northern audience that they had 'kept the statutes of Omri and . . . Ahab' (6:16).[32]

---

30. As Renaud observes (1987: 131), Micah expresses no critique of the cult here.

31. Carroll R. (2007: 113) contends that 'the present worship at the cult has misconceived God and, unavoidably then, has misconstrued what it is that he requires of them in their daily life together and before him.'

32. However, the reference to *my people* that closes this section favours the conclusion that its addressee is identical to that of 6:1–8, i.e. all Israel understood as north and south, but the addressee there is necessarily part of, but not exhaustively definitive of, YHWH's people. Ben Zvi (2000: 157) notes that 'a main feature in this unit is the fluidity and ambiguity of speakers and addressees. This is the result of the implied author's play on, and purposeful intermingling of, two difference scenarios: (1) YHWH's direct speech to the city and its inhabitants,

This unit is widely recognized as a judgment speech, and YHWH is the speaker throughout, except for the interjection in 6:9b. The structure of the unit is straightforward:[33]

6:9	Introduction and exhortation to heed YHWH's discipline
6:10–12	List of sins
6:13–15	Covenant punishments
6:16	Summary: habitual sin leads to definitive punishment

Comment

9. The *city* is presumably Jerusalem, for the reasons mentioned above and because the noun itself is definite.[34] Recognizing that YHWH addresses the city (its population is grammatically masculine and plural) at a crucial moment, Micah interjects that *respect for your [YHWH's] name* is *sound wisdom*, a sentiment close to that expressed in 6:8, especially in the light of the link between obedience and wisdom in Deuteronomy 4:6.[35] Those in Jerusalem who are wise will heed what God says and does to Jerusalem (the one who has appointed the rod is masculine and singular). This is a very relevant overture to a judgment speech announcing that Jerusalem will fall under the covenant's heaviest sanctions and become desolate, and the assumption that the rod of punishment (Job 3:18; Isa. 10:5, 24; 30:32) can be heard shows that the process of discipline has already begun.

(note 32 *cont.*) and (2) the prophet voice telling someone else – identified also as Israel – about YHWH's talk to the city.' See Andersen and Freedman 2000: 553–556 for further discussion of changes in gender, number, speaker and addressee in this section.

33. Similarly, Kessler 2000: 275 and others.

34. So Renaud 1987: 135; Kessler 2000: 277; Waltke 2007: 395; Smith-Christopher 2015: 199; etc. For an alternative view, see Andersen and Freedman 2000: 546, who think Samaria is equally plausible.

35. Furthermore, Deuteronomy makes 'reverence for YHWH' the first item in several descriptions of what a life consecrated to YHWH looks like; cf. Deut. 4:10; 5:29; 6:4; etc.

10–12. YHWH asks a series of rhetorical questions (he alone speaks in the first person in this section) that reveal the status quo in Jerusalem and in doing so constitute a strong critique of it. The practices mentioned have to do primarily with deceptive business practices, although the *violence* mentioned in 6:12a shows that the perpetrators will stop at nothing to enrich themselves. The *still* at the beginning of 6:10 makes YHWH's almost-exhausted patience an important undertone, and leads to the punishments in 6:13–15.

Almost every term here is unique in Micah, except for *deception*, which appears in 2:11. None the less, the activities that YHWH condemns are essentially the same as the land-grabbing in 2:1–4 but are pursued in the everyday venue of small transactions and personal interactions. Every phrase in this section has one, and sometimes two, terms that modify the subject in a negative way. Three times this term is *wicked*, and three other terms fall in the semantic field of 'deceit, falsehood'. *Violence*, for its part, is a very strong term (note its first appearance in Gen. 6:11) that 'is the polar opposite of *ḥesed*' which YHWH's covenant people should love according to 6:8.[36] These negative evaluations have to do with unjust commercial instruments (weights, scales, measures), deceitful speech, and the unjustly enriched perpetrators and their well-filled homes.[37] In much the same way that these objects and persons are part of the city, these moral wrongs characterize the city itself, as is evident from the possessive suffixes in 6:12 that link the city with *her* violent *rich men* and lying merchants.

This web of corruption violates not only the primordial directives of the eighth and ninth commandments, but many more that appear later in the Pentateuch (Lev. 19:35–36; Deut. 25:13–15

---

36. Dempster 2017: 169. Kessler (2000: 280) suggests that the 'violence' associated with a witness (Exod. 23:1 etc.) may be tied to a transaction, and so can be verbal rather than physical.

37. Waltke (2007: 397–398) proposes a number of textual emendations here, but the manuscript evidence for them is quite weak; cf. Gelston 2010: 106.

for just measures, weights and balances; Lev. 19:11 for false speech and dealings, etc.), especially the call to love one's neighbour as oneself (Lev. 19:18).[38] The picture that these accusations paint is thus of the Jerusalem elite's habitual, calculated and successful – but corrupt, sinful and cursed – exploitation and abuse of those who purchased wares and staples from them, all the while running roughshod over scriptural norms. Still more fundamentally, these merchants seem to believe that YHWH does not care about such sins, or that his holiness and justice are so weak that any consequences would be insignificant – yet he affirms the contrary: *Shall I acquit* such people? This fundamental theological error would cost them dearly, 'for all who do these things, all who practise injustice, are an abomination to YHWH' (Deut. 25:16).

13–15. These verses make clear the eventually inevitable connection between such hardened patterns of sinful behaviour and the curses of the covenant. Like Deuteronomy 28, this section addresses the sinful individual directly, with the singular *you* (cf. Deut. 28:15), and ties the punishment to his or her actions (*because of your sins*, 6:13). Verse 13 echoes the verb *strike* that introduces many of the covenant curses of Leviticus 26 and Deuteronomy 28, and God repays these oppressors in kind by beating them down (cf. Lev. 26:17; Deut. 28:22) just as they had crushed their victims economically, removing their ill-gotten gain and leaving them desolate. Verse 14 probably inverts the blessing from Deuteronomy 11:15 or applies the curse from Leviticus 26:26 (*eat but not be satisfied*) and develops that punishment to include hunger and the loss of food set aside, all in the context of violence presumably resulting from an armed invasion (Deut. 28). In verse 15 YHWH draws on several futility curses of Deuteronomy 28 to promise that the dishonest monetary gains these Judeans have collected will not profit them: they will *plant but not harvest*

---

38. Ben Zvi (2000: 159) notes that many of the items and offences mentioned here appear in Proverbs, including almost all the wrongs in 6:11 (cf. Prov. 11:1; 16:11; 20:10) and the 'house of the wicked' (Prov. 3:33; 14:11; 21:12), another link to the wisdom–fear of YHWH elements in Mic. 6:8–9.

(cf. Deut. 28:38), have *olive* trees but no olive *oil* (cf. Deut. 28:40), and have vineyards or crush *grapes* but not *drink* the *wine* (cf. Deut. 28:30, 39).

16. The section closes by describing Judah in terms that are very negative and which portend its doom.[39] A sizeable or important portion of Jerusalem's population had chosen to follow not YHWH's laws (the expressions 'keep statutes, walk in commandments', etc. are typically used for obedience) but *the statutes of Omri, and all the practices of Ahab's dynasty* (cf. 2 Kgs 17:19) – 'the worst kings imaginable within the discourse in general'![40] As a result, God will make Jerusalem, and by extension Judah, a horror (Deut. 28:37). The plight of its inhabitants will elicit astonishment (cf. Jer. 18:16; 19:8; 25:9; 29:18; 51:37), and they, *my people*, will bear the *scorn* and *reproach* that attends divine rejection (cf. the 'scorn' of Egypt, Josh. 5:9; of those who remained in Jerusalem after its destruction, Neh. 1:3; 2:17; in exile, Pss 44:13 [Heb. 14]; 78:4; 89:41, 50; in distress, Joel 2:17, 19).

The observation in 2 Kings 17:15 that the northern kingdom 'rejected YHWH's decrees and the covenant he had made with their ancestors and the statutes he had warned them to keep' captures the essence of the reference to Omri and Ahab. These kings were known for idolatry and the continuation of the deviant YHWH cult established by Jeroboam I (Omri, 1 Kgs 16:25–26; Ahab, 1 Kgs 16:30–31), but these phenomena are foregrounded only in Micah 1:5–7. Ahab, however, was also known for his strident opposition to Elijah (1 Kgs 18 – 19) and his violent seizure of the vineyard of Naboth the Jezreelite (1 Kgs 21). This episode mixes the false witness mentioned in Micah 6:12 and the illegal appropriation of

---

39. 2 Kgs 17 points out that Judah continued in these practices even after the same practices led to the destruction of the northern kingdom and the exile of many of its inhabitants in 722.

40. Ben Zvi 2000: 161. This comparison reflects indirectly a date well before the mid seventh century, when a comparison with Manasseh would have been more powerful. Andersen and Freedman (2000: 556) suggest that the king may be the anonymous third-person subject of *keeps* in 6:16a.

another's inheritance in Micah 2:1–2 (cf. 1 Kgs 21:3), and suggests that this comparison is meant to summarize Judah's practice as described across the book of Micah, as does Ahab's penchant for false prophets (1 Kgs 22:6–8; cf. Mic. 2:6–7; 3:5–8, 11).

The corrupt religion of Omri and especially of Ahab is not without relevance for Judah.[41] In addition to the critique of the north's cult made in 1:5–7, it is crucially important that just as true worship and faithfulness to YHWH produce a lifestyle of justice, fidelity and love, worship of false gods inevitably leads to self-serving injustice, unfaithfulness and violence. Especially since it follows immediately upon 6:8, the critique of Judah's sinful elite for commercial fraud and violence in this section is an implicit argument that they are living outside the covenant that YHWH established with their ancestors, and thus are without a real attachment to him. The parallel between Jerusalem and Samaria here echoes that in 1:5, a link that reinforces the imminent nature of Jerusalem's fall (since Samaria's fall is predicted immediately after that passage, in 1:6–7), and builds on the prediction of 3:12.

Meaning
Although some of the sins mentioned here are familiar (violence), this passage is notable for including more mundane, purportedly less serious sins such as dishonesty, especially in commerce and speech. The mention of Omri and Ahab underlines another danger, one that arguably lies *behind* such sins – that of putting other gods before God or creating him in our own image. The well-known account of Isaiah's vision of God's inexpressible and overwhelming glory in Isaiah 6 captures a reality that even faithful believers too easily forget. 'Teach me . . . that even my highest thoughts of Thee are but dim and distant shadows of Thy transcendent glory' (Baillie 1996: 73).

---

41. Greenwood (2014: 293) observes that 'The focus of the Deuteronomist's account [in 1 Kgs 16] . . . is the antagonistic relationship between the house of Omri and Yahwistic orthodoxy.'

C. Micah laments the guilt and imminent punishment of Judah (7:1–6)

Context

The speaker in this section is most likely Micah, since if Daughter Zion were the speaker, as she is in 7:7–10, she would presumably refer to herself, to the remnant and to sinners in Jerusalem quite differently. The situation is one in which, like 6:10–12, those who do evil are dominant, so that divine judgment is imminent (7:4a). Ben Zvi (2000: 166) argues strongly for including 7:7 in this unit, but it seems to fit better as part of 7:8–9 (see below).[42]

The genre most closely resembles a lament but includes other elements, such as complaint and reproach (Renaud 1987: 139; Ben Zvi 2000: 170). Ben Zvi expresses well its significance: it

1 Shapes a set of circumstances that are depicted in the most negative terms from the perspective of the speaker,

2 Characterizes directly or indirectly the speaker as a pious person opposed to the evildoers,

3 Characterizes the speaker as one with full confidence – despite the circumstances – in the saving or restoring action of YHWH, and

4 Attempts to develop in the audience an emotional attachment to the speaker.

(Ben Zvi 2000: 166)

Comment

1. The gravity of the situation in Judah, to be described here for the last time in the book, compels the prophet to bemoan his unhappy lot as witness to Judah's terrible condition. His lament forms a rough bracket, with the lament in 1:9–16, around the book. After verbalizing in a striking way his grief over the Judah of which he is part (this Hebrew expression for *Woe is me* occurs elsewhere

---

42. Jeremias (2007: 213–214) draws attention to a number of links between this section and chapter 3, which concludes the negative portion of the book's second cycle; Kessler (2000: 290) sees links between 7:1–4 and chapters 1–3.

only in Job 10:15), the prophet represents the situation in Judah with a metaphor: Judah is like a vineyard and a plantation in which, exceptionally, not a single grape or fig is visible to the harvester (cf. the famine of 6:13–15).

2. Verse 2 explains the metaphor in binary terms: the *land* (Judah), even all *mortals* (*'ādām*), are (hyperbolically[43]) entirely without persons who are *faithful* (the same root as *faithfulness* in 6:8) and *upright* (as in 2:7; 3:9). Rather, all inhabitants pursue one another with violent stratagems. *Bloodshed* was attributed to Jerusalem's leaders in 3:10, and the commitment to violence that the second half of the verse describes recalls that of 6:12. The widespread practice of hunting animals with a *net*, when applied to human prey, captures well the degradation and spite inherent in such treatment (Dempster 2017: 175), and this is exacerbated by the fact that *brother* preys upon *brother*. To put this sad situation in terms used elsewhere in the book, the remnant (Daughter Zion) is so small a minority that Micah laments its minuscule size and fears for its disappearance.[44]

3–4a. In a manner now familiar to the reader, Micah asserts that the elite are particularly guilty in this regard. Their insouciance with respect to evil manifests itself in the corruption of governmental and judicial decisions by bribes while the misuse of power and authority allows might to determine what is right. *The best of them* (a self-negating comparison) is *like a thorn bush*, and the *most upright* is like *a thorn hedge* (even worse, because made up of more than one bush!). Both are likely to draw blood when encountered!

4b. The consequence of the pervasive sin that this passage sketches is not delayed until its conclusion, but is placed in the middle of the passage (7:4b).[45] The reference to Jerusalem's *watchmen* in the context of *the day* refers either to them seeing the threat

---

43. Otherwise there would be no need to warn the just of the schemes of the wicked, as in 7:5–6.

44. See, in the same vein, Jeremias 2007: 215, who underlines the discontinuity between the remnant, represented by the solitary speaker, and the nation at large.

45. Contra Renaud 1987: 143, 7:5–6 is not part of the punishment.

which has been building (if literal watchmen, i.e. an objective genitive; cf. YHWH's patience in 6:10; similarly, Hos. 9:8)[46] or to the day they foresaw (if prophetic watchmen, i.e. a subjective genitive). In either case, *punishment* is coming.[47] The *disarray*[48] mentioned here occurs elsewhere only in Isaiah 22:5, an oracle against Jerusalem in Isaiah's oracles concerning the nations (Isa. 13 – 23) that portrays the Day of YHWH overturning and destroying Jerusalem. Both texts depict the effects of YHWH's judgment on hardened sinners, and even though relatively muted, the note of destruction is clearly present here.[49]

5–6. These verses develop the brother-against-brother nature of Judah's commitment to self before all else, showing that even the closest relations of blood and proximity are devoid of love and fidelity (contrast 6:8). Outside the household, *friend* and *neighbour* cannot be trusted, nor can one's spouse be trusted within it! This lack of fidelity in the closest relationship is then predictably traced outwards to the limits of the household. One's offspring (*son* or *daughter*) pose a danger, for they rise up against their parents, in violation of the fifth commandment. The end of the verse depicts a deadly household melee in which no member of a *family* is safe from the others.

This is the worst social situation imaginable, worse even than the lamentable situations described in 2:2, 9, where the enemies of a household are at least outside it, and 4:10, where they are outside

---

46. For the role of watchmen, see Ezek. 33:6; Nah. 2:1 [Heb. 2].

47. Dempster (2017: 174) notes the assonance that links the Hebrew terms for 'your punishment' (*pĕquddatkā*) and 'your disarray' (*mĕbûkātām*). Reicke (1967: 357) draws attention to the 'day of my [YHWH's] visitation' in Exod. 32:34, which although not eschatological is very significant.

48. *HALOT* 1.541 proposes 'confusion', but this lacks the stronger negative nuance present in 'disarray'. See van Rooy 1997.

49. The Day of YHWH, at least in a preliminary or incomplete stage, is most likely referred to here, albeit without that pair of words being used. See the comments of Wolff (1990: 207) in the same vein, and note the analogous phrase in Exod. 32:34, which refers to a non-eschatological judgment.

Israel/Judah. 'With this disintegration of the nuclear family the very foundations of the society are shaken.'[50] This kind of social and familial collapse is used elsewhere in the Ancient Near East to portend the end of the world, which underlines its seriousness while resonating with the eschatological nature of the coming judgment in 7:4b.[51] This is the darkest portrayal of Judah in the book, and so comes last. It is probably for that reason that the most developed portrayal of the remnant and of the means of its ultimate deliverance follows immediately in 7:7–20 (Dempster 2017: 174).

Meaning

Micah's sadness over the sinfulness he sees all around shows that his heart is closely aligned with his message. His sadness surely has to do with his fellow citizens' failure to enjoy life under YHWH's will and protection (cf. also 1:8–9) as well as his dismay at seeing God's will flouted and his holiness ignored. The situation is so grave that it threatens to ruin Judean society even apart from the divine punishment that will end it! It is difficult to encounter stark proof of sin's power, whether in ourselves or in others, without either losing hope or withdrawing in self-protective cynicism. Micah feels intense distress when he looks around him but maintains hope in God's commitment to justice, mercy and ultimate victory over evil as expressed by Daughter Zion in the next sub-unit (7:7). Paul's fervent desire to see the gospel reach the Corinthians' hearts (2 Cor. 5:20) did not exist despite, but because of, his conviction that they needed Christ (2 Cor. 2:4; 7:9). Confidence in the power and grace of God is imperative if we are to live and share the gospel without losing hope.

---

50. Renaud 1987: 141. Jeremias (2007: 212) calls it 'the dissolution of all order'.

51. Reicke 1967: 358, and see the examples cited in Andersen and Freedman 2000: 573–574. For example, in *Erra and Ishum II*, the complete lack of love between parent and child coincides with Erra's decision to 'finish off the land and count it as ruins . . . fell people and [I shall leave no] life, I shall not keep a single one back' (Dalley 2000: 297).

D. Daughter Zion's faith, deliverance and praise (7:7–20)

Context
This passage falls into two distinct parts: a speech of Daughter Zion and a reply to her (7:7–10, 11–13), and a prayer to YHWH (including a brief reply to its first petition; 7:14–20). YHWH is centre stage here, to say the least. Dempster identifies seven 'distinguishing divine characteristics' that come fully into view in this, the book's concluding section: 'pardon, forgiveness, temperance, *ḥesed*, mercy, conquest of sin, and its complete abolition' (Dempster 2017: 181). It draws together a number of the book's key themes as it draws its plot to a close.[52]

In terms of the book's plot line, this unit reinforces the impression that there are only three actors on the world stage: God, his people, and their enemies. The identities of the two latter groups vary over time and cannot be tied to neatly defined ethnic or national groups. Indeed, the descriptions of both groups in this unit focus on their proximity to or separation from YHWH as their Creator, King, Judge and (in the case of his people) Saviour.

The separation of this personification (Daughter Zion) from the sinners in Israel is perhaps the most radical means by which Micah redefines the people of God. Separate from sinners, characterized by faith and confident that God will refine her even through suffering (7:8 and following), Daughter Zion hopes in God's grace and commitment to save through his various covenantal commitments, especially to Abraham.[53] Furthermore, this disposition of faith and expectation is meant to create or strengthen the same allegiance to YHWH in the reader.

Di Fransico has helpfully explored, on the basis of numerous allusions to Exodus 15 in Micah 7, how this passage replaces the

---

52. See Wessels 2003 and Kessler 2000: 297–299 for discussion of this unit's relation to the rest of the book.

53. From the very beginning, this covenant's blessings were not ultimately determined by one's genealogical descent; e.g. Abraham's circumcision of foreign servants, Gen. 17:27, and his being a father of many nations, Gen. 17:5.

human enemy that pursued Israel in the exodus and especially at
the Reed Sea with the sin that now causes the punishment of the
Israelites (north and south) (Di Fransico 2017: 195). She shows that
this metaphorical presentation of sin as an enemy complements
that of redemption – that is, the delivery from the power of a
malevolent other (e.g. the liberation from exile and spiritual transformation in 4:6–8).[54] Vargon's arguments for Micah as the author
of the section are convincing and in agreement with the book's
claims (Vargon 2009).

The passage can be structured as follows:

7:7–10   Daughter Zion's faith in YHWH's justification and
            deliverance
7:11–13   Address to Daughter Zion: Zion to be filled, the
            world to be emptied
7:14–20   Prayer and praise to YHWH (7:14–15, 16–17, 18–20)

Comment

7. The conjunction on the 'I' presumes a connection with the
preceding unit, but an apparent change in speaker makes it likely
that here Daughter Zion responds to the description of historical
Jerusalem in 7:1–6 (taking for granted that she speaks in 7:8–9).[55]
Micah has not offered a prayer to which YHWH would respond (his
complaints and sadness are not addressed to God in 1:8 or 7:1),
whereas Daughter Zion has been heard by God (4:9), has uttered a
prayer to which she is confident YHWH will respond (7:7), and is
sure that her case is already known to him (7:9). These links are
strengthened by the wordplay between the last words of 7:7
(*yišmāʿēnî ʾĕlōhāy*) and the first words of 7:8 (*ʾal-tiśmĕḥî ʾōyabtî lî*)

---

54. The argument of Nogalski (2010) that Mic 7:8–20 is dependent upon
    Isa. 9 – 12 is not implausible per se, but his presumption that this
    part of Micah's book originated in the post-exilic period strains the
    credulity of the reader who understands the book as the product
    of the ministry of the prophet named in 1:1.

55. The feminine possessive suffix on *your God* in 7:10 lends some formal
    support to this interpretation.

(Dempster 2017: 181). Finally, differences in language and style distinguish 7:7 from what precedes it,[56] including the self-reflective tone of 7:7 that connects it with Daughter Zion's speech in 7:8–9. Daughter Zion's discourse covers several interrelated topics: her relationship with YHWH (7:7), her trust in his future deliverance (7:8–9), and his coming defeat of her enemy (7:10).

The language used by Daughter Zion identifies her with the ideal people of God, even though she is not yet fully delivered. In her current condition, not yet fully distinguished from the imperfect Jerusalem of 7:1–6 (also 3:10–11) within which she finds herself, she *watches expectantly for* YHWH, identifies him as her *salvation* and is confident that he will *hear* (i.e. answer) her petition. This is the only time that YHWH is the subject of the verb 'hear' in Micah, and since Zion's address to YHWH takes account of what YHWH or Micah has said to her earlier in the book (e.g. 4:10, 13), her affirmations here fit into a continuing dialogue with God. The characterization of Zion as faithful, even as she awaits deliverance, is deepened by the allusion to Exodus 15:2, 'Yah . . . has become my salvation', in Zion's *I will wait for the God of my salvation* (Di Fransico 2017: 192).

8. The earlier passages that deal with Daughter Zion make clear that her enemies are historical. These enemies include both non-Israelite nations (e.g. 4:10, 11–13) as well as ethnic Israelites (i.e. from north or south) who are morally and spiritually distinct from her (e.g. 2:2; the *you* of 2:3–5, 8–9; the corrupt rulers of 3:1–2; etc.).[57] All these enemies are what they are because of their attitude towards or treatment of the oppressed remnant or Daughter Zion, respectively, in different contexts. Accepting the proposal that the enemy is 'a typological figure representing the opposite of Daughter Jerusalem' (Dempster 2017: 183), the brief but dense characterization of Daughter Zion in 7:7 means that this enemy pays no heed to YHWH, does not recognize its sin, and is committed to realizing its self-determined destiny by its own efforts. This identity can be

---

56. So also Renaud 1987: 145.

57. Smith-Christopher (2015: 216) agrees: 'An internal enemy would be consistent with Micah's rhetoric throughout the book.'

true not only of Assyria and Babylon, but of any individual who does not share Zion's faith in YHWH and her acceptance of his condemnation as well as his grace.[58]

This enemy gloats over Daughter Zion (identical here to the remnant, but later enlarged by the integration of some foreigners in 7:11–12) in her current, lowly state of judgment, and reveals the desire to see Zion come to an end (cf. the nations in 4:11). Her fall presumably took place between 7:6 and 7:7, so to speak, and begins, according to other parts of the book, with Judah's exile (4:10) and abandonment (5:3 [Heb. 2]). It lasts beyond the so-called return from exile until Zion's restoration, which in Micah involves her supremacy over the nations (4:13), the arrival of YHWH's ruler (5:4–6 [Heb. 3–5]), the submission of some nations to YHWH's rule (4:1–4), and Zion's deliverance and justification from sin (7:7, 9). Both falling and being in darkness are negative, and both are due to the sin of the nation (including the remnant).[59]

9. This verse deals more explicitly than any other in Micah with the remnant's sin and God's wrathful reaction to it. Earlier in the book no sin was clearly attributed to the remnant, although its imperfection was hinted at by terms like *lame*, and sin was presupposed in YHWH's afflicting it (4:6). Here, by contrast, the remnant itself states that it has *sinned*, and it accepts as discipline the temporal consequences of that sin in the form of divine *fury*. But Daughter Zion's conviction that YHWH is perfectly just explains

---

58. The argument of Nogalski (2010: 133) that the enemy is Nineveh is too exclusive. Vargon's argument (2009: 610–615) that Assyria's early aggression against Israel is in view is more solidly rooted in history and therefore more plausible, but it too restricts the temporal horizon of the enemy in ways that various passages in Micah do not.

59. Darkness sometimes has connotations of imprisonment (Ps. 107:10; Isa. 42:7), but as part of the darkness–light pair that seems to be of secondary importance here; contrast Allen 1976: 395. While distinct from the Israelite 'enemy', the remnant (and Daughter Zion) are never said to be sinless in the present. But their sin will be overcome, a change represented by the metaphorical movement from darkness to light.

not only her readiness to recognize her sin, but also her firm faith that only YHWH can and will remove it as an otherwise insurmountable obstacle between them.[60] Her case is not laid out in detail, but its key elements have already been presented: her objective guilt (7:9), her knowledge that YHWH is the only Saviour (7:7), and her confidence that he will save her by removing her sin and guilt (7:9).[61]

The resolution of Daughter Zion's case is described in three ways. First, YHWH will *execute justice* for her, not by pretending she is innocent but in responding to her repentance and trust in him as Saviour (the reasons for this confidence are presented most clearly in 7:18–20).[62] Second, he will *bring* her *out into the light*, an exodus (cf. the same root in 2:13; 7:15) from the *darkness* of sin into pardon and acceptance that only he can grant. The third element develops in forensic terms the metaphor of the second one: Daughter Zion will *see* [experience] *his righteousness.* Unable to see in the darkness of judgment, Daughter Zion's 'seeing' involves coming into the *light* that is its opposite, spelled out here in terms of divinely granted *righteousness* that defines (negatively) the absence of the sin that, in terms of the preceding metaphor, was left behind in the darkness.[63] It is probably unnecessary to distinguish between a vindicating act and the result of that act, since God's vindication of Zion involves bringing her (positively) into conformity to 'a norm or standard expressed in a particular relationship'.[64]

---

60. Renaud (1987: 147) comments, 'This confession of sin opens the path of hope for Zion', and Kessler (2000: 302) contends that it is the heart of the book's concluding section.

61. Kessler (2000: 300) observes that the recognition of sin makes this case the converse of the one that YHWH brings against his sinful people in 6:1–8.

62. Jeremias (2007: 221) notes that the grounds for what Zion says here are developed across the unit, and especially at its end.

63. YHWH accomplishes *righteous deeds* in 6:5: note also the strong emphasis on forgiveness or the effacing of guilt in 7:18.

64. Seifrid 2000: 742, who notes that the feminine *ṣĕdaqâ* used here 'is generally concrete, signifying either a vindicating action . . . or the deeds which warrant the claim to justification'.

10. YHWH's saving acts in favour of Daughter Zion are simultaneously a judgment against her *enemy*, which had pursued her
destruction for its own, unjust purposes (cf. Gen. 12:3). Just as Zion
was covered in shame while awaiting YHWH's salvation (cf. the
expectant waiting in 7:7) and was mistreated and oppressed by
other Israelites and the nations alike, Zion's enemies (who express
their spite for YHWH in the sarcastic *Where is he, YHWH your God?*)
will suffer *shame* and humiliation in turn.[65] In this short section's
move from present to future, 'all roles are now reversed', for Zion
stands justified (rather than sitting under sin's punishment), while
the enemy that formerly shamed her is now shamed and no longer
a threat.[66]

11. Verses 11–13 present the radical enlargement of Daughter
Zion, now presented as a city, in terms of her dimensions and
population. The Jerusalem that was ripe for judgment was local
(*from the land* in 7:2), but this one is global. The speaker is most
likely the prophet, since YHWH would presumably refer to himself
as the one who will do these things.

The only plausible audience for this speech is the same feminine
singular entity at the centre of 7:7–10, that is, Daughter Zion,
addressed here as a personified city. Her (re)*building*, specifically of
her walls,[67] relates to the literal city in two ways. It contrasts
sharply with its construction by violent means (3:10; the only other
use of 'build' in Micah), but also with its literal destruction (presumably along with other cities of Judah in 5:11 [Heb. 10]; cf. esp.
6:16). The idea of 'extending' metaphorical Zion's *boundary* goes
beyond the idea of merely rebuilding to expansion, suggesting a

---

65. Di Fransico (2017: 192) notes that the waters cover the Egyptian
    forces (Exod. 15:5) just as shame covers the enemies of Daughter Zion
    (Mic. 7:10), and both passages use the same verb (*kāsâ*).

66. Andersen and Freedman 2000: 581. Being 'trampled like the mire
    of the streets' emphasizes 'the depth of the humiliation' rather than
    destruction (Wolff 1990: 223).

67. Jeremias (2007: 226) argues that these *walls* are not for a city's defence,
    but that sense cannot be excluded (Ezek. 13:5; 22:30; Ezra 9:9), although
    the term also refers to other kinds of walls, as Waltke shows (2007: 456).

reality that surpasses what Zion has already been, and this is developed in the following verse.[68]

12. The idea of *peoples* and *nations* coming to renewed and radically transformed Jerusalem has already appeared in 4:1–4, and non-Israelites are the most likely subject here.[69] However, this verse adds several elements to the description in chapter 4. First, it emphasizes these peoples' number, variety and distant points of origin. The phrase *sea to sea* expresses a worldwide extent, a further reason to see non-Israelites as the subject here.[70] Second, the choice of Egypt and Assyria is probably motivated by the role of each as Israel's paradigmatic oppressors (Babylon is still on the distant horizon, 4:10). The amazing nature of this peaceful influx of non-Israelites to restored Zion is all the more stunning because these long-time foes are foremost among them (cf. 4:3).

13. In contrast to restored Zion as a miraculously enlarged city welcoming people from across the globe, *the earth* will become *desolate* (the same term as *horror* in 6:16) because of the sins of those who inhabit it and do not come to Zion (the same logic applies to the Jerusalem of Micah's day, 6:13).[71] Taken together with 7:12,

---

68. So Ben Zvi 2000: 176.

69. If exiles are in view (cf. Deut. 30:4), the motive for return to Jerusalem is obvious, but 'return' (*šûb*) is not used, nor is 'from' (*min*), which would imply that they had gone there previously, as in Deut. 30. For arguments in favour of seeing this group as returning exiles, see Timmer 2015: 108. It is also possible to affirm with Dempster (2017: 185) that because these people come from across the world, both non-Israelites and exiled Jews come.

70. Cf. Ps. 72:8; Zech. 9:10. Boda (2016: 573) notes the very close links between the passages, as well as the fact that such global dominion is attributed in the OT either to YHWH or, as in those two passages, to his final messianic king (note also Mic. 5:4 [Heb. 3]).

71. The Hebrew word (*'ereṣ*) can be translated as either 'earth' or 'land', but 'land' is too small to be relevant in the context of people coming from far outside Judah to enter restored Zion. Contrast Micah's focus on the land of Judah in 7:2, in the context of his Jerusalem-focused lament.

this verse divides the entire human population into two sharply contrasted groups: those who enter Zion and have the same repentant, faithful disposition as Daughter Zion, and those who remain outside because of their sinful practices (much like the enemy of 7:8, 10; note also the similar accusation against Israel/Judah in 3:4).[72] This Daughter Zion–world dichotomy has already been sketched in 4:1–4, 11–13; 5:4–9 [Heb. 3–8], 10–15 [Heb. 9–14], but this presentation of it is the clearest in the book.

14. The last sub-unit of the passage, 7:14–20, draws together many of the key elements treated earlier in the chapter (the submission of the nations, the forgiveness of Daughter Zion's sins) and elsewhere in the book (YHWH as shepherd-king, the return from exile), but develops several of them in new ways. It also draws a broad covenantal frame around YHWH's work of salvation and guides the reader towards a response of praise and absolute trust in YHWH.

The unit is a prayer with an initial petition (7:14) which (unusually in Micah) is immediately met with a divine response (7:15). Affirmations of faith in God's supremacy over the nations follow (7:15–17), and the prayer closes with a meditation on his forgiving, merciful, compassionate and faithful character as demonstrated in the salvation of his people.

Daughter Zion is most likely the speaker throughout. Although this means she refers to herself in the third person in 7:14, that is hardly an insurmountable problem, since she clearly does so in 7:18–20, where a first-person-plural referent predominates.

The prayer's first petition asks YHWH to *shepherd* his *people*. The metaphor first appeared in the restoration passage of 2:12–13, where YHWH as the shepherd reunited the remnant of his people.[73] There

---

72. Renaud (1987: 144) also speaks of 'a chastisement of cosmic scope'. Waltke (2007: 455) concludes similarly, as do Andersen and Freedman (2000: 592) and Kessler (2000: 305–306).

73. The only other comparable use of the verb 'shepherd' is of YHWH's 'ruler' in 5:4 [Heb. 3]; other leaders of the group under his protection are also called shepherds in 5:5 [Heb. 4]. That passage shows the eschatological ruler to be in very close relationship to, yet distinct

the role of shepherd overlapped with the role of king, as YHWH liberates his reunited remnant people from captivity, guides and protects them on the way to Zion, and rules them (similarly, 4:6–7). This passage picks up that theme and adds the element of provision, and this purified Israel is now identified as YHWH's *inheritance*. This last element emphasizes that the remnant belongs to YHWH definitively and inalienably, although the concept involves both continuity and discontinuity with the nation of Israel in the light of the remnant theme and its realization in Daughter Zion (Pss 68:9 [Heb. 10]; 106:5).[74]

The petition does not mention the return from exile, perhaps because that is described in the earlier shepherd passage in 2:12–13, and instead speaks of YHWH's people as being *alone in a woodland*.[75] The *alone* implies security (cf. Num. 23:9; Deut. 33:28; Ps. 4:8; Jer. 49:31),[76] as does the absence of (other) people from a *woodland*, which is by definition uninhabited. Some English versions render the Hebrew term 'Carmel' as a proper noun that refers to the mountain itself, but it is probably better translated as 'fertile and tilled land'[77] because that rendering parallels *woodland* and because *Gilead* and *Bashan* are in the Transjordan and are suitable areas for pastures, whereas a mountain is not.

The second petition is that they might *graze* in Bashan and Gilead, two regions known for their excellence as pastureland. In the light of the reference to the exodus in 7:15 and the fact that

---

from, YHWH, who equipped him for his role. While 7:14 does not mention that royal figure, neither does it exclude YHWH's use of him to guide and provide for his people.

74. Note the unacceptable expropriation of one's inheritance in 2:2; see also Ps. 74:2; 106:5; Isa. 63:17; Joel 2:17.

75. See the arguments of Vargon (2009: 600–603) in favour of this conclusion. *Pace* Nogalski (2010: 138), the shepherd image here is neither ambiguous nor sinister.

76. Waltke 2007: 440; Smith-Christopher 2015: 220. Num. 23:9 and Deut. 33:28 are especially relevant, and contrast Lam. 1:1.

77. Vargon 2009: 603; cf. the various overlapping meanings for the word in *HALOT* 1.499.

Israel's settlement after the exodus began in Transjordan (Deut. 3:1–19), the comparison with *long ago* is most likely a reference to yhwh's guidance and protection of Israel (cf. Mic. 6:5) on its way through the Transjordan to Gilgal (this return to the exodus period also connotes Israel's unity; cf. Mic. 2:12–13). The allusion to Exodus 15:17 presents Israel's final restoration as a recapitulation of the first exodus, as yhwh 'brings' his people into the land and 'plants' them there permanently.[78]

15. God's response to this petition is brief but clear and potent. He affirms that in the same way that his superior power was evident in the exodus from *Egypt*, he will again show his *amazing deeds*. The one who will see these deeds is not specified but is not the *you* who makes the petition. While the exodus events are known to and have immense significance for Israel (cf. 6:3–5), Israel was not the only audience then, and what the nations heard produced fear and foreboding (Exod. 3:20; 9:16; 10:6; Deut. 2:25; Josh. 2:8–11). The focus on the nations in Micah 7:16–17 suggests that the nations are in view here as well, and this is corroborated by the same dynamic in the Song of the Sea (Exod. 15:11, 14–16) (Di Fransico 2017: 193; Timmer 2015: 108–109). Note especially Exodus 15:11: 'Who among the gods is like you, yhwh? Who is like you . . . doing wonders?', the last word of which has the same root as *amazing deeds*.

16–17. The speaker's response to yhwh's promise in 7:15 expresses the conviction, based on his statement that he will *show* (Hiphil *rā'āh*) the nations *amazing deeds*, that *nations will see* these deeds (Qal *rā'āh*). This confirms that the nations are the primary audience for yhwh's actions here. Compared with the exodus-conquest scenario evoked in 7:15, the nations here are modelled on the Egyptians and Canaanites of the past, but with a significant twist: there is no destruction or death, but rather submission and reverence. One might say that the nations are recast in the model of Rahab and her family![79]

This sub-unit presents the non-Israelites' reaction to yhwh's amazing deeds with a series of seven verbs that constitute a

---

78. Following the hints of Di Fransico 2017: 192.

79. Cf. Timmer 2016, esp. 167, 171–172.

definitive response. The aspects of this reaction include humiliation (*ashamed*), astonishment (*hand on their mouth*, deaf *ears*), subjugation (*lick the dust, come trembling*) and reverence for YHWH (*fear*) (Timmer 2015: 109–110; Vargon 2009: 606–610). YHWH's amazing acts reveal these nations' relative powerlessness, and as a result they abandon their resistance or aggression, adopting the radically different posture of submission. The meaning of the last few words, *be terrified and fear before you*, is difficult to determine. Dempster points out that Hosea 3:5 uses a similar expression[80] to describe Israel's eschatological conversion to YHWH, and that sense is appropriate here.[81] Although *fear before* at the end of the verse involves an unusual use of the Hebrew preposition often translated 'from', the phrase most likely means that the nations will revere YHWH.[82]

It is notable that the speaker never asks God to destroy these nations, even though that thought is hardly foreign to the book of Micah (cf. 5:9 [Heb. 8], 15 [Heb. 14]). Rather, she presents their reactions as part of a transformation which leads them to a posture of 'subservience to the Lord' (Vargon 2009: 609). This reflects the unit's logic that YHWH's enemies have already been destroyed (7:13) and the world is desolate, so that all who come to him later in the

---

80. Dempster 2017: 186 (the LXX translated the Hebrew as 'be amazed'). Vargon (2009: 609) notes similar uses of the preposition *ʾel* in Jer. 39:14; Ezek. 16:29. A sense like that proposed here is recognized by van der Merwe, Naudé and Kroeze (2017: 330), who note that the preposition can identify 'the goal of an act of observation or that of an emotional process'.

81. Allen (1976: 400–401) notes an interesting parallel with David's prototypical reign over 'people' and 'nations' as described in Ps. 18:43–45 [Heb. 44–46], which notably follows a section in which he speaks of the destruction of his 'enemies'. Ps. 18 exhibits a number of correspondences with Mic. 7:7–20 that invite exploration.

82. Kessler (2000: 308–309) and others conclude similarly. Van der Merwe, Naudé and Kroeze (2017: 362–363) note that Hebrew 'from' sometimes indicates 'orientation in space' and is frequently without its original 'primary sense of detachment'.

passage come not as opponents but as those who recognize him as unchallenged Sovereign.[83]

18. The final sub-unit of 7:18–20 completes Micah's character-ization of Daughter Zion (here *the remnant*). In the book's first cycle (2:12–13), we are told only that they were kept in a confined space from which God as king 'breaks forth' and leads them into freedom. In the second unit (4:1–8 etc.), YHWH restores them to health, leads them to Zion, and they bring good or ill (5:7–8 [Heb. 6–7]) to the nations in keeping with the Abrahamic promise (Dempster 2017: 237). Here they are described in terms of the salvation that YHWH will bring first to them, and through them to the nations (7:16–17).

Even more fundamentally, this section explains how God can maintain a relationship with his people, both Israelite and non-Israelite, without compromising his holiness. The problem of sin has been evident in nearly every passage of the book, so the conclusion of the book of Micah really is the conclusion or denouement of the drama of God and his human image bearers. While the priority of Israel is reflected in the fact that the full resolution of the problem of sin comes through the fulfilment of YHWH's covenants with Abraham and the nation of Israel, the inclusion of non-Israelites in the earlier, foundational covenant with Abraham makes this solution the same one that will undo their trust in their own power and reconcile them to God and his people.

This passage is rich with allusions to earlier Scripture, includ-ing Exodus 15 and Exodus 34:6–7 (see Table 2 on p. 225).[84] It is

---

83. Contrast Waltke's claim (2007: 462) that this is 'not the godly fear that leads to repentance and faith'. Since Rahab's faith in YHWH was the result of 'terror', 'melting' and 'dissolving of heart' (Josh. 2:9, 11), the nature of the process and the things that drive it (i.e. fear, terror, etc.) can be determined only by its outcome, not simply on the basis of vocabulary. Note also Isa. 8:13.

84. Kessler (2000: 309) notes that other passages, often informed by the earlier Exod. 34:6–7, are perhaps also cited here, including Num. 14:18 and Ps. 103:8–13.

Table 2 Allusions to Exodus 15 and Exodus 34:6–7 in Micah 7:18–20

Micah 7:18–20	Exodus 15	Exodus 34:6–7
[18]Who is a God like you?	YHWH is his name (v. 3) Who is like you among the gods, O YHWH? Who is like you, majestic in holiness, awesome in praise, doing wonders? (v. 11)	YHWH, YHWH (v. 6)
Pardoning iniquity		Forgiving iniquity (v. 7)
Passing over rebellion		(Forgiving) rebellion (v. 7)
The remnant of his inheritance		To thousands (v. 7)
[19]Let him/He will again show us compassion		A God merciful (v. 6)
Let him/He will subdue our iniquities		
Let him/He will throw all our sins into the depths of the sea	He has thrown horse and rider into the sea (v. 1) He threw Pharaoh's chariots and his host into the sea (v. 4) They went down into the depths like a stone (v. 5) Horse and rider he threw into the sea (v. 21)	(Forgiving) sin (v. 7)
[20]May you/You will show faithfulness to Jacob		(Abundant in) fidelity (v. 6)
May you/You (show) faithful love to Abraham	You have led in faithful love the people whom you redeemed (v. 13)	Abundant in faithful love (v. 6) Keeping faithful love to thousands (v. 7)
As you swore to our forefathers long ago	This is my fathers' God (v. 2)	

theologically significant that those aspects of Exodus 34:6–7 that stress God's anger against sinners in the second half of Exodus 34:7 are not cited here. Only two key terms occur twice: *iniquity* (singular in 7:18, plural in 7:19) and *faithful love* (7:18, 20), with the latter term appropriately closing the hymn.

Di Fransico (2017: 201) concludes from these uses of earlier Scripture in Micah 7 that

By reading the Micah passage in light of the Exodus allusions and references to the Song of the Sea tradition, 'sins' are personified as a physical enemy as daunting and oppressive as Pharaoh and his armies in Egypt. Pharaoh oppressed and enslaved the Hebrews; but to the audience of Micah 7, the destruction of their beloved Jerusalem and the subsequent exile and oppression is the result of their own wrongdoing and rebellion. Consequently, their own sins – the reason for their oppression – may be personified as a physical enemy that enslaves.

Although Daughter Zion's redemption has not yet been fully accomplished, she has no doubt that YHWH will complete his work of deliverance because of his gracious and compassionate character and his commitment to save. In addition to drawing upon God's saving character as displayed in Exodus, the echoes of Exodus 34 draw a parallel between the early history of Israel, who rebelled immediately after the exodus from Egypt (Exod. 32), and the Israel/Judah of Micah's day, whose sins were no less serious.

Verse 18 expresses Daughter Zion's wonder and astonishment at YHWH's willingness to save the guilty from the otherwise inevitable and ultimately destructive consequences of their sin. The concept of sin or guilt is present in every one of the seven descriptions that summarize YHWH's saving work. He *pardons iniquity, passes over the rebellion of the remnant* (cf. 1:5 [northern kingdom]; 1:13 [southern kingdom]; 3:8), and *does not keep his anger* (5:15 [Heb. 14]; 7:9) because he *delights in faithful love* (cf. 6:8; 7:2). Here that *faithful love* or goodness manifests itself in his commitment to save the undeserving and helpless.[85] The fact that only this phrase explains (*because, kî*) God's saving actions towards her underlines its importance: it is the *only* reason why God's anger does not drive him to destroy *the remnant of his inheritance* and why he forgives their sins.[86]

---

85. Romerowski (1990) argues convincingly that *ḥesed* refers to more than mere fidelity.

86. This reinforces the importance of its central position in the sevenfold list, noted by Dempster (2017: 182). The relationship of 'the remnant of

19. The three final elements of this description of the nature of YHWH's salvation also have to do with sin (cf. the same focus in 7:9). The confidence that God will once again demonstrate his *compassion* uses a verb that expresses divine grace and favour and therefore fosters hope and trust on the part of his people (Butterworth 1997: 1095). The adverb *again* may show an awareness of the fact that he has done so before, notably in not destroying Israel after the apostasy with the golden calf in Exodus 32 (the same root appears in Exod. 33:19; 34:6).

The next element, *subdue our iniquities*, implies that YHWH will overcome these sins' power, and not only their guilt.[87] This sanctification is necessary if Daughter Zion is to grow in conformity to YHWH's will as outlined in 6:8, for present sins no less than past ones threaten to undo her.[88] The seventh saving action, by contrast, anticipates that *all* the remnant's *sins* will be removed as far as possible from it, so far that they cannot be seen, much less retrieved. Like Israel's Egyptian pursuers, these sins, once done away with, will never again pose a threat to renewed Zion's relationship with God.[89] The *all* is emphatic, both because it is the only one in this seven-part series of saving actions, and because the final position of *all our sins* in the series gives it the last word.

YHWH's heritage' to Daughter Zion is presumably one of exact identity, as long as one remembers that non-Israelites have joined her and so are part of YHWH's 'heritage'.

87. In the light of Di Fransico's observations (2017: 200–201) that Egypt in Exod. 15 is coordinate with sin in Mic. 7, it is interesting that 2 Sam. 8:11 uses this verb of David's subjugation of non-Israelite nations, and that it describes humanity's mandate with respect to the rest of creation in Gen 1:28. The word falls within the semantic field of 'kingship, rule, supervision, dominion', according to Nel (1997). Whether 'subdue' is a metaphorical use of Hebrew *kābaš* depends in part on the relevance of its Akkadian cognate; see Gordon 1978: 355.

88. See the similar reflections of Allen (1976: 402).

89. This most likely has to do with the redemptive-historical dynamics of justification being based on Christ's then-future death and resurrection; cf. Rom. 3:25–26.

20. The list of acts that (partially) constitute the glorious effects of YHWH's saving power on the remnant is complemented by a covenantal interpretation of these hoped-for actions. This focus on YHWH's anticipated fidelity is based on his fidelity to his covenantal commitments to Israel from Abraham's time onwards, but also a recognition that these covenants have not yet come to fulfilment. However, Micah has indicated repeatedly how the promises of land, descendants and blessing promised to Abraham and his faithful descendants (Israelite or not) will come to fruition. 'Zion' will no longer be limited in terms of space and geography, so will be able to welcome *many nations* (4:1–4) from across the globe (7:11–12). Her newly arrived citizens, particularly those of non-Israelite ethnicity, will radically expand her population (it is important that Daughter Zion identifies herself as Abraham's offspring, rather than extending that title to all ethnic Israelites[90]). Similarly, the blessing promised to the patriarchs will reach its apogee in the full deliverance of the remnant from sin, opposition and all danger. Even the blessings promised to obedient Israel in the broken Sinai covenant, whose sanctions Daughter Zion feels even in Micah's day, will become reality as she is made increasingly able to obey and as YHWH's righteousness and light become increasingly definitive of her.

Meaning

This passage begins at the lowest possible point, with Daughter Zion aware of her sins and their destructive power (cf. 1:2–4), but ends at the apogee of the experience of salvation. It also integrates all the book's major theological themes, including the renewal of Israel and the integration of non-Israelites in the people of God. Zion's trust in YHWH's grace and her dependence upon his righteousness sustain her throughout her transformation, until she sees her enemies submit to God and her sins disappear in the ocean of his forgiveness. The second exodus pattern that the text follows reaches what is truly the final destination and full realization of God's saving plan, with his people in his presence celebrating his

---

90. See the similar reflections of Kessler (2000: 311–312).

grace and goodness. This is a fitting conclusion to the book, for it invites the reader to taste and see that the LORD is good, and so to know God better: 'it is in the process of being worshipped that God communicates His presence' to men and women (Lewis 1958: 93).